BRAZIL IN THE URUGUAY ROUND OF THE GATT

Brazil in the Uruguay Round of the GATT

The Evolution of Brazil's Position in the Uruguay
Round, with Emphasis on the Issue of Services

RICARDO WAHRENDORFF CALDAS

Routledge
Taylor & Francis Group

LONDON AND NEW YORK

First published 1998 by Ashgate Publishing

Reissued 2018 by Routledge
2 Park Square, Milton Park, Abingdon, Oxon OX14 4RN
711 Third Avenue, New York, NY 10017, USA

Routledge is an imprint of the Taylor & Francis Group, an informa business

Publisher's Note
The publisher has gone to great lengths to ensure the quality of this reprint but points out that some imperfections in the original copies may be apparent.

Disclaimer
The publisher has made every effort to trace copyright holders and welcomes correspondence from those they have been unable to contact.

A Library of Congress record exists under LC control number: 97037028

ISBN 13: 978-1-138-60772-9 (hbk)
ISBN 13: 978-0-429-46055-5 (ebk)

Contents

Abbreviations

ASEAN	Association of Southeast Asian Nations
BISD	Basic Instruments and Selected Documents (GATT)
BOP	Balance of Payments
BRP	Restrictive Business Practices
CAP	Common Agricultural Policy (EU)
CBM	Confidence Building Measures
CED	Construction, Engineering and Design
CF	Common Fund
CG-18	Consultative Group of 18 countries. It advised the Director-General of the GATT prior to his decisions.
DCs	Developed Countries
DEPE	Special Delivery of Economic Studies
DFA	Final Draft Act
DMP	Decision Making Process
DPC	Division on Trade Policy
EC	European Commission
ECLA	Economic Commission for Latin America
ECLA	United Nations Comission for Latin America
EEC	European Economic Community
EFTA	European Free-Trade Association
EOI	Export Oriented Industrialization
EP	European Parliament
EU	European Union
FDI	Foreign Direct Investment
FOGS	Functioning of the GATT System
G-10	Group of 10 LDCs who joined forces to prevent the entrance of the issue of services in the GATT or in the Uruguay Round
G-77	Group of 77. Coalition of LDCs created at UNCTAD (1964)
GATS	General Agreement on Trade in Services
GATT	General Agreement on Tariffs and Trade
GNS	Group of Negotiations on Services
GSP	General System of Preferences
IACO	International Civil Aviation Organization

IBRD	International Bank for Reconstruction and Development
ICO	International Coffee Organization
IDB	Inter-American Development Bank
IMF	International Monetary Fund
IMO	International Maritime Organization
INPI	Brazilian Institute of Intellectual Property
IPC	International Programe of Commodities
IPEA	Institute of Applied Economic and Social Research - Brazil
IPR	International Property Rights
ISI	Import Substitution Industrialization
IT	Information Technology
ITAMARATY	Brazil's Ministry of Foreign Affairs
ITO	International Trade Organization
LDCs	Less Developed Countries
LJSPA	Lyndon Johnson School of Public Administration
MFA	Multi Fibre Arrangement
MFN	Most Favoured Nation status
MIC	Ministry of Industry and Commerce (Brazil)
MINICOM	Ministry of Communications (Brazil)
MTN	Multilateral Trade Negotiations
MTO	Multilateral Trade Organization
NIC	Non-Industralized Countries
NIEO	New International Economic Order
NTBs	Non-Tariff Barriers
NTMs	Non-Tariff Measures
OAS	Organization of American States
OECD	Organization for Economic Cooperation and Development
OPEC	Organization of Petroleum Exporting Countries
PMA	Pharmaceutical Manufacturers Association
QRs	Quantitative Restrictions
QTBs	Quasi Tariff Barriers
S & D	Special and Differential (Treatment)
SEI	Special Secretariat for IT issues (Brazil)

SELA	Latin American Economic System
SEPLAN	Ministry of Planning (Brazil)
SOG	Senior Official Group
TDB	Trade and Development Board
TNC	Trade Negotiating Committee
TNCs	Transnational Corporations
TRIMs	Tariff Related Investment Measures
TRIPs	Tariff Related Intellectual Property Right Measures
UK	United Kingdom
UN	United Nations
UNCTAD	United Nations Conference on Trade and Development
UNCTC	United Nations Centre for Transnational Corporations
UNEP	United Nations Environment Programme
US	United States
USSR	Formerly the Union of Soviet Socialist Republics (Soviet Union)
USTR	Office of the United States Trade Representative
VERs	Voluntary Export Restraints
WIPO	World Intellectual Property Organization
WTO	World Trade Organization

Key Participants

Amorim, Celso	Brazilian Ambassador to the GATT (1991-93)
Batista, Paulo	Brazilian Ambassador to the GATT (1983-87)
Brock, William	United States Trade Representative (1980-85)
Bush, George	President of United States (1988-1992)
Collor, Fernando	President of Brazil (1990-92). He adopted a free-trade policy
Hills, Carla	United States Trade Representative (1989-92)
Huguenet, Clodoaldo	Head of Trade Policy Division at Itamaraty (GATT issues) and main supporter of Batista
Maciel, George	Brazilian Ambassador to the GATT (1979-82)
Neves, Tancredo	Elected President of Brazil, died before taking power. He was replaced by V.P. Sarney
Reagan, Ronald	President of United States (1980-1988)
Ricupero, Rubens	Brazilian Ambassador to the GATT (1987-91)
Sarney, José	President of Brazil (1985-90)
Setúbal, Olavo	Minister of Foreign Affairs (1985-6)
Sodré, Abreu	Minister of Foreign Affairs (1987-90)
Tarso, Paulo	General-Secretary of Itamaraty, and Minister of Foreign Affairs *de facto* during Sodré's Term (1986-90). Ambassador Plenipotentiary in the US-Brazil dispute on IT and Head of Brazil's Delegation at Montreal Meeting (1988)
Vargas, Getulio	President of Brazil (1930-45) & (1951-54)
Yetteur, Clayton	United States Trade Representative (1985-89)
Yerxa, Rufus	US Ambassador to the GATT

Acknowledgements

First of all, I would like to thank Dr. Andrew Williams, my former supervisor at the University of Kent at Canterbury (UK) without whom this book would not exist. He created and designed the International Political Economy (IPE) series which made this book possible. I should also like to thank Ashgate Publishing for their support and encouragement of the IPE project.

Besides Dr. Williams, I should like to thank all the staff at the Department of International Relations from University of Kent for creating a stimulating environment to carry out research. I am grateful in particular to Professor Groom, the Head of Department, to Dr. Stephen Chan, former Director of the London Centre of International Relations, and to Dr. Jarrod Wiener, for their useful comments.

I would like to show my appreciation to CAPES, the agency from the Ministry of Education which financed my studies at University of Kent. I couldn't have stayed in Britain for four years without their uninterrupted support. My parents gave me continuous encouragement throughout all the period that I was in Britain.

At University of Kent I made an excellent set of friends and people that I hope will always be in touch. Among them, I would like to mention Irene, Claudio, Ana, José, Catarina, Frank, Abu and Jerry.

At the LSE, where I carried out part of my field research, I met exceptional individuals that hopefully will always be part of my life. Among them, I would like to mention Luciana, John, Mariane, Thomas, Mirela, Ernesto, Chico, Debora, Ariel, Marcela and Richard. Professor Domingos Giroletti has been very active in the creation of the Brazilian Society, which helped organize social meetings and seminars. I owe my pleasant stay in London to all these individuals.

Dr. Charles Madison and Ms. Taylor helped to improve my English style in order to make the text clear and understandable to the reader. I owe to them my gratitude.

Ariel Zastsman was kind enough to help me to revise all the original text. This work requires not only patience and time but also commitment. He offered all the time he had available in a very generous way, which is the main aspect of his character, I am very grateful to him.

Bruno Reis helps me with the final editing work which was of excellent quality.

Finally, I would like to thank all those who agreed to receive me to give me an interview and offered advice, but preferred not to be mentioned in the text. A list of all the individuals interviewed can be found at the end of the book in the bibliography section. Needless to say that without their support, much of the work I carried out would be either incomplete or imprecise.

Introduction

The main objective of this book is to analyze Brazil's strategy in the Uruguay Round, focusing on the issue of services. Three different instances were chosen for analysis. The first was during discussions before the launch of the Uruguay Round. During this period, Brazil and India in particular led the Less Developed Countries (LDCs), and the Group of 10 (G-10), in obstructing the inclusion of services on the agenda. The second was during the launch and the first year of the Uruguay Round, when Brazil persisted with this policy. This second period is referred to as the initial position of Brazil in the Uruguay Round. However, it was also similar to Brazil's position before the launch of the Round.

The third, and decisive moment, was in Montreal in 1988, when Brazil supported the principles which guided an agreement on services. After this turning point, Brazil's position in the Round was increasingly supportive of an agreement, not only in services, but in all fields. Brazil's position in 1991, when it supported Arthur Dunkel's (then Director General of the GATT) Draft Final Act (DFA), is seen as a direct result of the position Brazil adopted in 1988 and maintained to the end of the Round in 1994. Consequently, this book will concentrate more on the period which preceded the change in Brazil's position during the Uruguay Round, from 1986 to 1988. After 1989 and at the end of the Round in 1992, Brazil's position did not change. The election of President Collor in 1990, a supporter of free-trade, only accelerated the process begun between 1986 and 1988. Indeed, the developments which occurred between 1986 and 1988 are considered to be of crucial importance to understanding Brazil's change of position in the Uruguay Round and thus merit a special emphasis in this book.

Organization of the book

This book is organized into six chapters. The introduction discusses briefly some theories that might have been behind Brazil's position in the GATT. These include a short review on the key points which supported Brazil's trade policies as well as the literature on the Less Developed Countries (LDCs) and the GATT Regime.

Chapter 1 of this book discusses the preparation for the Uruguay Round from 1982 to 1986, with emphasis on the differences of position between the US and Brazil on the issue of Services. During all this period Brazil maintained a consistent attitude against the discussion of services on the GATT or in the Uruguay Round. Chapter 1 seeks to explain the main facets of this attitude. Although it deals with the period which goes from 1982 to 1986, it concentrates on the 1982 Ministerial Meeting, when Brazil's position was made clear. This position would be exactly the same, namely, that GATT should not deal with services.

Chapter 2 describes Brazil's Decision Making Process. It concentrates on Itamaraty, the Brazilian Foreign Ministry, and by law, in charge of negotiating international agreements. Itamaraty also has a monopoly of Brazilian representation abroad. This implies that all the strategies of international economic negotiations, with the exception of the renegotiation of the foreign debt, are decided with the involvement of that agency. As a result, the prevailing beliefs at Itamaraty will have a deep impact on the way Brazil takes part in international trade institutions, such as the GATT or the UNCTAD.

Chapter 2 also discusses Brazil's attitude towards the Service Sector. In order to understand Brazil's position on the issue of services, it is necessary to learn why it was against the liberalization of the service sector. Since Brazil's diplomacy is basically multilateral, an understanding of the coalitions which Brazil took part in can help to explain Brazil's position in the Round.

The launching of the Uruguay Round is described in more detail in Chapter 3. For this reason, Chapter 3 concentrates on the Ministerial Meeting at Punta del Este, when the Round was officially launched. In this chapter, the Brazilian position is discussed in its main aspects: technical, political, ideological, among others. The link that Brazil made between services and other issues (such as textiles) is also described in Chapter 3.

An analysis of the evolution of Brazil's position during the discussions within the Group Negotiating on Services (GNS), up to the point of Brazil's support for the final results, which were embodied in the Draft Final Act (DFA) of 1991, proposed by Dunkel, can be found in Chapter 4. From 1991 to 1994, when the negotiations ended, there was no change in Brazil's position. The draft proposed by Dunkel was in essence the same text, with few changes, that was approved. Chapter 4, therefore, offers this overview of the changes - or evolution, as Itamaraty prefers - of Brazil's position.

Chapter 5 is concerned solely with the reasons which contributed directly and indirectly to Brazil's change of position in the Uruguay Round. This chapter is divided into two parts. The first part analyzes the domestic factors which influenced the change in Brazil's position. The second part concentrates on external factors which may have influenced changes.

Chapter 6 offers a summary of the book. It also offers a conclusion about Brazil's position in the Uruguay Round, the attitude of Brazil's Foreign Affairs agency, Itamaraty, and about Brazil's trade policies. It contains some suggestions of new studies for researchers and scholars interested in issues linked to trade policies and developing countries and international organizations.

It must be pointed out that this book does not deal with the issue of Intellectual Property Rights (IPRs), nor the conflict between Brazil and the US on Information Technology (IT). Both are considered to be beyond the scope of this book. The LDCs' call for a New International Economic Order (NIEO) and Brazil's position within UNCTAD are also beyond the scope of this book, although bibliographical references are provided in end notes.

Protectionism and Brazil's Trade Policies [1]

Import Substitution Industrialization (ISI)

The reasons for protectionism vary considerably. A classical supporter of protectionism is Friedrich List, who proposed the Theory of the Infant Industry.[2] LDCs sympathized with List's arguments because they also believed that infant industries should be protected.[3] This argument fitted LDCs who thought they were different from DCs, and, therefore, free-trade could not apply in the same way.[4] LDCs also were convinced that free-trade was a zero-sum game. Moreover, they wanted to create an industrial structure, and they did not think they could achieve this through free-trade. Other arguments were also used together with the infant industry. The most common argument to explain protectionism is that it raises the number of those employed in the production of the goods for which the country has no comparative advantage.[5]

Moreover, some protectionist tools, such as tariffs, may attract FDI, and therefore, increase domestic production. If there were complete liberalization, the sectors in which the country had no comparative advantage would disappear. As a result, if a country wanted to develop a certain sector, there must be protection to attract FDI, such as tariffs. There is a strong prejudice against foreign products, but - paradoxically - there is no prejudice against the control by foreigners of companies within the country.

Another argument in favour of protectionism, is that tariffs may help to increase the revenue of governments.[6] In countries which do not have a developed industrial background, tariffs levied on imports are an important source of government revenue. This explains why some countries do not want to decrease the level of tariffs. In Brazil this was not a decisive factor, since tariff shares of tax revenue fell continuously throughout the century.

A more powerful argument used in favour of trade barriers is to correct a BOP deficit. In many cases, LDCs depend on few products to obtain foreign currency. They believe that exports of these products are not enough to avoid a BOP deficit. Thus, some governments from LDCs countries have decided to impose tariffs in order to reduce imports by increasing their final price.[7] It has been argued by supporters of protectionism, that tariff barriers allow some countries to avoid the costs of reforming the economy. In fact, the burden of reform is transferred from importing countries to exporting countries. However, the costs of such a practice, such as the rent effect, are not taken into account.[8]

There are two main forces which drive protectionism. The first is based on power politics and aims to increase national wealth. The second is the pursuit of domestic policies regardless of external interests. These forces are not exclusive, and when they work together they become a drive towards protectionism.[9] In Brazil, these forces worked together in the IT policy.

Another explanation is that economic nationalists see protectionism as an end in itself.[10] The reason is that economic nationalists assume the superiority of industry over agriculture and commodity production.[11] Brazil's Representative in the GATT (1983-1987), Batista, is an example.[12] Batista represented a view which prevailed in Brazil during his tenure at GATT. Indeed, Itamaraty's rationale was based on ISI policies and economic nationalism.[13] ISI became synonymous with economic development. Trade policies emphasized protectionism and export promotion. ISI can be defined as "an attempt to replace commodities, usually manufactured goods which were formerly imported with domestic sources of production and supply. The typical strategy is first to erect tariff barriers or quotas on the importation of certain commodities then to try to set up a local industry to produce the goods that were formerly imported...".[14]

The ISI is considered as a sequential process working its way from light consumer goods to heavy industry and capital goods.[15] Thus, ISI replaces the imported goods for domestic production. Later on, it achieves the production of sophisticated machines, such as capital goods. However, this process has to be used with caution, because not all countries have started ISI with consumer goods; some of them started ISI through heavy industry and later on they achieved the production of consumer goods.[16]

Despite this, one can assume that in LDCs, ISI appeared to have followed a similar pattern of three stages,[17] although some have not yet reached the last stage. In the first stage, the local production of light manufactured and consumer goods replaces the imports of these goods. In the second stage, consumer durable and transportation means are produced locally. During this stage the intermediary sector receives a boost. The production of simple machinery, such as machine tools and industrial equipment, starts during this stage. In the third stage there is an expansion of existing industries, which produce the most sophisticated goods. Thus, intermediate products are available locally. Besides, capital goods start to be produced during this stage. The export of manufactured goods also begins during this period.[18]

Among the reasons that may lead a country to adopt an ISI Policy Balance mentions the disruption in trade caused by wars or by a great economic depression. Other causes which could be mentioned are economic nationalism, lack of foreign currency to cover all the basic imports of a country and deterioration of trade terms. All these factors can lead to inward-looking strategies.[19]

The main rationale of ISI is that if one country imposes tariffs in order to protect existing domestic industry or to favour its establishment, the net result will be positive, for two main reasons. Firstly, tariffs attract investments. Thus, several industries will be set up. Although the supporters of ISI acknowledge that those industries may be not as efficient as existing industries, they believe that in the long term they will become internationally competitive (infant industry argument). Secondly, the industries created after the establishment of tariff protection will help the country to save foreign currency. These two positive factors together will allow the LDCs, according to the ISI model, to achieve self-sustained growth (the "take-off") and to escape the condition of underdevelopment.[20]

In order to reach this goal, LDCs adopt higher tariff barriers in the area of consumer goods, where the process of ISI starts. It does not mean that there will be no tariff barriers in other products. This means that they will be higher in consumer goods than in capital goods or in intermediary goods.[21]

However, there are three consequences of an ISI which may not have been predicted by policy-makers. First, once it has started an ISI has a spill-over effect on other economic sectors. Thus, when a company is created to receive the benefits of tariff protection, it will have to import the machines which are not available on the domestic market. As a result, the replacement of imported consumer goods by national products will increase the dependence on imports. If one thinks in terms of a world market, the country will become more interdependent with foreign markets to import capital goods than it was before the start of the ISI process. Second, once the ISI has started it will stimulate new ISI as a result of the demand for imports and for intermediary goods and machines. This occurs because when an industry of consumer goods is established it has an obligation to buy a minimum percentage of its components in the internal market. This creates a reserved market and the local firms take advantage of this fact. Third, the self-sufficiency projected by ISI supporters will be achieved in the long term, if at all.[22]

To these consequences, Todaro adds five others. First, the beneficiaries of ISI are TNCs which take advantage for themselves of the high tariffs. Second, ISI attracts capital intensive firms with low employment effects. Third, the BOP of LDCs is worsened because TNCs send their part of the profits abroad. Fourth, the over-valued exchange rate adopted because of the ISI decreases the competitiveness of commodities and of manufactured goods exported by the country. Finally, ISI blocks further industrial development because it increases prices and it decreases the quality of intermediary goods used in the process of industrialization.[23]

Conclusions

However, these existing theoretical frameworks fail to explain fully the behaviour of LDC's middle powers, such as Brazil, in the world economy. Middle powers are those countries which have more resources than most countries, and sometimes become quite influential in international relations. Nevertheless, the literature on middle powers still presents some gaps that this book expects to help to fill.

This book suggests that influence varies from issue to issue. Therefore, the influence of a country in a given issue is based on several factors, such as the interest of the country in the issue being discussed, in the resources employed in that particular matter, in the availability of experts and technical information on that topic and, last but not least, in the personality, values and beliefs of the negotiator of the country as well as the agency from which he receives his instructions. In this case the way in which the agency is built and works will have a very important impact on the outcome of the negotiations, because some agencies from certain countries are more centralized than others. Brazil is a particulary interesting case, because the decentralization of its agency allows its negotiators to take personal views and positions which go beyond their original instructions.

It is true that Brazil had a trade practice based on protectionism. This would, of course, limit the scope of the position that a negotiator could sustain in the course of the negotiations, since tradition is a very difficult barrier to overcome, because when the negotiator did not receive a clear instruction from his agency he would tend to adopt a conservative position, which, in the case of Brazil would mean support for protectionist views. Protectionism - as well as free-trade - then becomes a self-stimulating mechanism, where previous positions, tradition and inertia become the explanation of future positions. This explains why protectionism was the ideology which prevailed in Brazil for many years, but it does not explain why Brazil moved to free-trade or at least to "pragmatism". Here a series of aspects start to appear and become more relevant than others.

One of these factors is how the decisions are taken in each country. Who is in charge of what and is responsible for the final decisions. In this book, in which we concentrate on Brazil, the focus will be on the Brazilian decision-making process. Decisions in Brazil regarding international trade are not taken either by the Trade Minister or by the Finance Minister, as might be expected, but by the Ministry of Foreign Affairs (Itamaraty). As a result, trade issues in Brazil are decided exclusively by the agency in charge of foreign affairs and any conflicts are solved by diplomats who are in charge of all phases of the process. Itamaraty not only represents the country, but also formulates the decisions going beyond what is specified by Brazilian law. Another interesting aspect is that in most cases Brazilian Presidents rarely directly supervise Itamaraty, leaving the agency in the hands of the Minister, in most cases a former Ambassador. This, needless to say, guarantees a degree of autonomy which would be the envy of its counterparts around the world. This book also suggests that Itamaraty had a hidden agenda, which was to exercise hegemony among Third World countries or to be the Leader of the Third World. This is consistent with Itamaraty's older ambition of getting a permanent seat in the United Nations, another side of Itamaraty's hidden agenda.

This kind of hidden agenda leads us to another issue: that of leadership. In this book, it is suggested that some states have more influence than others in shaping the formation and agenda of regimes: the leaders or counter-leaders.[24] However, this does not mean that there is a leader state which will dictate norms or impose its views in all fields. It is possible that states which are not leaders obtain favourable results in particular issues-areas.[25] Changes in the distribution of influence among leaders may lead to changes in regimes, at least in the rules and procedures. Therefore leadership is crucial.

Leadership, understood as the capacity of inducing followers to act for certain goals that represent their motivations and values, is based on several factors. Among these factors can be mentioned knowledge, tradition, expertise, seniority, and the ability of the state to mobilize other states to defend its interests. Thus, leadership is a skill which requires a degree of entrepreneurship. It is possible that LDCs obtain favourable results in particular issues-areas.[26] Thus, influence changes in each particular area and has directly favourable results in particular issues-areas. Therefore, a state which is very influential in a certain area may not be in another area.

However, it is also important to point out that any kind of automatic link is rejected in this book. Both states and regimes have a relative autonomy to take decisions. Thus, this approach rejects the pure structural perspective which focuses its analysis in the economic structure of the world economy because it does not give enough emphasis to political aspects. This is specially true in the case of the GATT. The structural approach considers the GATT was not relevant to liberalize the world economy. However, without the decrease in tariffs promoted by the GATT, it is difficult to imagine that there would be the same level of transnationalization of the economies as there is nowadays.

End Notes

1.   This section does not include new-protectionism. See: Lieberman, 1988, S. *The*

Economic and Political Roots of the New Protectionism. Totowa: Rowman & Littlefield, pp.125-167.

2. The main idea is that all companies have a learning curve. It is the role of the state to protect the national industries while they are in this learning process, or in their 'infancy'. See List, 1983, *The Natural System of Political Economy.* London, Cass.

3. When they have grown, protection can be abolished. See El-Algraa, 1989, *op.cit.*, pp.139-142.

4. Pomfret, 1991, *op.cit.*, pp.196-199.

5. Evans, P., 1974, *The Politics of Trade. The Evolution of the Superbloc.* London, Macmillan, p.9.

6. Pearce, R., 1970, *International Trade.* London, Macmillan, p.157.

7. Brazil did it with luxury products, with tariffs of 100%.

8. The rent effect is the economic returns (profits) obtained by the producer which are superior to market conditions.

9. Evans, 1974, *op. cit.*, p.9.

10. Gilpin, 1987, *op.cit.*, p.185.

11. Ibid. However, with the advent of the service sector, this view will be modified, as it will be seen later.

12. Batista's statement is in Tachinardi, 1993, *op.cit.*

13. Fontaine, 1970, *op.cit.*

14. Todaro, 1977, *Economics for a Developing World: An Introduction to Principles, Problems and Policies for Development*, London, Longman, p.300.

15. Ballance; Ansari; Singer, 1982, *The International Economy and Industrial Development: The Impact of Trade and Investment on the Third World*, Brighton, Wheatsheaf, p.40.

16. This is the case of the ex-USSR.

17. Edwards and Teitel, 1986, *Introduction to Growth, Reform and Adjustment: Latin America's Trade and Macroeconomic Policies in the 1970s and 1980s.* Chicago, University of Chicago, p.42.

18. Edwards and Teitel, 1986, *op.cit.*, p.43.

19. Todaro, 1977, *op.cit.*, p.300.

20. About a take-off theory: Rostow, W., 1963, *The Economics of Take-off into Sustained Growth: Proceedings of a Conference held by the International Economic Association.* London, Macmillan.

21. For two reasons: first because consumer products are the first phase of ISI model and because purchase of capital goods (national or foreign) can be considered an investment and, therefore, should be stimulated.

22. See Little, R., 1970, *Industry and Trade in some Developing Countries: a Comparative Study.* London, New York, Oxford Press.

23. Todaro 1977, *op.cit.*, pp.305-306.

24. An indicative of influence in the GATT is the Consultative Group of 18 countries (CG-18). See Curzon & Curzon, 1974, *op.cit.*

25. See: Kivimaki, T., 1993, *Distribution of Benefits in Bargaining Between a Superpower and a Developing Country, A Study of Negotiating Process between the United States and Indonesia*, Helsinki, Finish Society of Science and Letters.
26. Ibid.

1. The Preparations for the Uruguay Round with Emphasis on the US' and Brazil's Position on the Issue of Services

Introduction

This chapter has two main aims. The first is to describe the US position and analyze Brazil's negative reaction in the GATT towards the negotiations prior to the launching of the Uruguay Round. As an example of Brazil's negative attitude in the GATT, this chapter concentrates on the issue of the inclusion or not of services in the GATT framework, during the preparation of the Uruguay Round.[1] The second main objective of this chapter is to describe Brazil's position on services in the Uruguay Round after the Ministerial Meeting in 1982.

Indeed, until the beginning of the 1980s Brazil considered the GATT a 'rich man's club'. In the period preceding the launch of the Uruguay Round, from 1982 until 1986, the main aspect of Brazil's attitude was to oppose any attempt by other countries to widen GATT's scope. The issue of trade in services is a case in point. Brazil used its bargaining power which had arisen from its multilateral diplomacy and its role as one of the leading LDCs to try to block the inclusion of services in the GATT framework. These efforts by Brazil are the subject of this chapter.

The negotiations preliminary to the launching of the Uruguay Round are described here for three main years: 1982 - when the Ministerial Meeting was arranged; 1984 - when the results and proposals of the 1982 Ministerial Declaration were discussed; and 1985 - when several meetings were organized in order to prepare the launching of the new Round. The Meeting at Punta del Este in 1986 which launched the Uruguay Round will be discussed

1

in the next chapter.

The 1982 Ministerial Meeting

An overview of the Ministerial Meeting

Brazil's condemnation of GATT's recommended trade policies could not be more clear than in the discussion about the introduction of services in the GATT framework. Services will illustrate the changes in Brazil's position on the Uruguay Round of GATT.

Officially, the main objective of the 1982 Ministerial Meeting was to consider problems affecting the world trading system.[2] The system was considered to be in danger.[3] The solution envisaged was a renewed consensus in support of the GATT and its strengthening. However, there were differences on how to achieve this. To Brazil, the need to upgrade the world trading system did not mean the inclusion of new issues in GATT. Brazil believed that first GATT should deal with old issues which were escaping GATT rules, such as agriculture and textiles. However, some Developed Countries (DCs), - such as the US -, believed that to strengthen the GATT it was necessary to include in the GATT areas which were not yet covered, such as services.[4]

The 1982 Ministerial Meeting did not herald substantial changes in the GATT. Indeed, in February of 1982, the Consultative Group of Eighteen (CG-18) - to which Brazil belonged - met to prepare the agenda for the 1982 Ministerial Meeting. During the talks within the CG-18 - the most influential policy-making forum of the GATT - the EC, Brazil and India refused to accept the US request to start negotiations for an agreement on trade in services[5]. The talks also failed to produce an agreement on agriculture. Indeed, the Report of the CG-18, prepared by the General-Director of the GATT, Dunkel, to the Council of the GATT, did not mention services and noted that it was not possible to arrive at a consensus on the content of a work programme in agriculture.[6] As CG-18 decisions shaped GATT policies, the lack of agreement on agriculture in the CG-18 anticipated the problems that the 1982 Ministerial would face.

The positions adopted by Brazil and the EC on services help us to understand the failure of the 1982 Ministerial Meeting to broaden GATT's scope to include services. They confirm why Brazil is considered an important member in the GATT. In fact, Itamaraty was aware that the 1982 Ministerial Meeting would only be a first step towards a complete removal of the barriers to trade in services. Brazil was convinced that any concession made would allow a complete change in the rules of GATT, including the introduction of services in its framework.

Brazil was fearful of the insistence of the US in introducing services in the GATT. In particular, it feared that the discussions on services in GATT would be used to bring Foreign Direct Investment (FDI) under the aegis of the world trade system through the back door. In the end, a compromise was found. National studies would be carried out by Contracting Parties interested in services. The Ministerial Declaration noted that studies should be used to consider whether multilateral action would be appropriate.[7] The findings of the national studies carried out by each country would be discussed during the 1984 GATT Session. This aspect of the 1982 Declaration reflected the dispute between the US, and Brazil and India, concerning the inclusion of services in the GATT.[8]

The fact that Brazil supported a study of the service sector was not a change of attitude. Many reasons can be cited to explain this position but the most important is that LDCs were united against the introduction of services in the framework of the GATT, but they were not uniformly opposed to a study of services. Indeed, several countries supported the studies, such as South Korea, Singapore, Chile, Pakistan and Egypt. Although the EC opposed the immediate inclusion of services in the GATT, they accepted the conduct of the study as proposed by the US. Brazil also received positive stimulus to support the service studies. These included loans from the US Treasury to help during the debt crisis, support from the US in the IMF to renegotiate Brazilian debt, and permission to use subsidies to stimulate its exports.[9]

The reason for the US support for the study was clear from the beginning of the 1982 Ministerial Meeting.[10] The US government wanted to present the 1982 Meeting as a success to its internal opponents and respond to the pressure from private service industries.[11] There was protectionist pressure in Congress, and Reagan wanted to show that the world trading system was working and advancing in new sectors, such as services.[12] The service sector was also the main employer in the American economy in the 1980s. Of one hundred jobs in the economy, sixty five were in services.[13] It was natural that the US wanted to promote this sector where the US economy seemed to enjoy a comparative advantage.

Indeed, the service sector was playing a vital role in the US economy. The US became the biggest exporter of commercial services in the world[14] and service exports were covering part of the deficit on imports of goods. Thus, the US did not want to leave this sector without any regulation. They believed that if a free-for-all situation prevailed, LDCs would take advantage to establish Non-Tariff Barriers (NTBs). In this case, national regulations would prevail over international rules.

The Brazilian Position

At the beginning of the 1980s new issues began to be discussed in international fora. Services, in particular, became one of the main points of discussion, since there exports were presenting high rates of growth of about 14% per annum.[15]

During the negotiations for the 1982 Ministerial Meeting and during the Meeting itself Brazil demonstrated that it did not share the point of view held by the US. Ambassador George Maciel[16] had opposed the call for the 1982 Ministerial Meeting, because he was aware that the US would use the Meeting to try to propose a reform of the GATT with the inclusion of new issues.[17]

Maciel was not convinced of the advantage of including new issues in the GATT.[18] He believed that it was necessary first to amend GATT rules to incorporate services before including them in a new Round, since the GATT had no provisions in its articles to deal with services. Maciel maintained that it was important to find a common definition of services and of studying the new sector in depth before including it in the new Round proposed by the US.[19] Brazil emphasized that before launching a new Round, old issues should be resolved first, such as Voluntary Export Restraints (VERs), NTBs, trade of agricultural products and the Multi Fibre Arrangement (MFA).[20] In short, Brazil opposed a new Round. But, if a new Round were to be launched, it should include the unresolved issues, which were of particular interest to LDCs, and not the new issues of interest to DCs. Brazil was ready to discuss services outside the terms of the GATT.[21]

Itamaraty was aware that it did not have enough influence to prevent the launching of a new Round. But Brazil could try to block the inclusion of new issues in the new Round. Indeed, Brazil opted for obstructing such negotiations, adopting a defensive position, and using all its defensive power.[22] Brazil looked for the support of other LDCs which opposed the launching of the new Round in an attempt to abort it. If this was not possible, at least these countries would make an effort to prevent the inclusion of new issues. Thus, Brazil formed a coalition of ten LDCs, the Group of 10 (G-10).[23] The membership of the G-10 would vary, but there were five countries that would remain as its core: Brazil, India, Egypt, Argentina and Yugoslavia.[24]

Brazil took advantage of its position in the influential CG-18 to block any attempt to discuss services at GATT.[25] When the issue of services was raised, Brazil would ask for a break in the discussion, arguing that the issue of services was not covered by the GATT, and therefore should not be discussed within the GATT.[26] As a result, Brazil successfully prevented the CG-18 from beginning to discuss an agreement on services, as proposed by US officials. This was clear in the CG-18 report mentioned above. On the other hand, Maciel believed that a study on services would not undermine the position adopted by Brazil for several reasons. First, the studies were not binding. Thus, Brazil imagined that it could overcome the 1982 Ministerial Declaration by not presenting the study at all. As it happened, Brazil ignored the Declaration on carrying out the studies. Indeed, by the end of 1985 only DCs had submitted studies to be analyzed by the GATT secretariat.[27]

Furthermore, in Brazil's view, even if it were obliged to present a study, the text of the 1982 Ministerial Declaration was ambiguous enough to allow the study to be conducted by other organizations, in which case Brazil would ask UNCTAD to conduct the study, since both shared the same views on trade issues. Moreover, in 1982 Brazil was in a bad financial situation due to the debt crisis. Thus, Brazil was in a vulnerable position and could not confront the creditor countries.

Although most of the Brazilian debt was owed to private banks, Brazil counted on the goodwill of the US and of other DCs to obtain credits from the IMF and World Bank. Brazil expected support from DCs in refinancing its debt with the Paris Club. It was for this reason that the Brazilian delegation included the Finance Minister, alongside the Head of Itamaraty. Thus, financial problems explain why Brazil was willing to reach a compromise solution. The US took advantage of this to apply pressure on Brazil.[28]

Brazil did not want the collapse of the 1982 Ministerial Meeting. Its collapse would stimulate retaliatory measures from DCs. Indeed, the US Trade Representative, William Brock, threatened such measures in the case of an unsuccessful outcome of the Ministerial Meeting. An unsuccessful outcome for the US would mean not including services in the Declaration.[29]

Moreover, the US proposal of study groups seemed to be the least of all possible evils. If the alternatives were between a possible disruption of the GATT or a study on services, Brazil would opt to conduct a study. Itamaraty's approach was to support multilateral institutions. This occurred even if Itamaraty had strong reservations about an institution, as was the case of the GATT. Besides, Brazil did not want to fight a losing battle, as it was clear that there was no unity among LDCs over the issue. From Brazil's perspective, it would be wiser to concentrate its efforts in the battle that would come later: the introduction of services within the GATT framework.[30]

The inclusion in the Declaration of a commitment to conduct studies on services played into Brazil's hands, since it wanted to win time. Brazil was not in a position to fight any proposal from the DCs without support from other LDCs. Thus, Brazil opted to wait and see how things would develop. Brazil imagined that after some years the US interest in the inclusion of services in the the GATT would decrease. Furthermore, Brazil had a strong arsenal of legal and technical arguments which it was willing to deploy against the introduction of services in GATT. Brazil knew that to rewrite the text of the GATT would open Pandora's box, a situation that no country wanted, not even Brazil. These were only two of the many weapons that Brazil was planning to use against the inclusion of services in the GATT. Another argument was the union of LDCs against the introduction of services in the GATT. We will now explore the US position in more detail.

The US Position in the 1982 Ministerial Meeting

The US had very high expectations of the 1982 Ministerial Meeting and adopted a very ambitious approach which included multiple objectives.[31] The main goals of the US can be summarized as follows:

a) The US wanted to stimulate trade liberalization in the 1980s. This included two subsidiary goals. The first was the opening of the markets of countries which adopted protectionist policies, such as the majority of LDCs. Second, the US wanted to bring in issues which were outside the scope of the GATT, such as agriculture;

b) The US wanted to discuss FDI and trade in high technology goods;

c) The US believed that it could attract LDCs if it offered to end the MFA and the expansion of preferential tariff rates to LDCs in exchange for the opening up of their markets;

d) In the services sector the US wished to establish a programme that would analyze the barriers in that sector, in particular in terms of market access, and the GATT rules in that area.[32]

The US believed it had a comparative advantage in the export of such products since it had been the leading exporter of commercial services since the 1970s.[33] US service exports were growing at a higher rate than merchandise exports. Indeed, while the export of services represented 31.8% of the global exports of the US in 1960, at $ 9.22 billion out of a total of $ 28.86 billion, they had reached 34.5% of the total in 1980, at $ 118.21 billion compared to global exports of $ 342.48 billion.[34]

Moreover, this sector accounted for a larger proportion of jobs in the US. While employment in the service sector in 1960 was equivalent to 56.2% of all civilian employment, this rate had risen to 65.9% in 1980.[35] The service sector in the domestic economy was also growing considerably and from 62% of the GDP in 1970 it reached 68% in 1987.[36] This helps to explain the US interest in bringing international trade in services under the GATT discipline.

However, services were not included originally in the GATT framework and most LDCs believed they should not be included. Thus, the US had two options: to amend the GATT Agreement, which required unanimity of its members - or to include services straightaway in a new Round. Reagan opted for the second alternative. He felt that a new Round could help to defeat the protectionist trends in the US Congress and at the same time give a boost to the world economy. However, Reagan was convinced that it was necessary to include an issue in the new Round that would assure the support of the Congress. The choice, for obvious reasons, fell on the service sector. The problem then was to convince LDCs of the viability of introducing services in a new Round. In order to discuss these issues the Ministerial Meeting of 1982 was called.

The goals of the US to reform the GATT and to include the 'new is-sues' were not accepted by LDCs.[37] LDCs had other plans for the 1982 Ministerial Meeting. LDCs saw an opportunity in the 1982 Meeting to re-quest that previous commitments made by DCs, such as the Programme of Action (1963), Part IV (1965) and the Enabling Clause (1979) should come into effect.[38] Thus, LDCs wanted to increase their privileges in the GATT, with a strengthening of the Special and Differential (S&D) treatment.[39] The LDCs did not want to hear about 'new issues' and were ready to polarize the issue into a North-South debate.[40]

Brazil also noted the fact that there was no harmony among DCs con-cerning the new Round, since the EC was not convinced of the necessity for such Round.[41] If a new Round were to be launched, the EC would refuse to discuss the end of subsidies to agricultural programmes, because it would imply the end of the Common Agricultural Policy (CAP).[42] The EC was not sure about the introduction of services and they shared the LDCs point of view that studies should be conducted. Diplomats have suggested that there was an informal agreement between Brazil and the EC. Brazil and India would not press for the end of the subsidies in agriculture and the EC would not press for trade liberalization in services.[43] The EC was lukewarm on the prospects of liberalization in a sector it did not know well.[44]

At the end of the Ministerial Meeting, the US proposed a compromise. The countries interested in discussing services would prepare national stud-ies on the subject. They could exchange information through the GATT or through any relevant international organizations. This was a concession by the US to the LDCs, who wanted to discuss services within UNCTAD and not in the GATT. The EC, on the other hand, agreed to study the issue of subsidies on agricultural products and a committee was created in the GATT to work with the aim of liberalizing trade in agricultural products.[45] One of the priorities of the US, the end of export subsidies for agricultural products in the EC (CAP), would be very difficult to achieve. However, the creation of a study group in that area would be considered a step forward by the US. The second priority of the US, to include the new issues, would require strong diplomatic efforts.[46] Moreover, the US could argue that the inclusion of services in a study group announced by the Declaration would point to the fact that GATT would be in charge of it.

The US also wanted to liberalize trade in the LDCs. With this goal, it launched the Brock Initiative, which was based on an exchange of concessions. The LDCs would open their markets and in exchange the US would commit itself to keeping its system of preferences intact and not adopting the system of graduation. The US had no illusions on the issue of liberalization in the LDCs and it expected results in the long term. Another goal of the US was the adoption of a safeguards option. This would conclude the negotiations begun in the Tokyo Round. These proposals would make up the US position on GATT reform.[47]

The Ministerial Meeting: main results

The views of the US and of the LDCs were not compatible, at least in the short term. This explains the weak results of the 1982 Ministerial Meeting, and also the watered-down Declaration. In agriculture there was a convergence of views between the US proposals and the LDCs goals, but they faced strong opposition from the EC. The result was the creation of a committee, the GATT Committee on Trade and Agriculture, to study market access, agricultural subsidies, and exceptions to or infringements of, the GATT rules in the agricultural sector. This committee would recommend measures to liberalize agricultural trade.

On services, the GATT Ministerial Declaration suggested national studies on the issue. The 1984 Session would discuss if multilateral action should be undertaken in that area. The Declaration mentioned that a study of world trade in textiles would be carried out in order to analyze the possibility of applying GATT rules to that sector. On safeguards, it was agreed that a code would be adopted by the contracting parties not later than their 1983 Session. On the issue of market access, the contracting parties created a group to study all quantitative restrictions and other NTBs which prevented the circulation of goods, in particular exports from LDCs.[48]

The Declaration is open to two interpretations. The first is a literal one: only what the Meeting achieved at that time would be considered. From this perspective, the Meeting achieved nothing concrete. As a result, it was an absolute failure. This was the view adopted by Australia, which refused to sign the final Declaration, considering it meaningless.[49]

However, another view can be adopted. If one considers not what was achieved at the Meeting, but the momentum it created, the Meeting was not a complete failure. In this perspective the 1982 Ministerial Meeting can be seen as a first step towards the launching of a new Round. Even in the discussions on services, by far the most controversial issue, together with agricultural subsidies, the 1982 Declaration is seen by some authors as a starting point and a first step towards eventual multilateral action.[50]

In any case, the frustration due to the high expectations generated by the 1982 Declaration weakened the stature of GATT and stepped up pressures on the GATT system to produce results.[51] In this context the defensive position adopted by Brazil and by other LDCs led to a paralysis of the Decision-Making Process (DMP) in the Ministerial Meeting and subsequent meetings.[52] It meant that the major powers were not capable of imposing their own goals on other States. One should also not forget that the LDCs were coordinating their positions within two coalitions; the Group of 77 (G-77) in UNCTAD and the G-10 in the GATT. It is clear that the lack of consensus among DCs increased the ability of the influential LDCs, such as Brazil and India, to play a defensive role at the 1982 Ministerial Meeting.

Indeed, an important conclusion that can be drawn from the Ministerial Meeting is that when the main players in the GATT - the US and the EC - do not share the same view of what should be done, the likelihood of a consensus expressed in a final Declaration is very low, as the commitment on agricultural subsidies illustrates. The lack of consensus among the US and the EC decreases the possibility that one of them might behave as an initiator. The existence of a coherent opposition by other parties which are not as powerful but are well-organized can prevent the main players from behaving as initiators.

This confirms the hypothesis that a lack of agreement between the main players increases the bargaining power of LDCs. Aho and Aronson also suggested that the negotiation of services did not flourish due to the opposition of LDCs.[53] Thus, the 1982 Meeting is a clear example of the negative influence of Brazil and India who led the LDCs in opposition to the launching of the new Round and to the inclusion of services.[54] However, there were also some positive contributions from Brazil in the 1982 Ministerial Meeting. Brazil insisted that the DCs should make their trade practices conform to the GATT rules. Brazil wanted the end of subsidies for agricultural exports and the abolition of NTBs. Brazil also supported the end of the MFA and the liberalization of trade in tropical products.

Some authors have suggested that the US took advantage of Brazil's difficult financial situation in order to include services at the end of the 1982 Ministerial Meeting.[55] According to this view, Brazil would have accepted debt relief from the US Treasury in exchange for allowing the study on services. British newspapers also suggested that Brazil supported the inclusion of a study of services in the 1982 Declaration in exchange for loans from the US Treasury. They also suggested that the US would press the IMF to support a financial agreement with Brazil.[56]

However, Brazil believed that it could ignore the *communiqué* released in the Ministerial Meeting and not prepare a study on services. One should note that the US had made it clear that if no compromise was achieved, it would discuss services in other fora with like-minded countries. Brazil took this threat seriously, even if it was of difficult implementation.

During the negotiations on services, of which the 1982 Ministerial Meeting was only the start, Brazil was aware that there are limits to the influence of LDCs. The goal of regulation of trade in services became a central issue of the US foreign economic policy in the 1980s. Thus, a compromise would have to be achieved. The alternative would be a breakdown of the GATT.

GATT officials believed that Brazil and India's intransigence in refusing to include services in the new Round almost led to the breakdown of the GATT, such was the influence of these countries in the negotiations. Indeed, some authors consider that Brazil, India, Argentina and Indonesia and a few other middle-level powers tended to be the most influential countries in the GATT negotiations.[57]

The fortieth session of the GATT (November 1984)

Context

After 1982, Brazil and India blocked all attempts to discuss services in the GATT until the 1984 meeting. In 1983, the US sought to organize an informal discussion in the GATT concerning which aspects of services should be included in the national studies allowed by the 1982 Ministerial Declaration. Brazil and India led a procedural struggle over the use of the GATT facilities, the attendance of members of the GATT Secretariat, and later the preparation of minutes. The disputes continued through 1983 and 1984 and included the exchange of views on national studies.[58] This illustrates the climate which prevailed in the GATT over services.

After 1982 Brazil tried to increase the role played by other international and regional organizations. In 1982, Brazil supported decision 250 of the Trade and Development Board (XXIV Session) of UNCTAD. This decision stipulated that when dealing with issues related to protectionism and trade, attention should be given to the sector of services.[59]

The G-77, with the support of Brazil and India, sponsored a discussion on services through the Guatemala meeting on services in trade in January 1983. At the V Ministerial Meeting of the G-77 in Buenos Aires (28th March to 19th April 1983), the LDCs examined the issue of services. At this meeting LDCs pressed for UNCTAD to be given charge of analyzing the importance of services to LDCs. It was suggested that UNCTAD should establish a programme which envisaged multilateral cooperation among LDCs and a greater participation of LDCs in international transactions in services. The effort was linked to the attempt by Brazil to take the discussion on services outside the GATT.

In UNCTAD VI in Belgrade (June 1983) the issue was raised again under item 10 of the agenda, which mentioned issues in the area of international trade in foods and services. In spite of the failure of UNCTAD at Belgrade,[60] Itamaraty insisted that UNCTAD was the right place to discuss services.

Brazil proposed discussing the issue within the Trade and Development Board (TDB) Sessions of 1984, which resulted in Resolution 286 (XXVIII Session) on 6 April 1984. This Resolution reaffirmed Resolution 250 of the TDB in which the service sector would be emphasized.[61] In its XXIX Session the TDB would suggest further work for UNCTAD in this field.

The political activism of Brazil on services did not limit itself only to UNCTAD, the G-77 or the Trade and Development Board. Brazil also involved other organizations, such as the United Nations Economic Commission for Latin America (ECLA), in parallel discussion on services.[62] However, the most important political action by Brazil relating to the discussion on services in the GATT was the Latin American Economic Conference held by Heads of States in Quito, Ecuador, in January 1984. At this meeting, Latin American and Caribbean countries confirmed decision 153 of the Latin American Council which established a concerted position concerning discussions on services in international organizations or other multilateral fora.[63]

In May 1984, the LDCs released a joint paper questioning the credibility of a new Round without any progress on the studies being carried out in GATT, which included agriculture, safeguards, dispute settlement, services, and S&D to LDCs.[64] This first step in the coordination of efforts by Brazil in support of its position against a new Round, or against the inclusion of services, occurred in May 1984.

Itamaraty was also supportive of the Latin American Economic System (SELA), of which Brazil was one of the founding members. Created to support Latin American countries against "foreign economic aggression", this group sponsored a meeting in August 1984 to set a common position of Latin American countries on the discussion of service issues promoted by UNCTAD in September 1984 and by GATT in November 1984. However, until 1984 Brazil had not presented its studies to UNCTAD. Thus, when the UNCTAD report was published in 1985, Brazil was not among the 29 countries which answered UNCTAD's questionnaire.[65] It should be pointed out that the illusions of Itamaraty about UNCTAD were not widely shared even in Brazil. Some diplomats from Itamaraty had warned that UNCTAD meetings were too superficial.[66] Now, we should examine what was happening in the US.

The New protectionism and its origins[67]

Some authors consider that the recent drift towards the new protectionism represents a serious threat to world welfare.[68] However, the protectionist pressures in the 1970s and 1980s had a different characteristic from protectionist pressures in the 1930s. Firstly, it was the different international political context. In the 1930s, great powers had different approaches to trade policies. In the 1980s, although it could be argued that there were still different approaches between DCs, after the war there was a basic consensus that free-trade is better than protectionism.[69]

A second main difference among protectionism and the new-protectionism is that the first referred to tariffs, and the second refers to the Non-Tariff Barriers (NTBs), Quotas, and Voluntary Export Restraints (VERs). Finally, the main aspect of the new-protectionism is the shifting in comparative advantages.[70] In brief, this occurs due to changes in knowledge and technology. Low technology products which were produced in DCs started to be manufactured in LDCs. High levels of unemployment in the

1970s generated increased pressure for protection.[71] The fact that the GATT already provided escape clauses in its text[72] gave its members the possibility of limiting imports without adopting formally protectionist measures.

The pressures from special interests in DCs found fertile ground in which to flourish due to the interaction of several factors. The above mentioned shift in comparative advantage from DCs to LDCs, the breakdown of the Bretton Woods agreement in 1971, the macroeconomic instability of the 1970s, the oil crisis (in 1974 and in 1979) and the changes in the world market structure.[73] The increased exports of manufactured goods from LDCs, and in particular from the so-called NICs.[74] This had a specially strong effect in the US and Canada,[75] which had relatively open markets[76] while the EC could use the fact that it was trying to build an internal market to 'select' its imports. The success of the LDCs in increasing their exports of manufactured goods made them very easily identifiable as the enemy.[77]

During the Carter Administration (1976-1980), the level of intervention of the state accelerated at an alarming pace, and hardly an industry which asked Carter for protectionist assistance had to walk away empty-handed.[78] Reagan, who supported free-trade, believed that this trend should be stopped. A new Round which included new issue, could halt the protectionist trends, and the protectionist lobby in Congress, and give a boost to US exports of services, since there was a shared belief that the US had a comparative advantage in services.[79] However, to include services in the new Round it was necessary for the US to achieve a consensus in the GATT. The US already had support from Canada and Japan. The EC opposed including services in the new Round on the grounds that the sector was too large and difficult to define.[80]

The 40th Session of the GATT's Contracting Parties should be seen, therefore, within this effort carried out by DC and in particular by the US government to decrease the influence of special interests in favour of protectionism[81] and to try to forge a 'new consensus' in favour of free-trade, now with support of the service industries.

The fortieth session of the GATT: main developments

The 40th Session of the GATT, in November 1984, discussed national studies of the service sector of 13 countries.[82] These countries presented studies on the importance of the service sector to their economies. Brazil refused to present its study. Belgium, Australia, and France presented their studies in the second half of 1984. Although most LDCs did not present their studies of services in their economies, they made their position clear.[83]

First, LDCs stressed that services either in DCs or in LDCs were a very heterogenous sector of the economy. Second, the classifications and definitions of what activities could be considered as services differed in several aspects. Third, there was no definition of services that was widely accepted. Fourth, goods and services were so linked that it was difficult to say where the service sector started. Sometimes one service sector mixed with another service sector. Fifth, due to these different classifications and technical difficulties, the statistics on services were not reliable. Even if they were reliable, they could not be comparable across several countries. Sixth, what was considered to be a private service in one country may be part of the public sector in another. The ownership of services changed according to the political and economic system, and also due to social demands and interests. Moreover, some common features should be found between several service sectors in order to allow a comparison between different countries. Thus, Brazil pointed out that while these technical difficulties had not been overcome, it could not discuss whether multilateral action was possible.[84]

DCs challenged the arguments of the LDCs on many grounds. Firstly, a definition of services depends on the goal that is being pursued. Secondly, the non-existence of harmonized definition of services did not prevent a discussion about the convenience of multilateral action in that sector. Thirdly, the national studies and the exchange of information carried out by the GATT secretariat could allow standardization of the different statistics and data from different countries. At the end of these studies, a common definition could be found.[85] Indeed, the studies carried out by the GATT included features of the service sector; a conceptual framework; statistical problems; and national and international regulations governing some service sectors. Also, without taking sides on the political aspects of the discussions, they mentioned the problems identified in relation to international transactions in services and issues raised in connection with multilateral action on services.

However, Brazil and India were not interested in listening to these arguments. They continued the blocking strategy.[86] Ambassador Paulo Batista[87] opposed the inclusion of services in the new Round on three different grounds. At an economic level, Brazil argued that the theory of comparative advantage could not be applied to services. At a legal level, Brazil maintained that GATT does not cover trade in invisible goods, such as services, but only visible trade. Besides, Brazil also maintained that, at a political level, services should be controlled by national citizens for security and cultural reasons.[88] Brazil also argued that there was already an international organization, the World Intellectual Property Organization (WIPO), specifically dealing with issues that DCs suggested should be tackled by the GATT.

Furthermore, Brazil used the 1984 meeting of the GATT to concentrate on the problems of the LDCs, the GATT should discuss trade and its linkage to other issues such as finance. This created a North-South polarization in the GATT, as had already happened in UNCTAD. Brazil argued that the DCs had not fulfilled the promises made in the 1982 Meeting towards LDCs. In fact, in 1984 Brazil and India adopted a similar hard-line position to that they had adopted in 1982. They blocked the discussions on services in the GATT, arguing that it was not the right forum to discuss the issue.[89] Brazil publicly criticized the US insistence on including services in the GATT as exceeding the mandate given by the 1982 GATT Ministerial Meeting. However, Batista denied that services were being used as a North-South issue.

The answer of the US delegation to this blocking strategy was that unless services were included in the agenda of the GATT through a formal Group of Studies, the US would withhold its contributions to the GATT budget, more than 14% of the total. As a result of this disagreement about the role of services in the GATT, one day of the Sessions of the GATT had to be cancelled. However, the proposal of the US to establish a group of studies on trade in services was rejected by Brazil and India. At the end of the GATT Session a compromise was reached. The Chairman of the GATT Council, Felipe Jaramillo, proposed that GATT members move to set up formal meetings to exchange information about services and trade in counterfeit goods. This was already envisaged by the 1982 Declaration. Moreover, the US delegation managed to include in the agenda of the 1985 Session of GATT a discussion on the convenience of a Round including services. After the removal of the deadlock, the GATT budget for 1985 could be approved.[90]

The results of the fortieth session of the GATT: November 1984

At the end of the 40th Session, a consensus was not reached on the inclusion of services in a new Round.[91] It was only after a threat by the US to withhold its contribution to the GATT and to withdraw its preferences to LDCs that a compromise was found. This fact was admitted by the GATT secretariat, which mentioned in its report of the 40th Session that it was not possible to achieve an agreement between LDCs and DCs on the inclusion of services in the GATT. Instead, the Contracting Parties adopted a compromise.[92]

First, the Chairman of the Contracting Parties would organize the exchange of information sought by the 1982 Ministerial Meeting based on a uniform format. Second, the GATT secretariat would provide the support necessary for the process. Third, the Chairman of the GATT would report to the members of the GATT on progress made. Fourth, the members of the GATT would review the results of the national studies at its next Session, in 1985, and consider whether multilateral action should be launched. Moreover, the Director-General of the GATT would also send a letter to 14 international organizations, including UNCTAD, requesting information on services.

Although it seems that the gap between the final agreement and the US proposal was minimal, to Brazil the difference was vital. The initial US proposal was to assume that services would be included in the GATT. Brazil's position of establishing an exchange of information about services limited GATT to a forum of debates. Furthermore, with the compromise to continue the exchange of information and to postpone until 1985 the question whether services should be included in the next Round, Brazil achieved at least four political victories.

First, Brazil created a cohesive and distinct block of Third World countries in the GATT.[93] Moreover, Brazil and India managed to postpone the launching of a new Round for at least one year, without taking any position on the issue. They demonstrated that they could depend on the support of the G-10. Indeed, the G-10 managed in 1982, and again in 1984, to achieve what had seemed impossible: to block the US proposal to launch a new Round which included services.

Another victory by Brazil and India was to transform the issue of services into a North-South divide. This assured some support from other LDCs even though they were not sure about the issue, but decided to follow the leadership of Brazil and India. However, this victory of Brazil and India would not last long. The dispute was just starting and the US wanted to re-establish its leadership in world affairs, including trade issues.

Nevertheless, Brazil had other plans which differed from the agreed conclusions of the GATT. Brazil approved a protectionist law on Information Technologies (IT), which came into effect on 30 October 1984. The Law was the Brazilian answer to the attempt by DCs to widen the scope of the GATT to include services. The 1984 Law on IT covered not only micro-computers, but also data processing and telecommunications. This was a signal by Brazil to other countries that it believed that the opening up of its service sector to foreign firms was out of the question.

GATT Meetings during 1985

Context

The climate for negotiations at the 41st Session of the GATT could not have been worse. The US was not satisfied with the outcome of the last Session in November 1984. The US felt that Brazil and India were trying to reduce the GATT to the same kind of confrontational and blocking politics they used in the UNCTAD, and the US decided not to allow this. Therefore, from the beginning of the meetings, the US decided to adopt confrontational tactics. The US Trade Representative Clayton Yeutter, stated that: "We simply cannot afford to have a handful of countries, responsible for 5% of World Trade, dictate the destiny of a large number of countries who deal with 95% of that trade".[94]

The US also threatened to withdraw its tariff preferences to LDCs if they continued to block the inclusion of services in the new Round.[95] It was in this climate that the discussions over the inclusion of services in the new Round started. In fact, its fate had already been sealed. By the time that the important discussions in the 41st Session of the GATT started, the US had already obtained full support from all DCs, including the EC which had been undecided at the beginning of the process.[96]

Furthermore, the US started to adopt a policy of "divide and rule", negotiating with moderate LDCs for an acceptable compromise, alienating Brazil and India - "the radicals" - in the process. This is a very interesting development, because the US was trying to find other LDCs to replace Brazil and India as spokesmen for the LDCs. This new policy of the US in the GATT would undergo its main test during the GATT Meetings of 1985.

During 1985, eight meetings were held to exchange information on issues in the services sector.[97] They started in January and went on till November 1985.[98] The aim of these meetings was to summarize the studies conducted by the contracting parties interested in discussing services, up to the 41st Session. The issue of services was also discussed by the CG-18. In its report to the 41st Session, the CG-18 noted the erosion of the multilateral trade system and mentioned the different perspectives which prevailed among DCs and LDCs.[99] The main point of this report was that the LDCs would accept the launch of a new Round if it was restricted to goods. However, the US considered that this would not be sufficient to launch a new Round. Thus, no consensus was achieved on which issues should be included in a new Round.[100]

Brazil and India used these meetings to try to demonstrate that it was impossible to apply the GATT principles to services, and that other organizations were already competent to deal with them.[101] In fact, the LDCs were employing the same tactics already used in UNCTAD. It was in this climate that the discussions on the inclusion of services in the new Round began. The negotiations in 1985 started in an atmosphere of division between DCs and LDCs. Moreover, the process of the erosion of confidence in the trade regime continued, due to the deterioration in the observance and, thus, the efficiency of GATT discipline, as the CG-18 admitted.[102] Nevertheless, the international economic context was more promising. Since 1982, there had been a steady recovery in the DCs. This helped Brazil to increase its exports. As a result, its financial situation in 1985 was not as bad as it had been in 1982. This increased Brazil's bargaining power in that it did not depend as much as it had in 1982 and 1983 on foreign loans. Although it continued to negotiate a stabilization programme with the IMF, the situation was more favourable to Brazil.

Brazil's financial situation in 1982 could be summarized as follows: Brazilian reserves were negative at a critical level of $553 million. Since then, they had increased to reach $5.6 billion in 1985.[103] Brazil's trade situation had also presented some improvements. In 1981, Brazil had a surplus of only $1.2 billion in its trade balance. With a low level of reserves and a poor trade performance in 1981, Brazil was not ready for the increase in US interest rates, as the 1982 debt crisis illustrated.

However, at the end of 1984 and the beginning of 1985, the situation had undergone significant changes. Indeed, since 1982 Brazil had adopted a policy of mega-surplus and it achieved a surplus of $13.1 billion in 1984. This contributed to the improvement in Brazil's situation, and, as a result, its bargaining power increased. Thus, one could say that during the GATT negotiations of 1985 Brazil was in a better situation than it had been during the 1982 Meeting when Brazil declared default on its foreign debt.

Furthermore, as Brazil was not enthusiastic about a new Round, time was on Brazil's side. As a result, Batista continued to block any relevant decision on services, as he had done in 1984. Brazil's strategy was openly obstructionist in this period and was maintained for as long as possible.[104] However, it had a high political cost for Brazil since it isolated Itamaraty from other moderate LDCs. As a result, the cohesiveness of the LDCs at the GATT suffered serious rupture. The G-77 became less cohesive, active and vocal as there were growing tensions inside it.[105]

Developments in 1985

During 1985 Brazil's position was that a new Round was not necessary. The first task should be to implement the work proposed by the Tokyo Round. This included tariff concessions (in tropical products) to LDCs, agreed by the Tokyo Round, but never implemented. Moreover, Brazil felt that there were some areas which were not covered by the GATT, such as textiles (MFA) and agriculture, where there was considerable work to be done.[106]

Nevertheless, Brazil would support a new Round if its objectives included the end of the protectionist measures and the opening of markets of DCs. Brazil also encouraged discussions on commodities such as sugar, where several protectionist regimes remained. As a result, Brazil and India led the LDCs against the new Round. They would oppose a new Round if it concentrated on trade in services or in high technologies. However, it was more difficult for them to resist the pressure for a new Round.[107]

Japan and the US persuaded the EC to support the new Round, despite opposition from France and Italy. The EC accepted the two main demands from the US: the inclusion of cereal exports and services in the discussions.[108]

The first step by Brazil to influence the new Round occurred in January 1985, when a group of 23 LDCs drew up a list of subjects they would like to see included in a new Round.[109] Services were excluded from it. These pre-conditions included a commitment by DCs to roll back protectionist measures inconsistent with GATT rules and a promise not to adopt new protectionist measures. The 23 LDCs also required an increase in access to the markets of DCs. This meant that DCs should reduce their trade barriers to products from LDCs. The point of view of these 23 LDCs was expressed on 7 June 1985 in a statement made by the Indian Ambassador, on behalf of the 23 LDCs.[110]

The negotiations seemed to have made some progress in June, during an informal meeting of trade ministers, hosted by Sweden, in Stockholm. At this meeting Brazil's Minister of Foreign Affairs, Setúbal, supported a moderate position and accepted a new Round. Trade Ministers accepted that services could be discussed if negotiations were carried out separately from goods, following the principle of parallel but separate negotiations.[111]

However, these discussions should take place in a forum different from the GATT. Discussions on liberalizing trade in goods could start simultaneously.[112] Contributing to this change in Brazil's position was the US threat of signing bilateral agreements with like-minded countries. The US was already holding talks with Canada, Israel and with ASEAN countries. The US threatened to create a Super-GATT, which would include countries ready to discuss liberalization in services.

Setúbal proposed the twin-track approach and had the support of 23 LDCs. It meant that the talks on services would be conducted by a different set of negotiations from those involved in the GATT talks on goods. Brazil proposed UNCTAD as a forum. The US rejected this suggestion. Setúbal pointed out that GATT rules would not apply in the negotiations on services and reaffirmed a roll-back of protectionist measures and a standstill by DCs as its pre-conditions for starting negotiations on services.[113]

Brazil's position was confirmed during the meeting of the CG-18. However, the US rejected the Brazilian twin-track proposal and insisted that both negotiations on goods and services should be conducted under the umbrella of the GATT. The pre-conditions were also rejected. As a result of these irreconcilable positions, the meeting of the CG-18 finished without any agreement.[114]

Batista decided to radicalize his position again. This was apparent when the GATT Council met on 17 July 1985 to discuss the preparation of a new Round During the meeting the EC presented a draft calling for a meeting on 9 September of senior officials to prepare a new Round including goods and services. Batista presented a resolution proposing a meeting of seven officials in September, to discuss the possibilities of a Round of talks on goods. In October, another group of officials would meet to discuss trade in services. There would be no linkage between the two discussions.[115]

Batista 'clarified' Brazil's previous position in favour of negotiations on services outside the GATT and stated that some countries had submitted proposals to discuss issues which were alien to the competence of the GATT, that is services. In another, Batista was even more specific and stated that it could not accept the discussions of the new issues, such as services, outside the specific confines adopted by the Ministerial Meeting of 1982 and reaffirmed by the contracting parties in 1984.[116] Again it was not possible to find a consensus between the position of Brazil, and that of the DCs. Batista refused all compromise proposals from the US including one which stated that participation in preliminary talks would not commit a country. The US proposal was very specific and suggested that all the GATT principles and concepts should be applied to negotiations on services straightaway, which Brazil considered impracticable.[117]

The postal ballot and the 4th special session (30/09 to 02/10)

As a result of the deadlock, there were few options available to the US calling for a new Round. If the US kept negotiating under GATT rules, it would have to make concessions to Brazil and India, since the GATT decisions were traditionally taken by consensus.

There was an alternative, however. Any Contracting Party could call a Special Session of the GATT if it had the support of a majority of its members. It means that for such a Session to be held the minimum of 46 of the GATT members (90 in all) would have to support it. The US enquired if it would have the support of enough members in order to secure the minimum required.

As a result, the US started a marathon of meetings and private consultations to ascertain the position of each country in the GATT and to find out if it had sufficient support. Votes counted and checked, the US concluded that it had the support of the European countries, of the LDCs of the Pacific Rim and of most Latin American countries. When the US was convinced that it could achieve the majority of votes, it concluded that it was better to call a Special Session of the GATT to establish an agenda for the new Round, than to face the delaying tactics of Brazil and India. When the US called the Special Session it felt sure that it had obtained the required votes, because no one was going to press for a vote simply to demonstrate that they could be voted down.[118]

After the US's success in the postal ballot, the 4th Special Session of the GATT was convened. The US obtained an important victory during this Special Session, which took place between the end of September and the beginning of October, 1985, when the proposal that the issue of services should be included on the agenda was approved by a sufficient majority.

An unexpected development of the Special Session was that the French did not have instructions from their government to support the establishment of a Preparatory Committee. Thus, it was necessary to effect numerous consultations between Geneva and Paris in order to harmonize the position of the EC.

DCs agreed on an agenda for the new Round, but Brazil rejected the final text. It was then agreed during the Special Session that a Senior Officials Group (SOG) would meet in October to discuss procedures for the launching of the Round. The SOG group would report to the annual meeting of the GATT in November.[119]

The consequence of this US victory cannot be underestimated. Only three times before in its almost forty years of existence had a Special Session been convened by the GATT. The US showed that it did exercise leadership in the GATT. The prospects of a new Round were also revived and it increased the possibilities of including services in the negotiations, with or without the support of the group of Brazil and India. Finally, it showed that there was a clear majority of countries in the GATT, including LDCs, who believed that trade liberalization was more important than the issue of inclusion of services in the trade negotiations. As a result, the US President could demonstrate to Congress that the fight for free-trade was not lost. Thus, it could try to limit the actions of the protectionist lobby there.

The Protectionism in the US

Due to the depth of the recession of 1982, the pressure for protectionism in the US increased substantially. Some authors consider that those pressures had no precedent in the post-war era.[120] The protectionist pressures came from most domestic producers, but in particular from those who were not well prepared to face foreign competition. This seems to be the case for the textiles and clothing sector. This apparent inability to face international competitors can be traced to different factors. First, some industrial sectors do not invest in innovation, and their methods of production or their products become obsolete. Second, low productivity, strong unions, or unskilled workers may give international competitors an advantage, if they have a modern industry. Third, the existence of countries where certain goods can be produced at lower labour costs means that domestic producers cannot compete with such countries. In any of the three cases, the likely result in the absence of protection is structural change in the industry, loss of jobs or both.

However, this process does not occur smoothly. The association of domestic producers facing external competition joined forces to demand protection for their industries from Congress. At the same time, unions also demanded protection from Congress (the imposition of tariffs) to protect their members. Sometimes such lobbies caused an irresistible pressure in the US Congress, since the groups, such as unions who want protection, are, in general better organized than groups who benefit from free-trade, such as consumers. This generates pressure for protectionist legislation.

In years of recession the pressure on Congress to adopt protectionist measures increases. This was reflected in the US position to include services in the GATT to widen domestic US support for free-trade. Indeed, the domestic lobby in services wanted to include it in the GATT and worked as a counterweight to the domestic special interests in specific fields (viz., textiles), which were against the liberalization of the US markets to imports.

The Senior Official Group (SOG)

The SOG was agreed during the 4th Special Session which met during the month of October to discuss the launching of a new Round.[121] The objectives of the SOG were to examine the prospective multilateral trade negotiations and their modalities according to the Ministerial Declaration of 1982 and changes in the trade environment since then, in order to ensure that the GATT was responsive to these changes.[122]

The SOG Meetings began by reviewing the objectives of future multilateral trade negotiations. These included: the strengthening of GATT principles and the credibility of GATT's legal framework as a whole, expansion and liberalization of trade, and implementation of the Ministerial Work Programme of 1982. The SOG discussed the implementation of commitments agreed in the 1982 Ministerial Declaration, such as standstill and roll-back measures. Moreover, the SOG also considered how to include S&D treatment to LDCs and how to stimulate these countries to make efforts to liberalize. The SOG would also focus on more polemical topics, such as whether or not to include services in any future negotiations.

Indeed, during the meetings of the SOG in October and part of November, the DCs - read the US, Japan and the EC - stepped up pressure for the launch of a new Round, and insisted on an immediate inclusion of services. This was not acceptable to Brazil and India who blocked agreement in the Group. Thus, there was no agreement in its final report, as its rapporteur sadly noted.[123] Therefore, no compromise was reached and due to this divergence of views, the US threatened to launch a new Round of negotiations outside GATT's framework. The US government considered that Brazil and India were adopting obstructionist tactics and were blocking the launching of the new Round of trade talks. This was basically true.[124]

If negotiations on services were launched outside GATT rules, the countries which refused to take part in them, such as Brazil and India, would not receive the benefits of the negotiations. The US government also threatened to exclude Brazil and India from the General System of Preferences (GSP). Other countries which could have been excluded from the GSP were Yugoslavia, Egypt, Angola, and Argentina. The GSP was very important for Brazil and the threats by the US to exclude it were taken seriously and were a powerful argument in convincing Brazilian diplomats on several occasions.[125] The threats of the US were also a way of trying to soften the position of LDCs before the meeting of GATT on 25 November. Before agreeing on a new Round, Brazil and India wanted guarantees that the agreements established, such as the Declaration of the 1982 Ministerial Meeting, would be respected.[126]

Basically, Brazil and India wanted guarantees from the DCs in four areas.[127] Firstly, no rules would be adopted to restrict imports from LDCs which did not conform to GATT rules. Secondly, all the existing restrictions in the DCs inconsistent with GATT rules would be eliminated on a short term basis. Thirdly, the protection of industries in DCs ("safeguards") would be subject to strict rules which would be applied in a non-discriminatory way - and not selectively as was the case. Fourthly, Brazil and India wanted to ensure that preferential treatment, such as GSP, would not be used again as a bargaining chip by DCs.[128]

The 41st GATT session (November Meeting)

As these conditions had already been basically accepted in November 1985 during the Meeting of the Contracting Parties, the EC, Brazil, India, South Korea, and Switzerland agreed that a Preparatory Committee would be charged with organizing the procedures for and the issues of the new talks, without pre-conditions on the subject of the discussions. In return for this concession, Brazil and India secured the guarantee that any country which wanted to be excluded from the negotiations on services would be allowed to do so. The agreement established that a new Round would be launched in September 1986.[129]

Nevertheless, the agreement was too vague, and did not specify the inclusion of services in the new Round. The formula arranged allowed a Preparatory Committee to be created without mentioning the issue of services. Therefore, Brazil and India could still claim - as they did - at the end of the work of the Preparatory Committee that services were not part of GATT's framework.[130]

In spite of this different interpretation of the agreement, in September 1986 there was a Ministerial Meeting where a new Round was expected to be launched. Between the GATT Session of 25 November 1985 and the 1986 Ministerial Meeting a compromise had to be found. The place for this compromise was the Preparatory Committee. Nevertheless, in December 1985 Brazil and other LDCs met in New Delhi to coordinate their positions in the Preparatory Committee and in the new Round of talks. The main conclusion of the meeting was that services should be excluded from the new global trade negotiations.

An overview of Brazil in the GATT in the 1980s

From the preparation of the Ministerial Meeting of 1982 to the 41st Session of the GATT in November 1985 Brazil maintained the same position on services in the GATT.[131] Initially, Brazil refused to discuss the inclusion of services in the GATT. One should realize, however, that Brazil was exercising a maximalist position which was not compatible with either its economic, or political power. Indeed, although Brazil had a large economy - one of the twenty largest in the world - its foreign trade represented little more than 1% of world trade. Furthermore, the debt crisis of 1982 had badly affected Brazil's financial situation. A higher proportion of Brazil's export surplus had to be used to service foreign debt. It also increased its vulnerability to OECD countries. Indeed, Brazil was dependent on the goodwill of OECD, and in particular of the US, to obtain a comprehensive agreement from the IMF. Brazil also sought support from the World Bank and from the Paris Club. In both cases a good relationship with OECD countries was a condition *sine qua non* to obtain loans.

In the political sphere the situation was not much better. Brazil and India were influential leaders of the G-77. However, the G-77 was divided on whether to include services within the GATT. Some LDCs, such as South Korea, Thailand, Malaysia, Singapore and Taiwan, made it clear that the issue of the inclusion of services in the GATT was not crucial to them. Therefore, they would not confront the DCs because of services. Although some Asian countries - such as South Korea - had protective practices in some areas of the service sector (viz. banking and insurance), they would be ready to make concessions if this would mean an opening of markets to their competitive exports.

Brazil took advantage of the consensus mechanism operating in the GATT to block any decision on the inclusion of services in GATT's framework. Brazil also benefited in its confrontation on the issue of services by way of its prominent position in the influential Consultative Group of Eighteen (CG-18). This position, as has been stressed throughout this chapter, was a result of the "infiltration period" during which Brazil tried and succeeded in obtaining access to key positions in the GATT structure. The CG-18 is the best example, other examples are: the Chairmanship of the Trade and Development Committee (in 1972), the Chairmanship of the Council of Representatives (in 1975) and the Chairmanship of the Contracting Parties (in 1976).

In 1979, however, a rupture in Brazil's attitude towards GATT seemed to have occurred. In that year, Brazil made public its dissatisfaction with the international trading regime and with GATT in particular, in an article published by the Trade Policy Research Centre. The article - Brazil's proposal on GATT reform - was written by Brazil's Ambassador to the GATT, George Maciel, who had the full approval of the Brazilian government. It represented a revolution for the standards of Brazilian diplomacy which had been more used to behind the scenes agreements and discreet lobbying policies. Indeed, Brazil's negative position between 1982 and 1985, when the negotiations on the launch of the Uruguay Round were being carried out, reflected several aspects of Brazil's vocal attitude.

Firstly, Brazil made it clear that it wanted changes in the world trading system and in GATT in particular. Secondly, Brazil could no longer ignore the principles of GATT as it had done since 1948. Worst of all, GATT was probably there to stay, and Brazil would have to learn how to live with this fact. Thirdly, Brazil believed that if the GATT was there to stay it did not mean that it should solely serve the interests of DCs. Brazilian officials were convinced that they could turn the existence of a majority of LDCs in the GATT in its favour. In short, Brazil wanted to transform GATT into a new UNCTAD. To achieve this objective, however, it was necessary to test the strength of LDCs in the GATT. Brazil and India assumed that they could command a majority of LDCs in GATT as they did in UNCTAD.

Nevertheless, the decision by the US to call a Special Session of GATT in September/October 1985 showed that there was no majority to be commanded. In fact, Brazil had the support of few countries in Latin America, Asia or Africa. Moreover, it was clear that there was no clear alignment in GATT. Each country in GATT voted according to its particular interests.

Therefore, the insistence of Brazil in blocking the inclusion of services in GATT during the period 1982-1985 can only be explained by three factors. The first of these are ideological reasons (economic nationalism). The second is that although Brazil did not want the inclusion of services, it did want the discussion of market access for its products on the markets of DCs. In other words, Brazil wanted the end of protectionism in OECD countries in order to expand its exports and service its debt.

Thirdly, Brazil believed that the sudden opening of its service market, which corresponded to half its GDP, would be a disaster in terms of jobs and production. Fourthly, Brazil was aware that it had to work within the GATT. The alternative would be bilateral and multilateral agreements by the US from which Brazil would receive no advantage.

This explains why Brazil accepted an open agenda for the preparatory negotiations of the new Round. This was a face-saving formula adopted to reconcile the interests of both the US and Brazil. Although it showed that Brazil and India did not command a majority during the preparations for the new Round, it prevented Brazil from changing the principles of its trade policy. The first act of Brazil's battle against the inclusion of services in the discussions was finished, and Brazil and India had lost it.

It was hard for Brazil to accept that the ideological values on which it had based its economic growth since the Second World War, protectionism and ISI policies, had lost their importance. Brazil believed that its intransigence and hard-line positions were the best ways of defending its national interest and its security. However, the Meeting at Punta del Este was a lesson to Brazil. Not only would Brazil have to adapt its ideology and position in the GATT to fit the new realities, for example, that no country could isolate itself for too long a period of time; also there would be a new Round, which would include negotiations in services. Although these would be technically outside the GATT framework, it would be obvious that it would be linked to the GATT in many ways. The procedures were just one example. An eventual agreement on services would certainly lead to the liberalization of trade in services, which Brazil was not yet ready to accept.

Brazil also learnt that despite its significant influence in the GATT, it did not command a majority in the GATT, as it did, together with India, in UNCTAD. The attempt to bring the block politics of UNCTAD to GATT resulted in failure for Brazil. The formal separation between negotiations in services and goods did not guarantee that there would not be any trade-offs between these two fields. The compromise achieved at Punta del Este in separating these two sectors represented Brazil and India's political intention of not negotiating them together with goods, but has no legal or contractual value.

As a result, all the efforts of Brazil and India to block the negotiations on services in the GATT in order to discuss them in another forum were a waste of diplomatic effort by Brazil and represented a misunderstanding of how the GATT system works. Brazil was wrong when it thought it could use the same kind of bloc politics it used successfully in UNCTAD within the GATT. This also showed a misconception of GATT's purposes and negotiating procedures. This topic will be discussed in the next chapter.

Conclusions

This chapter concentrated on the preparations for the Uruguay Round. It focused on the discussion on whether to include or not the service sector in the Uruguay Round. As trade in services had not been included within the GATT originally, it became a 'new issue'. As a 'new issue' certainly it generated, as was to be the case, a political dispute, within which each country would try to influence the outcome of the negotiations. Basically, there were four main groups in this dispute. The first is the US, and DCs in general, who believed that they could gain in terms of trade liberalization in services.[132] The second main group included the G-10. This group was formed by countries who believed they had everything to lose and nothing to gain with trade liberalization in services. As a result, they were against the discussion of services either in the GATT or in the Uruguay Round, because in both cases trade liberalization in services was implicit, which they did not accept. There was a third group with contradictory positions. It included both LDCs which were supporters of trade liberalization of services and LDCs which believed that the multilateral trading system was at risk if it did not include trade in services, as the US wanted. Finally, there was a fourth group which did not support the trade liberalization of services but felt that a multilateral set of rules even in GATT was better than no rules at all, because they were vulnerable to pressure from the US (for example, South Korea).

The main point in this chapter is that Brazil maintained basically a coherent position in the GATT against the inclusion of services in the Uruguay Round. The main reasons mentioned by Brazil to explain its position against such inclusion was the fact that GATT had ignored old issues, such as agriculture and textiles, which had remained outside its reach. Batista supported the view that it was necessary first to bring this issue to the GATT before discussing the expansion of GATT to new issues, such as services.

Brazil was also convinced that it had nothing to gain from trade liberalization in services because it believed it had no comparative advantage in this sector. This belief was based on the personal perception of Brazil's main negotiator, Batista. It was not based on any concrete evidence, since Batista had refused to carry out the studies proposed in the Final Declaration of the 1982 Ministerial Meeting.

This is the most interesting aspect of the Brazilian position in the GATT against services. Brazil's representative in the GATT, Batista, never tried to learn what could be gained from trade liberalization in services. Even if one accepts that Brazil had no comparative advantage in any service sector, which is hard to believe, it does not imply that Brazil would not gain anything from trade liberalization.

This reinforces what is said in the last chapter about the role of the personality of the representative in the GATT in the outcome of the trade negotiations. Another proof of this fact is that Batista could have carried out studies at UNCTAD, but he refused to do so. As a result, he had to negotiate services without knowledge of its impact in the case of a sudden liberalization.

Another conclusion of this chapter refers to the Group that Brazil supported at the GATT, the G-10. The G-10 managed to block or obstruct the service discussions in the GATT for a period of almost five years, from the beginning of 1982 until the end of 1986. This illustrates the influence that some LDCs, such as Brazil and India, had in the GATT system.

End Notes

1. The discussions on the opportunity of creating a set of multilateral rules for services was already present in the International Trade Organization (ITO). However, the situation at that moment was inverted: the Less Developed Countries (LDCs) wanted multilateral rules against Restrictive Business Practice while the US was against them. A historical study on the inclusion of services in a multilateral trade organization is out of the scope of this book.

2. GATT, 1983, *GATT Activities in 1982*. Geneva, GATT. pp.7-8.

3. Ibid, p.8.

4. See: Oxley, A., 1990, *The Challenge of Free-Trade*. London, Harvester Wheatsheaf.

5. The international agreement in services would cover: banking and insurance, civil aviation and transborder data flows.

6. GATT, 1983, *BISD 1981-1982*. Geneva, GATT. pp.77-82.

7. GATT, 1983, *op.cit*, pp.24-25.

8. See: GATT, 1983, *BISD 1981-1982. 29th Suppl.* pp.9-22.

9. Lima, 1986, *The Political Economy of Brazil's Foreign Policy: Nuclear Energy, Trade and Itaipú*. Nashville, Vanderbilt University p.137, and Abreu, 1992, *O Brasil e o GATT*. Rio de Janeiro, PUC. p.19.

10. For an official view of the US position, see from the former US Trade Representative: Brock, W., 1982, "A Simple Plan for Negotiating on Trade in Services". In *The World Economy* 5 (3), pp. 229-240.

11. Coffield, S., 1984, "International Services-Trade Issues and the GATT, pp.70-71. In Rubin, S. & Graham, T. (eds.). *Managing Trade Relations in the 1980s*. Totowa (N.J.), Rowman & Allanheld.

12. See: Low, Patrick, pp.202-206, 1986, *Trading Free: The GATT and US Policy*. New York, Twenty Century Fund Press.

13. OECD, 1982, *World Economic Outlook, Historical Statistics (1960-1980)*, p.35.

14. GATT, 1989, *International Trade 1988-1989*, p.34.

15. GATT, 1989, *International Trade 1989-1989*. Geneva, GATT.

16. George Maciel was Brazil's Ambassador to the GATT until 1983. He was then replaced by Batista. See Chapter 1.

17. See also: Maciel, G., 1986, "O Brasil e o GATT". In *Contexto Internacional n.3*, Janeiro-Junho, pp.81-93, esp. p.83.

18. See: Maciel, 1986, *op.cit.*, pp.84-85.

19. See: Brazil.Itamaraty, 1983, *Relatório. 1982*. Brasilia, MRE.

20. Abreu, 1992, *op.cit.*, pp.19-20.

21. Abreu, 1992, *op.cit.*, p.19 and Maciel, 1986, *op.cit.*, p.84.

22. Abreu, 1992, *op.cit.*, p.20.

23. For details of the G-10, see Chapter 2.

24. The G-10 included Argentina, Brazil, Cuba, Egypt, India, Nicaragua, Nigeria, Peru, Tanzania, Yugoslavia.

25. On the importance of the CG-18, see: Low, P., 1993, *Trading Free: The GATT and US Trade Policy*, p.277. New York, The Twenty Century Fund Press. Note 2 (Chapter 9).

26. Confidential interview with a GATT official.

27. GATT, 1985, *BISD. 1984-1985. 32 Supp*.Geneva, GATT. pp.70-84.

28. Abreu, 1992, *op.cit.*, p.21.

29. *The Guardian*, 16/11/82.

30. Lima maintains that Brazil's position of supporting the studies weakened the LDCs coalition. I disagree. The G-10 coalition has always been a limited coalition. Lima, 1986, *op.cit.*, p.338.

31. See Rubin, S. & Graham, T. 1984, *op.cit.*, p.11.

32. See: Glick, L., 1984, *Multilateral Trade Negotiations. World Trade After the Tokyo Round*. Totowa (N.J.), Rowman & Allanheld. pp.152-154.

33. GATT, 1989, *International Trade 1988-1989*. Geneva, GATT. p.34.

34. IMF, 1991, *IFS Yearbook 1990*. Washington, IMF. p.732.

35. OECD, 1982, *World Economic Outlook. Historical Statistics (1960-1980)*. Paris, OECD. p.35.

36. GATT, 1989, *op.cit.*, p.23.

37. See: Winham, G., 1989, "The Pre-negotiation Phase of the Uruguay Round". In *International Journal* 44, pp.280-305.

38. Martone & Braga, 1988, *Brazil and the Uruguay Round*. São Paulo, USP. p.39.

39. See: Wolf, M., 1984, "Two Edged Sword: Demand of Developing Countries and the Trading System". In Bhagwatti, J. and Ruggie, G.(eds.). *Power, Passions and Purposes: Prospects for North-South Negotiations.* Cambridge, MIT.

40. See: *Le Monde* 5/11/82.

41. See: *Folha de São Paulo* 6/11/1982.

42. About the position of the EC, see: Wiener, J., 1994, *Making Rules for Agriculture in the Uruguay Round of the GATT. A study in International Leadership.* Canterbury, Kent University (PhD Thesis).

43. Confidential interview with a Brazilian Ambassador.

44. Martone & Braga, 1988, *op.cit.*, p.39.

45. GATT, 1983, *BISD. 1981-1982. 29Supp.* Geneva, GATT. pp.9-22.

46. See: Graham, 1984, *op.cit.*, p.11.

47. Glick, 1984, *op.cit*, pp.151-165.

48. TRIMs and high technology goods were not included in the Declaration. See: GATT, 1983, *BISD. 1981-1982. 29Supp.* Geneva, GATT. p.29.

49. Glick, 1984, *op.cit.*, p.162.

50. Krommenacker, 1988, "Multilateral Services Negotiations: From Interested Bilateralism to Reasoned Multilateralism in the Context of the Servicisation of the Economy". In Petersmann, E. & Mehiard, H. (ed.). *The New GATT Round of Multilateral Trade Negotiations: Legal and Economic Problems.* Dauntree (Hol.), Klewer Law and Taxation Publishers. Vol.5. p.457.

51. Glick, 1984, *op.cit.*, p.164.

52. Krommenacker, 1988, *op.cit.*, p.457.

53. Aho & Aronson, 1985, *op.cit.*, p.20.

54. Martone & Braga, 1988, *op.cit.*, p.39.

55. Schott & Mazda, 1986, "Trade in Services and Developing Countries" in *Journal of World Trade* 20 (3), pp. 253-273, p. 270.

56. *The Guardian.* 25/11/82.

57. Aho & Aronson, 1985, *op.cit.*, p.95.

58. Feketekuty, 1988, *op.cit.*, p.320.

59. UNCTAD, 1985c, *Services and the Development Process.*Geneva, UNCTAD. pp.1-3.

60. See Sachs, I., 1985, "Trade and Development: A Prospective View of UNCTAD". In Cutajar, M., *UNCTAD and the South-North Dialogue. The First Twenty Years.* (pp. 243-259). Pergamon, New York, p.243.

61. UNCTAD, 1985c, *op.cit.*, p.3.

62. UNCTAD, 1985, *op.cit.*, p.IX.

63. UNCTAD, 1985, *op.cit.*, p.69.

64. Finlayson & Weston, 1990, *Middle Powers in the International System.* Ottawa, North-South Institute, p.24.

65. UNCTAD, 1985c, *op.cit.*, p.4.

66. Maciel, who was the Head of Brazil's Delegation to UNCTAD III (Santiago:

1972), had reported to Itamaraty in 1972 that the discussions at UNCTAD were superficial. Confidential interview with another Brazilian Ambassador. The idea that UNCTAD had not achieved anything substantial was already circulating at Itamaraty in the 1970s. See also: Rothstein, R., 1979, *Global Bargaining. UNCTAD and the Quest for a New International Economic Order*. Princeton, Princeton University. p.181.

67. On New Protectionism, See: Greenway, D., 1983, *International Trade Policy From Tariffs to New-protectionism*. London & Basingstoke, The Macmillan Press; Lang, T. & Hines, C., 1993, *The New Protectionism. Protecting the Future Against Free-trade*. London, Earthscan Publications; Ball, J., 1987, *The Causes of Rising Protectionism*. London, British-North American Research Association; Low, P., 1990, *The GATT System in Transition: The Relevance of "Traditional" Issues*. Rio de Janeiro, PUC; Lieberman, S. 1988, *The Economic and Political Roots of the New Protectionism*. Totowa(NJ), Rowman & Littlefield; Lazar, F, 1983, *The New Protectionism. Non-Tariffs Barriers and their Effect on Canada*. Ontario, The Canadian Institute for Economic Policy Series; Krauss,M. 1979, *The New Protectionism. The Welfare State and International Trade*. Oxford, Basil Blackwell; Grilli, E. & Sassoon (eds.), 1990, *The New Protectionism Wave*. London, Macmillan; Greenway, D., Hine, R. O'Brien, A. Thornton, R. 1991, *Global Protectionism*. New York, St. Martins Press; Salvatore, D. (ed.), 1987, *The New Protectionism Threat to the World Welfare*. New York, North-Holland.

68. Salvatore, D.(ed.), 1987, *The New Protectionist Threat to World Welfare*. New York, Elsevier Science. p.21.

69. This does not mean, however, that protectionism has gone. Japan and the EU (ex-EC) still adopt protectionist measures.

70. See: Greenway, D., 1983, *International Trade Policy. From Tariffs to New Protectionism*. London, Macmillan.

71. Greenway, 1983, *op.cit.*, p.159.

72. In particular Art.VI (for dumping), Art.XII (balance of payment) and XIX (serious injury). See GATT, 1986, *The Text of the General Agreement on Tariffs and Trade*. Geneva, GATT.

73. Ball, J., 1987, *The Causes of Rising Protectionism*. London, British-North American Association, p.19.

74. There are no lists of NICs which are accepted by all authors, but all lists do include the Asian Tigers, Brazil and Mexico.

75. Canada also had some of its exports limited to the NTBs. See: Lazar, F., 1981, *The New Protectionism. Non-tariff Barriers and their effects in Canada*. Toronto, James Lorimer & Co.

76. See: Grilli, E. & Sassoon, E.(eds.)., 1990, *The New Protectionist Wave*. London, Macmillan, p.13.

77. Grilli & Sassoon, 1990, *op.cit.*, p.19.

78. Krauss, M., 1979, *The New-Protectionism. The Welfare State and International Trade*. Oxford, Basil Blackwell. p.37.
79. Grilli, E. & Sassoon, E.(eds.), 1990, *The New Protectionist Wave*. London, Macmillan Education. pp.25-26.
80. Grilli & Sassoon, 1990, *op.cit.*, p.25.
81. On recent protectionist trends in DCs, see, Greenway, D. & Hine, R. & O'Brien, A. & Thornton, R. (eds.)., 1989, *Global Protectionism*. New York, St. Martin Press.
82. These include: Canada, Denmark, EU, Finland, Germany, Italy, Japan, Sweden, Switzerland, Norway, Holland, US and UK.
83. GATT, 1985, *BISD. 1984-1985, 32 Sup.* Geneva, GATT. pp.75-76.
84. GATT, 1986, *op.cit.*, pp.75-76.
85. GATT, 1986, *op.cit.*, p.77.
86. Martone & Braga, 1990, *op.cit.*, p.198.
87. Brazilian Ambassador to the GATT from 1983 to 1987.
88. Martone & Braga, 1988, *op.cit.*, p.199.
89. *Financial Times*. 27/11/84.
90. *Financial Times*. 29/11/84.
91. Feketekuty, 1988, *International Trade in Services*. Cambridge, American Enterprise Institute. p.320.
92. GATT, 1986, *BISD 1984-1985. 32 Supp.* Geneva, GATT. p.71.
93. *Financial Times*. 3/12/84.
94. *Washington Post*. 15/11/85.
95. Nicolaides, 1989, *Liberalising Services Trade Strategies for Success*. London, Routledge, p.81.
96. Barros Netto, 1987, *op.cit.*, p.8.
97. GATT, 1986, *GATT Activities in 1985*. Geneva, GATT. p.19.
98. GATT, 1986, *BISD. 1984-1985. 32 Supp.* Geneva, GATT. p.72.
99. GATT, 1986, *op.cit.*, pp.44-45.
100. See: Barros Neto, 1987, *op.cit.*, p.9.
101. Koekkoek, 1988, Trade in Services, the Developing Countries and the Uruguay Round. In *World Economy*, p.124.
102. GATT, 1986, *op.cit.*, p.45.
103. IMF, 1993, *IFS. 1992*. Washington, IMF. p.243. (January).
104. Confidential interview with a Brazilian diplomat.
105. Finlayson & Weston, 1990, *op.cit.*, p.24.
106. Martone & Primo Braga, 1988, *op.cit.*, p.40 and Abreu, 1992, *op.cit.*, pp.26-27.
107. Maciel, 1986, *op.cit.*, p.81.
108. Martone & Primo Braga, 1988, *op.cit.*, p.40.
109. These included: Argentina, Bangladesh, Brazil, Burma, Cameroon, Colombia, Cuba, Cyprus, Egypt, Ghana,India, Ivory Cost, Jamaica, Nigeria, Pakistan, Peru, Rumania, Sri Lanka, Tanzania, Uruguay, Yugoslavia, and Zaire.

110. GATT Doc. L.5818: Improvement of World Trade Relations.
111. Oxley, 1990, *The Challenge of Free Trade*. London, Harvester Wheatsheaf, p.132.
112. Maciel, 1986, *op.cit.*, p.89.
113. Barros Netto, 1987, *op.cit.*, p.9.
114. GATT, 1986, *BISD 1984-1985 32 Supp*. Geneva, GATT. pp.44-45.
115. GATT Document 1985. C/W/479. 22/07/85.
116. GATT Doc. 5852. 22/07/85.
117. GATT. Document 5838 (09/07/85). Trade in Services. Information on behalf of the US.
118. Oxley, 1990, *op.cit.*, pp.133-134.
119. GATT, 1986, *BISD 32nd Session 1984-1985*. Geneva, GATT. p.9.
120. Graham, 1984, *op.cit.*, p.9.
121. GATT, 1986, *BISD 1984-1985 32nd Supp*. Geneva, GATT. p.9.
122. GATT, *Focus. Newsletter*. October/November 1985. p.1.
123. See: GATT, *BISD 1984-1985. 32 Sup*. Geneva, GATT. pp.14-15.
124. Confidential interview with an Ambassador from a developing country to the GATT.
125. See: Lima, 1986, *op.cit.*, p.137.
126. See: Maciel, 1986, *op.cit.*, p.88.
127. The Document is: 'Recent Developments in International Trade Negotiations and their Consequences for the GATT, and Status of Implementation of Ministerial Work Programme'. Statement by the Representative of Brazil at Council Meeting on 17 July 1985 (agenda item n.2).
128. Brazil's Position is in GATT Doc. 5818, 07/06/85 and GATT Doc. 5852, 28/07/85.
129. GATT, 1986, *BISD. 1984-1985. 32 Sup*. Geneva, GATT. p.10-11.
130. GATT, 1985, *Press Release n.1377*. 29/11/85. p.1.
131. For a short review of the different views on services see GATT, *Press Release n.1395*. 10/09/86. p.3.
132. Either because they believed they had comparative advantage in trade in services, or because they could increase the efficiency of their economy as whole with trade liberalization in services.

2.   The Brazilian Decision-Making Process (DMP) Related to the GATT

Introduction

The objective of this chapter is to analyze the Decision-Making Process (DMP) in Brazil related to the GATT and in particular its position towards the issue of services. This chapter is divided into four parts.

The first part of this chapter studies the Decision-Making Process (DMP) related to international trade policies, with an emphasis on the roles of different ministries. It also assesses the impact of other domestic factors, such as the role of Parliament, which might have affected Brazil's perception of the GATT.

The second section of this chapter describes the two mental frameworks which prevailed at the Ministry of Foreign Affairs (Itamaraty) related to the GATT. It analyzes the structure of Itamaraty during the Sarney government and the role of its related departments and divisions in the Decision-Making Process (DMP). Finally, it gives an idea of the DMP at Itamaraty in action. The third part of this chapter describes Brazil's position concerning the issue of services. The fourth part discusses Brazil's actions related to the formation of alliances in order to support its views against the inclusion of services in the GATT.

Brazil's international trade policies

The Principles on which Brazil's International Trade Policy is based: The traditional view

This is a summary of the principles underlying Brazil's trade policies, which prevailed from 1947 to 1987, and which will be discussed throughout the book: [1]

- The principle of maximizing Brazil's growth and employment level;

- The belief in ISI and in infant industry arguments; [2]

- The idea that the world trading system was both created and regulated by Developed Countries (DCs) to serve their interests;

- The interests of Brazil were not necessarily best served by the interests of the DCs in trade issues;

- The notion that in order for a State to achieve the status of DC, it needs to protect its national interest so as not to allow such a State to become an easy target for threats from DCs;

- The notion that the State bureaucracy knows the national interests best and is best able to guide the private sector;

- Imports make the country vulnerable to pressure from other countries. Thus, the ideal situation is to transform Brazil into a self-sufficient economy in as many sectors as possible.

According to these basic principles, it is not difficult to conclude which theory of international economic policy prevailed in Brazil between 1947 and 1987. The Liberal School can be dismissed for three main reasons. First, Brazil never adopted an open trade regime.[3] Indeed, Brazil has been historically a protectionist country.[4] Second, Itamaraty believed international trade was a zero-sum game. Third, the government is the primary actor responsible for fixing the level of openness of the economy.[5]

Therefore, economic nationalism and protectionism offer the best explanation for Brazil's attitude in the GATT. First, it accepted that the state is autonomous, with its own perspectives and goals, as Brazil's case suggests. Second, Brazil adopted ISI policies in order to increase the level of employment and domestic production, as the supporters of mercantilism suggest. Third, Brazil believed that by adopting certain domestic measures, such as the protection of the domestic IT market for national firms, it could decrease its foreign dependence and increase its global power. Finally, Brazil adopted several postures in the GATT in order to protect its national interests, as the Mercantilist School also advocates. Indeed, speeches from Paulo Batista from 1983 to 1987[6] make many references to national interests.[7] The fact that the State itself could define what is, and what is not, in the national interests, increased its power vis-à-vis private groups.[8]

The role of Parliament in foreign economic policy in Brazil

In Brazil, as everywhere, most politicians are not very interested in foreign affairs. They find the subject too complex and believe that decisions related to foreign relations should be taken by specialists, that is, diplomats at Itamaraty.[9]

Although international treaties in Brazil have to be approved by Congress, in most cases the Senate endorses the proposals put forward by the President or Itamaraty. Until recently, the Chamber did not have a group of advisers to advise MPs on the advantages or disadvantages for Brazil ratifying international treaties.[10] Moreover, Itamaraty managed to obtain not only a monopoly of Brazilian representation abroad, but also excellence in the study of international relations in Brazil.[11]

As a result, the discussion of foreign affairs reached the public through the press or the Chamber in an emotional way. Local MPs were aware of this and they used this emotional perspective to obtain votes. In the Chamber, MPs were divided into two groups: the nationalists (centre-left), who attacked the US, and the democrats (centre-right), who attacked the ex-USSR and communism. It was in this simplistic way that foreign affairs were discussed in the Chamber. The Amazon, the US-Brazil dispute in IT, military agreements and the International Monetary Fund (IMF) were the most controversial topics. They generated more passion and speeches than rational discussions.

In the Senate the situation was different. It was more influential than the Chamber because it fell within the scope of the House to approve international treaties. However, the lack of experts in foreign affairs in Brazil limited the capacity of Senators to influence foreign policy. In order to overcome this handicap, some Senators who were interested in foreign affairs used to hire experts to help them on complex topics. This explains how they were able to discuss subjects concerning international law or foreign affairs. But this aptitude was much more common in the Senate than in the Chamber and it by no means reflected the normal pattern. Congress, in general, had a marginal impact on Brazilian foreign policy. As a result, the influence of public opinion and Congress in the GATT negotiations was nil.[12] Most Brazilians shared the official view that if services became part of GATT, Brazil would remain forever an LDC. Therefore, it was necessary to fight this attempt by DCs to change the rules of international trade in their favour. Congress did not influence the change of Brazil's attitude in the GATT.

However, ISI was losing support inside and outside Itamaraty every day. Some MPs, for instance, Roberto Campos, criticized the lack of future and rationale for the Itamaraty's pro-Third World policy, a logical result of the ISI. The unpopularity of this policy in Brazil helped Paulo Tarso to consolidate his power at Itamaraty.[13]

The role of the President and of the Head of Itamaraty

The death of the President Elect, Tancredo Neves, in 1985 caused a national commotion. Some jurists claimed that the President of the Supreme Court should take power and call new elections. This view did not prevail, but it impaired the image of and caused some damage to Sarney, who assumed office with great trepidation.[14] Sarney took power and maintained the Cabinet chosen by Neves. Neves had chosen a Cabinet which was a reflection of the different sectors which composed the PMDB-PFL Alliance. For Itamaraty, Neves had chosen Olavo Setúbal; for General Secretary of Itamaraty, Neves had selected Paulo Tarso.[15]

Sarney had no experience of foreign affairs. He had been a journalist in the underdeveloped State of Maranhão, his home state. He pursued his career by way of clientelism and loyalty to local political bosses.[16] Thus, when Sarney took power as President he did not have much to say on foreign affairs. This was to be an important aspect of Brazil's position in the GATT. Indeed, Sarney's lack of knowledge meant that he would delegate the discussions related to Brazil's position in the GATT to Itamaraty. It is thus assumed here that Sarney had little influence on foreign affairs, in particular on issues related to the Uruguay Round.[17] Setúbal, first Head of Itamaraty in the Sarney Administration, also had no expertise in foreign affairs. He was the owner of Itaú Bank, which was expanding its activities to the field of IT in order to benefit from Brazil's IT Law. Although Setúbal had no experience in foreign affairs, he brought a business oriented style to Itamaraty and also a dose of pragmatism.[18]

It should be noted that Itamaraty always enjoyed a degree of relative autonomy within the State.[19] This means that historically decisions were taken at and by Itamaraty without the direct participation of the President.[20] This occurred because most decisions at Itamaraty assumed a previous knowledge of the issues discussed.[21] This trend increased with Sarney as a result of his lack of expertise in international affairs.[22]

However, this does not mean that the President ignores what happens at Itamaraty. It means that, in Brazil, the President may influence Itamaraty only in limited ways. The most important is the nomination of the Minister, followed by the General Secretary, who is - in the words of an ex-Minister - a provisional Minister.[23] Indeed, by choosing the Head of Itamaraty the President gives an indication of his beliefs. However, it is not enough to nominate the Minister to establish a foreign policy. It is necessary that the President chooses someone with knowledge or strong views in foreign affairs, which does not always happen.[24]

If the President chooses as Minister someone with a clear view in foreign affairs he will be sure that Itamaraty will have a new policy to follow. But this does not imply that this new policy will be followed in the way that the President and the Minister of Foreign Affairs would wish.[25] This occurs because Itamaraty has autonomy on how to implement the policies. Moreover, international negotiations are carried out by diplomats and rarely by the Head of Itamaraty himself. Thus, sometimes the Minister is just informed of the results of the negotiations. He may take part in them if the issue becomes too polemical to be decided by diplomats.[26] On the other hand, when the President chooses someone as Minister not on the basis of his views or knowledge of foreign affairs but due to party or personal links, the President's influence over Itamaraty may decrease. There is the risk that the President may lose control of the Itamaraty apparatus.[27]

In Brazil, generally speaking, if the President is interested in foreign affairs and wants to impose his views, he has to appoint someone familiar with the functioning of Itamaraty who shares these views. Secondly, he has to follow developments in selected fields. The system of briefing, however, may be tedious if the President is not keen on foreign policy. Sarney eventually did participate, but not on matters concerning the GATT.[28] In short, most Brazilian Presidents, with a few exceptions, have little interest in foreign affairs.[29] Sarney was not among the exceptions.[30] Thus, in order to analyze Brazil's position in the Uruguay Round, it will be assumed here that Itamaraty monopolized this issue.[31] Thus, we will focus on Itamaraty's Decision-Making Process since other Ministries were not powerful enough to interfere in the formulation of Brazil's policy to the GATT, with the exception of the Ministry of the Economy.[32]

Ministries involved in trade issues and the GATT

Before analyzing how Itamaraty makes decisions concerning international trade policy and Brazil's position to the GATT, it is necessary to identify other people in charge of DMP in Brazil's international trade policy.[33]

In Brazil, until 1990 there were two ministries responsible for economic matters. The first was the Planning Ministry, the second was the Finance Ministry. In general, the Planning Ministry was in charge of macroeconomic decisions, such as which strategy to adopt against inflation, and of formulating proposals linked to development such as industrial policies. It was also charged with informing economic agents of the President's priorities.[34]

The Finance Ministry was in charge of the technical aspects of the implementation of the budget. However, the important budgetary decisions would be taken depending on the relative power of the Planning or the Finance Minister and their respective relations with the President. After 1990, the two Ministries were combined into the Ministry of Economics which made it the most powerful Ministry in the government. Previously, therefore, there had not been one, but two Ministries where decision-making power was located, the balance varying according the persons who headed them. Delfim Netto was individually the most powerful economic Minister.[35]

However, in international trade policies, there were not two, but four Ministries technically involved in discussions. These included the Planning Ministry (SEPLAN), the Ministry of Commerce and Industry (MIC), the Ministry of Agriculture and Itamaraty. The extent to which each Ministry was heard would always depend on the power of the Minister in charge, but some of them were not very influential at all. Although farmers were very powerful in Parliament, in the DMP of the Ministry of Agriculture they were very weak.[36] The Ministry of Agriculture was rarely invited to meetings where Brazil's position in GATT was discussed.[37] In spite of its name, the MIC is not involved in the DMP in international trade policy but only in domestic programmes or programmes to support exports (BEFIEX). MIC was influential on specific products such as the export of coffee, sugar and alcohol, through the specialized agencies in charge of them.[38] It did not play a relevant role in the discussion of Brazil's position in the GATT. The MIC represented the *status quo* and supported the ISI model; it had no diplomatic skills.[39]

The two agencies which remain as the main actors in international trade policy were the Ministry of Finance and Itamaraty. The formal tools of trade policy are almost entirely in the hands of the Finance Minister.[40] He is also in charge of the foreign debt and other financial negotiations. Itamaraty has a monopoly of all external negotiations (except financial issues), in accordance with Brazilian law.[41] As a result, it has coordinated all negotiations in the GATT with the representatives of other ministries and the private sector. The Trade Policy division of the Economic Department of Itamaraty is the primary office involved in multilateral trade affairs.

There is also a Committee (CONCEX) in which officials from many Ministries take part.[42] In fact, there is a kind of division of labour between Itamaraty and the Finance Ministry. Itamaraty is in charge of multilateral negotiations while the Finance Ministry looks after domestic aspects of trade policies, delegating execution of some issues such as subsidies to exports (BEFIEX) and industrial policies to other Ministries, in particular the MIC.[43]

Sometimes the lines where international trade policies finish and domestic trade policies start disappear and disagreements between the Finance Ministry and Itamaraty arise. An example of these disputes concerned subsidies on exports. While Itamaraty was making a strong defence in Geneva during the negotiations of the Subsidies Code of the rights of LDCs to subsidize their exports, the Ministry of Finance announced that it would phase it out.[44]

This intra-agency dispute shows two different things. The first is that each agency behaves according to its own logic and rationale. The Finance Ministry takes an economic/financial view, in general linked to a short term perspective. It is willing to settle for short-term solutions. Experienced in negotiations, Itamaraty would balance Brazil's actions against long-term consequences for the country's foreign policy objectives and their political impact on Brazil's negotiating ability. It would rather begin with maximizing propositions than settle for less.

Second, the intra-agency dispute shows the autonomy of each agency. It confirms our initial hypothesis that each agency in Brazil has its own area, each one trying not to interfere in the other field. The only way of solving this conflict would be through the intervention of the President himself.[45]

These two aspects explain how Itamaraty negotiated services at the Uruguay Round regardless of the opinions of other Ministries.[46]

It is important to note that this study is centred in the main people who decisively influenced the DMP. In this sense, our analysis will focus on an elite - those who had the capacity to and did influence the DMP in the field of Brazil's position in the Uruguay Round of the GATT. In Brazil's case, contrary to most countries, this elite is found at Itamaraty. Therefore, we will analyze the DMP of Itamaraty on foreign trade issues as it is formulated in international fora. Before doing so, however, we will summarize the characteristics of Brazil's DMP relative to the GATT.

Characteristics of Brazil's Decision-Making Process (DMP) towards the GATT and to the Uruguay Round

The main characteristics of the DMP in Brazil which are used as premises in this book are as follows:

1) Trade negotiations attracted no public interest in Brazil. They were closed (parochial) and controlled by the Executive;[47]

2) The President was not interested in the Uruguay Round;[48]

3) There was a weak process of consultation with other agencies from other Ministries. Generally, Itamaraty took the final decision;

4) Brazil is the only country where the Foreign Office, not the Trade or Finance Ministry, is in charge of trade negotiations;

5) Notables within Itamaraty disputed the control of the DMP;

6) The concentration of decisions in few hands at Itamaraty;[49]

7) Negotiations which could reduce Brazil's ability to create laws or policies were considered to be against its sovereignty;[50]

8) DMP at Itamaraty is more reactive than inactive, reacting to facts originated by the US and the EC;[51]

9) It is difficult for analysts to follow Brazil's position in the Round due to the complexity of the issues involved;[52]

10) Brazil's Decision-Making Process lacks transparency;[53]

11) Special interests are not very powerful. They use state agencies to apply pressure. Export interests remain weak in challenging the coalition in favour of ISI policies;[54]

Decision-Making Process (DMP) at Itamaraty

Itamaraty's view of the GATT

Due to the 1982 debt problems, Brazil entered a period of economic crisis. However, there were different views within Itamaraty about how to overcome it. Itamaraty was divided into three on this issue:

a) the 'pro-UNCTAD' or 'pro-LDC' group,

b) the reformist group ('pragmatists') and

c) others.[55]

The first group represented the traditional view. It prevailed in Itamaraty during part of the 1960s and all of the 1970s. This group supported an increase in exports to Third World countries and a maintenance of protectionist measures and ISI policies. They also believed in the infant industry argument. Ambassador Paulo Batista, Brazil's representative at GATT (1983-87), was an influential member of the group.[56] This group put great emphasis on industrial development, if necessary through ISI policies.

They believed that Brazil had an industrial vocation.[57] They followed the line of the United Nations Economic Commission for Latin America (ECLA), maintained in UNCTAD, through Prebisch, its first General Secretary.[58] Itamaraty became one of the most outspoken of the LDC's demands for changes in the international economic order and took an active part in the elaboration of the agenda of the first UNCTAD.[59] Brazil concentrated its diplomatic efforts with UNCTAD as its main forum, a situation which prevailed until the 1970s. For this reason, the group is also called pro-UNCTAD. They sympathized with UNCTAD, and saw GATT as the "rich man's club", although Brazil was one of its founding members.[60] Thus, the group had a negative attitude towards Itamaraty's participation in the Uruguay Round. Brazil's representative to GATT, Batista, was thus often said to be the man who tried to sink the trade negotiations.[61]

The pro-UNCTAD group believed that the risk of a trade war was small, even in the case of the collapse of the Round.[62] They were against the inclusion of services in the GATT, and they only agreed to discuss it in the Uruguay Round under the dual-track procedure.[63] They were against the ending of the Round in the Bush Government arguing that it was not advantageous to Brazil.[64] Batista maintains that the Final Draft Act (FDA) imposed limits on Brazil's ability to legislate in services, without an improvement in the conditions of access by Brazilian products abroad.

Batista considers that Brazil is interested in the multilateral system due to the many products it exports and the several markets it trades with. However, he is convinced that the preservation of the trade system should not be made at the cost of less investment in Brazil and less access to foreign technology. Batista does not propose anything new to be done at the GATT except to maintain or expand Special & Differential (S&D) treatment.[65] He does not believe in free-trade and he supports the view that the US proposed rules to the new issues because it wanted to freeze the comparative advantage its economy had in those sectors.[66] He saw trade negotiations as a zero-sum game, as did most LDCs.[67] The reformist group had as its natural leader Ambassador Paulo Tarso,[68] General Secretary of Itamaraty (1985-1991), and *de facto* Minister of Foreign Affairs from 1987 to 1990.[69] This group believed that Brazil could not adopt defensive attitudes in the GATT, as it had done during the Tokyo Round.[70] In this Round Brazil only secured S&D treatment to LDCs and profited passively from the application of the Most Favoured Nation (MFN) clause, but offered practically nothing itself. Tarso views trade negotiations as deregulation, that is, one country barters deregulation measures against another. Tarso noted that the problem of legality of negotiations in the GATT plagued Brazil for many years.[71]

Tarso believed that the economic model which prevailed in Brazil from 1950 to 1980 had run its course. The era of North-South dialogue had also finished. He supported deregulation and the end of all invisible protectionist measures such as NTBs. He noted that Brazil's tariffs reached 150% in certain cases and proposed to bind Brazil's tariffs to 30% in the GATT. He believed that Brazil could adapt to external competition.[72] In short, he believed that free-trade was better than protectionism although he did not dare to say so openly. He preferred to say that there was no more place for economic autarkies. The last to exist was opening up to foreign trade, and so too should Brazil.[73]

As one can see these two views offer different proposals of what should be done to overcome the economic and financial crisis due to growing foreign debt. This dissertation will show how the two groups fought to impose their respective views of Brazil's future: Batista represented the traditional view (economic nationalism and protectionism), while Tarso supported the opening up of Brazil's economy (liberalism).

The Decision-Making Process (DMP) at Itamaraty related to the GATT

As the DMP related to GATT was concentrated in Itamaraty, the principal model used in this analysis is the Single-Agency model.[74] The main point to this model in this book is that besides dealing with agencies our research will deal with sub-agencies within Itamaraty, which compete with one another for influence. Inside Itamaraty, one agency dominates the DMP: the Economic Department.[75] This was the focus of power in Itamaraty on GATT issues before and during the Uruguay Round.[76] Technically, Itamaraty is divided into three sections, all of them secondary to the Minister: the Diplomatic Missions (Embassies and Permanent Missions), the General Secretary, and the Consular Offices.[77] These are set out as follows:

Basic structure of Itamaraty
– Figure 1 -

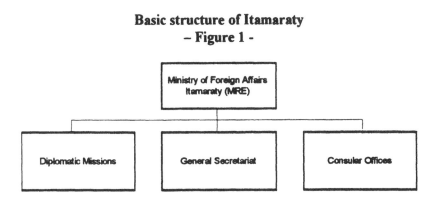

The Minister is therefore, theoretically, in charge of keeping in touch with Brazilian Diplomatic Missions abroad (viz. Brazil's Permanent Mission to the GATT). However, this did not occur. In fact, Brazilian Diplomatic

Missions contact direct, by telegram, the General Secretariat of Itamaraty.[78]

The Minister may ask to see the telegrams exchanged if he is particularly interested in a certain issue.[79] For this reason, power tends to concentrate in the hands of the General Secretary and not the Minister.[80] This is important because the authority of the General Secretary may be increased when the Minister is not a diplomat and thus is not interested in the issues affecting Itamaraty. Indeed, when the Minister is a diplomat, power is divided between the Minister's Cabinet and that of the Secretary-General.[81] If the Ministry is occupied by politicians such as Setúbal (1986) and Sodré (1987-1990), part of their power will tend to be lost to the General Secretary, then Tarso. Both indeed lost their power to Tarso, but in particular Sodré, who replaced Setúbal.[82]

To give an idea of the importance of the General Secretary, he controls four Committees, including the influential Promotions Committee and eleven Under-Secretaries and Offices altogether. The Under-Secretaries were created during Tarso's administration and strengthened his position at Itamaraty vis-à-vis the Minister.[83] Of the eleven Under-Secretaries and offices reporting to the General Secretary, the most influential concerning the Uruguay Round is the General Under-Secretariat for Commercial and Economic Affairs. It is divided into three departments and one Special Division as follows:

Decision-Making Process (DMP) related to the GATT
- Figure 2 -

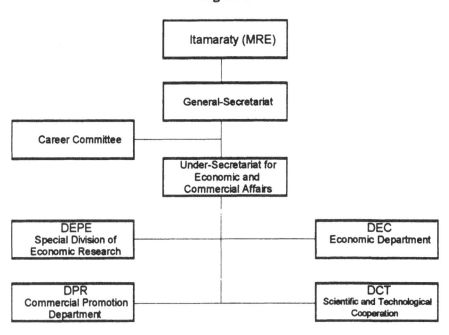

Tarso nominated Thompson Flôres, an original member of his group, for the position of Under Secretariat.[84] Then, Tarso started a process of co-option of members of the old pro-UNCTAD group to his group. This was necessary because if Tarso wanted to impose a new policy related to GATT, he needed support from ex-members of the influential Economic Department. Rego Barros, who originally supported ISI policies and had a strong bias against GATT,[85] was co-opted to Tarso's Group. During the period he remained as Head of the Economic Department from 1985 to 1987, he supported Batista. He had replaced Proença Rosa, also a member of the Batista Group. After 1988, he became Under Secretary of Economic Affairs, and a converted supporter of free-trade.[86]

The Economic Department was by far the most powerful of all Departments under the Under Secretariat for Economic Affairs. This fact can be illustrated by the number of divisions reporting to that Department. Certainly however such a criterion could be disputed if it were the only evidence demonstrating that the Economic Department was the most influential Department.

Nevertheless, some evidence of that influence can certainly be accepted. Other departments reporting to the Under Secretary were: the Special Division for Economic Studies (DEPE), equivalent to a department but without any Committee; the Department of Commercial Promotion, where Tarso comes from, with control over four Divisions; the Department for Scientific and Technological Cooperation to which three Divisions were seconded; and the Economic Department, itself in charge of seven Divisions. No other department in Itamaraty had so many important divisions under its control as the Economic Department, which included the Latin American Economic Commission. This is illustrated in this diagram:

Structure of the Minister of Foreign Affairs
– Figure 3 -

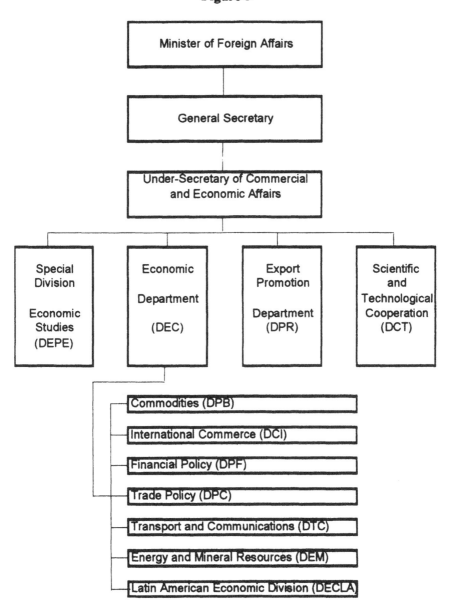

The structure is self-explanatory, but two points deserve some comment.

Central to this book is the Division on Trade Policy (DPC), in charge of giving instructions to Brazilian diplomats in the GATT. Another factor to be noted is that there is a Latin American Economic Division. This division is out of place for many reasons. Its content is too broad. It could be split into different categories: Mercosul, ALADI, etc.[87] If considered from a political or geographical perspective it should be located in the Under Secretariat for Bilateral Political Affairs, under a special Division of the American Department. From an economic perspective, it would make more sense to include it in the Under Secretariat for Multilateral and Special Political Affairs, under the Department for Special International Issues, for instance.[88]

The best explanation for its existence is that it is part of the ideology which permeated the Itamaraty, a direct heritage of the ECLA. Certainly it contributed to strengthen the idea of Latin America as a region with a common history and common problems, exploited by DCs. The most obvious result of this perspective is the defence of ISI policies, which prevailed in Itamaraty until the mid-1980s, in particular in the Economic Department.[89]

The role of personalities in the Decision-Making Process (DMP) related to the GATT: Main Brazilian policy-makers

In the mind of Itamaraty, Geneva was a high profile position and Itamaraty would never send a diplomat there who was not considered to be one of the best available.[90] Indeed, Saraiva Guerreiro, an ex-Head of Brazil's Mission in Geneva became Minister. George Maciel, who succeeded him, was very influential at the GATT, and was invited to work for the GATT in many positions.

Among Brazilian representatives to the GATT, Maciel was the most important. Indeed, Maciel was the high point of Brazil's contribution to the GATT system.[91] He had a deep knowledge of GATT legal affairs and was considered the main Brazilian expert on GATT at Itamaraty. A negative aspect of this fame was that Itamaraty could not dictate instructions to Maciel about what Brazil's policy to GATT should be. While Maciel was Brazil's representative, the DMP related to the GATT at Itamaraty was reversed. He was the representative and originator of Brazil's policy to the GATT.[92]

During the 1982 Ministerial Meeting, when discussions began on the possibility of including services in the GATT, Maciel was still Brazil's representative. He was against the inclusion for juridical and technical reasons.

Maciel believed that GATT had no legal competence to deal with services. Indeed, there was nothing in the GATT framework which mentioned that it should deal with services. Maciel thought that even if the rules of GATT were altered to incorporate services, these could not be included immediately in the GATT system because GATT's principles were created in the post-war era to deal with goods.[93] Maciel also believed that GATT principles would have to be revised to deal with services. Thus, he did not share the US position that GATT principles could be extended automatically to services. This is an important aspect of Maciel's position because he opposed the introduction of services with arguments of a technical nature, and not on ideological grounds.

The replacement of Maciel by Batista in 1983 brought a new style to the GATT negotiations. With an economic background, Batista decided to ideologize all economic discussions in the GATT. With his nationalist views, Batista brought to the GATT the block politics used by Brazil in UNCTAD. At Itamaraty, he was respected by some, and feared by most for his bulldozer style. He was known for his strong personality and for his coolness. In a negotiation he would not allow an emotion or sign of weakness to appear. If necessary, he knew how to be inflexible.[94]

As Maciel had already done, Batista also managed to reverse the DMP related to GATT, and Batista himself became the main formulator of Brazil's policy towards GATT. Certain circumstances contributed to the maintenance of Geneva as the main formulator of Brazil's policy to the GATT, as opposed to Brasilia. Services were a new subject and diplomats did not know what they meant or how to deal with them. Moreover, nobody knew where Brazil's interest in the subject area lay. In the absence of an agency inside or outside Itamaraty to define the national interest, Batista took the work into his own hands and defined it by himself. However, Batista played safe. He extended the arguments used to justify protectionism in Brazil to services: infant industry, lack of competitiveness of Brazilian firms and ISI policies.[95]

It seems, however, that Brazil lost an opportunity to learn a lot about services after the 1982 Ministerial Meeting. The 'Final Declaration of the Ministerial Meeting' suggested the elaboration and circulation of national studies on services in the GATT.[96] Irrationally, Batista refused to prepare a national study. The refusal to prepare studies was the initial feature of Batista's position in the GATT on services. Batista would make Brazil's opposition to discuss services the essence of his performance as the Brazilian Representative to the GATT.[97]

The costs of a tough position like this are high for any country, but in particular for an LDC, such as Brazil. It required a perfect coordination with other countries which shared a similar point of view. However, few countries were ready to support Brazil in a cause that was not very clear and only ten countries joined Brazil in this obstructionist policy.[98] On this issue, Batista's personality did not help. There was a feeling in the GATT that Batista might be a brilliant intellectual with a powerful personality, but he was not a diplomat.[99] Diplomats from the US (and from Brazil as well) saw him as a troublemaker.[100] They noted that instead of organizing support for Brazil's concerns with regard to services, Batista undermined the alliances which Brazil had previously built-up in the GATT, in particular with Latin American countries, of which Itamaraty used to be the spokesman.[101]

Batista was the leader of the group who had suspicions about the GATT at Itamaraty. He followed the nationalist perspective which had prevailed in the 1950s and supported UNCTAD as Brazil's main forum, and not the GATT, and for this, his group is called pro-UNCTAD. They fear a deeper integration of Brazil in the world economy and do not believe in free-trade. They support the ISI model. They also see in each international event a capitalist conspiracy with the participation of the US in order to keep LDCs in a subordinate position in the world system. The only means of breaking this subservient position of LDCs is through the adoption of ISI policies, such as those preached by UNCTAD.

Batista's radical views caused dissatisfaction within Itamaraty. His attitude as the Brazilian Ambassador to GATT also caused concern. Some diplomats considered Batista to be too much of a centralizer, and even authoritarian in his manner of treating his subordinates.[102] However, Batista had some support from diplomats in key-positions within Itamaraty. Hence, only someone in a high position, and with as much ability and intellectual prestige as he had, could challenge him. Few people filled all these requirements. Internationally, Brazil's position was very delicate. The 1984 Brazil Law of IT brought criticism from many countries, but the US was the most outspoken about its protectionist character. The US was concerned that Brazilian law could be imitated by other LDCs, in IT and in other sectors as well. Moreover, there was a perception that Brazil was a country outside international law due to its lack of protection in Intellectual Property Rights (IPRs).[103]

Brazil started to be in conflict with the US because of IPRs. The US was surprised at the piracy existing in Brazil and was disappointed with the lack of will of the Brazilian government to curb it. Thus, the US put Brazil on a watch-list and threatened sanctions against its products if there was no flexibility in the application of the Law on IT and if there was no progress with respect to IPRs, in particular in the area of software.[104]

At the GATT, after strong pressure from the US, and also due to the call of a Special Council in 1985 through a postal ballot, Batista agreed that a new Round would be launched in 1986. But he continued to maintain a tough position against the inclusion of services in a new Round, as the Report of the Chairman of the Contracting Parties Group illustrates.[105]

The unheard group which existed in Itamaraty, who disagreed with the tough line adopted by Batista at the GATT, concluded that they had had enough. It was necessary to change Brazil's position in the GATT because Batista was creating an unnecessary conflict with the US. This group - led by Tarso - decided to launch a campaign against the nationalist group, led by Batista. Generally speaking, these two diplomats are good examples of the different schools of thought which existed in Itamaraty.[106]

Tarso, as General Secretary, organized a pragmatist group who supported a wider integration of Brazil into the world economy. He noted that some of the conflicts with other countries, such as that with the US, were created and increased in magnitude by the pro-UNCTAD group in order to emphasize the differences in outlook between Brazil and other countries. Tarso tried to resolve disputes in such a way that Brazil might benefit from the world economy. Tarso considered that Brazil has limited resources and should avoid entering into international disputes in order to concentrate its bargaining power at important moments. He was aware of the dangers associated with protectionism, and was convinced of the advantages of an open trading system, but he was not a free-marketeer. He believed that an open trading system would benefit LDCs more than a world economy dominated by protectionism. But he noted that power was important in the world economy, and took it into account. He knew that powerful countries, for example the US, can use sanctions against other countries, while Brazil cannot. For this reason, his group was called pragmatist.[107]

However, the practical challenge faced by this group was how to interfere in the DMP and to influence Brazil's policy in the GATT. Tarso was the Head of the Export Promotion Department (DPR). This Department did not have the same influence as the Economic Department (DEC). However, through a competent performance, Tarso promoted Brazil's exports abroad, and as a result of his professional approach, Brazil's exports increased considerably during the period that Tarso headed the low-profile DPR.[108]

Tarso was ambitious but he had a major handicap: he did not share the values and ideologies which prevailed at Itamaraty. He had been promoted to Ambassador and this can be considered a direct result of his hard · work, although other factors, such as contacts, also probably helped. He was not only interested in securing a good posting abroad as Ambassador; he also wanted to impose his views and replace the old nationalist perspective prevailing in Itamaraty. He had lived in the US and knew how an open economy can work properly in the absence of protectionist policies.[109]

Contrary to the majority of Brazilian diplomats, Tarso had no prejudices against the US. He admired its democratic system and institutions. He did not share the ideology which prevailed at Itamaraty that the US was the cause of all international conflicts. He was determined to succeed in his diplomatic career, but he was not ready to change his views as some in Itamaraty had done in the past. Besides his competence, hard work, and the results he obtained when he headed the DPR, he also had other points in his favour. He knew how to motivate his staff through delegation of work. Although not an intellectual, but a very skilled entrepreneur, he attracted the best minds inside Itamaraty. He was well used to the structure of Itamaraty and was aware that some of those who were working under the prevailing ideology would be ready to change if another ideology or a better perspective was offered.[110]

He could also count on political support outside Itamaraty and knew how to use it, if necessary. Indeed, he was a close friend of several Ministers and his father had worked with President Elect Neves. Neves nominated him to be General Secretary at Itamaraty. When Neves died, he was confirmed in his position by Sarney. He managed to develop relations with the new President, which helped him to survive the Ministerial reform in 1986, when the Minister of Foreign Affairs Setúbal left.[111]

Tarso had all the requirements that a new challenger needs to succeed: a key-position at Itamaraty (General Secretary), the best people, motivation and courage. He was ready to put them into action, and he did. To obtain support for his views, the head of any Department at Itamaraty has to promote all its staff otherwise he will be abandoned by them and by potential subordinates. This is the case because if diplomats in Itamaraty realize that other diplomats worked for a head of department and did not obtain promotion, they would not be willing to work for him. They would rather work with an Ambassador heading a Department who can, and will, obtain promotion for his subordinates.[112]

It is not very difficult for a Department head to obtain the promotion of his staff. As has already been shown in the first structure of Itamaraty, the Career Committee, which decides who is to be promoted amongst Itamaraty's ranks, is subordinated to the General Secretary and not to the Minister of State. This ensures that promotions of Ambassadors will be considered as internal affairs of Itamaraty, and outside interference will be less than would be the case if the Career Committee was directly subordinated to the Presidency or to the Cabinet of the Minister.[113]

As a rule of thumb, all department heads manage to secure promotions using a prosaic method. In theory, promotions are decided by voting for the candidates they favour, whereby Ambassadors elect the candidates that they consider to be most suitable for the vacancy being considered. In practice what happens is an exchange of favours (*troca-troca* or *quid pro quo*). The Heads of Department agree between themselves who their candidates are; having decided, beforehand, who the candidates to be elected are, they go to the meeting and deliver their votes. A Head of Department who is opposed to this system will become marginalized from the DMP in Itamaraty and will lose all his staff, since he will be unable to secure their career in Itamaraty. That is why Heads of Department in Itamaraty accepted this system even if they were against it. The main defect of this system (or its advantage, from a cynical view) is that it reinforces the *status quo* of those who are at the top (the Heads of Departments) and does not allow a circulation of ideas.[114]

The future Ambassadors are diplomats who have to share the values and perception which prevail. In Brazil, these are the ISI model and protectionism. When these new Ambassadors reach the top positions, they maintain the system they know, and as a result of this system of promotion, staff tend to be disciplined and hierarchical. Creative thinking is not stimulated. Old values tend to crystallize making change difficult, as the existing policy stance tends to be taken for granted. The fact that Itamaraty has a decentralized structure has no effect and the old values tend to prevail.[115]

As a result, when Tarso became General Secretary he had to face many obstacles. He had to confront Departmental heads who had not been appointed by him, but who still had considerable power within their respective Departments. He also had to deal with the most powerful force in Itamaraty: inertia. Most diplomats prefer to leave the things as they are. Why change? A conservative policy is the key to a successful career.[116] Tarso was also challenged on political grounds: what proof was there that a moderate policy towards the US would be better for Brazil than a confrontational policy? Thus, Tarso brought to Itamaraty the fear of the unknown. Who could tell what might happen to Brazilian industry as a result of an open-door policy? And what if Brazilian companies confirmed that they were indeed uncompetitive compared to foreign firms?

Tarso also had to cope with the results of past success. Brazil had one of the highest rates of growth this century due to, among other factors, the policies of ISI. Why run the risk of destroying the industrial sector in the name of free-trade? Would free-trade be better for Brazil than the policy of ISI? These doubts were in the minds of all Brazilian diplomats during the 1980s, when Itamaraty began to undergo the most significant U-turns in its ideology on economic development.[117]

However, Tarso had some cards up his sleeve. In 1986, he promoted an individual from his group, Azambuja, as General-Under Secretary for Administration and Communications in charge of promotions. With this nomination, Tarso became the most powerful individual at Itamaraty, including Minister Sodré. He could then promote individuals who shared his views about the new direction Itamaraty should follow, and remove individuals from key-positions, viz., Batista. Tarso could choose the Heads of Departments, as he did. This was vital, in particular in the case of the all powerful Economic Department. This Department was led in 1986-1987 by Rego Barros, who was biased against the GATT.[118]

Tarso succeeded in attracting Rego Barros to his group, as Under-General for Economic Affairs, replacing Thompson Flores, an old ally. When Rego Barros left the post of Head of the Economic Department open, Tarso nominated Guimarães Neto, who was in favour of the opening up of the Brazilian economy.[119] He could also nominate future Ambassadors, and thus gain support for his policies or at least fail to promote his enemies. This happened in the case of Huguenet - a supporter of ISI and the right-hand of Batista at Itamaraty. Huguenet was the Head of the strategic Trade Policy Division (DPC) of Itamaraty. Although hierarchically inferior to Tarso, Huguenet decided to play hard. He, and Batista, became the two policy-makers in charge of the GATT. As the DPC was the division in charge of preparing the directives, it was possible for them to organize the directives without consulting other officials. Huguenet was the support needed by Batista to legitimize his position in the GATT in Geneva. With the support of the Head of the Economic Department, Huguenet could transmit instructions directly to Geneva on the attitude Brazil should adopt in the GATT and in the Round.[120]

However, Huguenet's star started to fade when the Head of the Department was replaced. He could not count on the support of the new Head, chosen carefully by Tarso. Moreover, Huguenet also had to think about his future. If he wanted to be Ambassador, he had to accept orders, as the game was played, and he knew the rules. When Huguenet realized that the changes at Itamaraty would last, his personal position evolved and he was incorporated into Tarso's group.[121]

This is ironic, since Huguenet initially had adopted an active position against services. In 1986 he used to give lectures to Brazilian entrepreneurs in the construction sector urging them to take positions against the inclusion of services in the Round. His argument was that services was an infant industry.[122] This shows the degree of emotion in the discussion of services in Brazil. Huguenet had been nominated by the President to prepare the report of the Inter-ministerial Group on Services (GIS), which would guide Brazil's position in the GATT. Instead of promoting serious studies, Huguenet launched a charm offensive to convince service firms of the unfeasibility of including services in the GATT, before the studies had been started. Not only did Huguenet not carry out studies on services but he announced the conclusions of the GIS before the studies were made. Indeed, in April, months before the GIS formally finished its work, he said that the inclusion of services in the GATT could jeopardize opportunities for Brazilian firms, abroad and in Brazil.[123] As a good diplomat, Huguenet must have known that it is not proper conduct for a rapporteur to make comments on an issue which is still being studied. The simple conclusion is that the studies were biased. The study could only reflect the official position of Itamaraty and more precisely his personal position. Indeed, as the head of the DPC, Huguenet was the person in charge of carrying out the studies. Instead of studies, Huguenet made a compilation of existing laws and legislation in many service sectors.[124]

Tarso then used the methods at his disposal. He had promoted his staff and as heads of departments he had put individuals who shared his views. Now was the time to weaken Batista. Tarso could nominate Ambassadors and he took advantage of this fact to offer a position to Huguenet, who accepted. However, after the launch of the Round Batista's position continued the same and sanctions from the US were drawing nearer. What could be done about it?

It was now the turn of Batista to be in a difficult position. Batista knew that domestic support for ISI policies was decreasing. At Itamaraty, many Ambassadors started to doubt the wisdom of the obstructionist policies adopted in the GATT. Moreover, at Itamaraty the Bandwagon effect operates both ways. If diplomats see that a change will occur they do not want to be associated with the old positions. Batista used his contacts to remain Brazilian Ambassador to GATT; he was aware that Brazil was becoming isolated at GATT. A group of LDCs formed the Group of 22, over which Brazil had little or no influence. But he wanted to complete his work. He accepted the inclusion of services in the Uruguay Round if these were not conducted under the aegis of the GATT. The solution reached, the Trade Negotiating Committee, was satisfactory because Batista could present it as a vindication of his position.[125]

Even after the launching of the Round, Brazil's position at the GATT had not changed at all. Batista continued to obstruct the negotiations in the Group of Negotiations on Services (GNS). Due to the decentralization of Itamaraty, it was possible for a Brazilian Ambassador to maintain his views even if the directives he had received followed the opposite path. Batista's cases, there was just one solution: his removal and replacement by an Ambassador who espoused the new views which prevailed in Itamaraty and who could restore Brazil's influence in the GATT. The person chosen to do this was Rubens Ricupero, not by coincidence the first non-technical diplomat to be sent to head the Brazilian Mission in Geneva.[126]

Ricupero was sent to Geneva for his personal qualities. He was a calm, skilful negotiator; flexible and conciliatory. He was the kind of person who not would raise his voice in an argument, if it was possible to enter into an argument with him. He was the quintessential diplomat. He would never argue, always trying to negotiate. If Batista was said to be a bulldozer, Ricupero was considered a negotiator. He did not radicalize his position for ideological reasons; he always tried to find a compromise. He was responsible for putting Brazil at the centre of the negotiations again. He brought Brazil back from its isolated position in 1987 and rebuilt alliances, in particular with Latin American countries. This does not mean that Ricupero was soft as a negotiator. He knew how to express disagreement when it was necessary. But these rare cases reflected a compromise which was not being respected.[127]

Itamaraty in action: A hierarchical and disciplined structure

In general, Brazilian diplomats are considered to be highly competent and professional by their peers from other countries. Ex-British Ambassador John Shakespeare considered Brazilian diplomats to be some of the best in the world, after the British, the French and the Italians.[128] He considered his opinion to be shared by his fellows in the Foreign Office. The same can be said of Brazil's representation in international organizations, be they specialized or not. Even if the opinion of Ambassador Shakespeare can be said to be sympathetic to Brazilian diplomats, there is no doubt about the professionalism and competence of Brazilian diplomats.[129] The explanation for this performance is the DMP in Itamaraty. It can take two forms: before and during an international event.

When there is a conference, a diplomat who, in general, will already be working in that field is chosen to represent Itamaraty. The prospective delegate then receives the agenda of the Meeting and has to draft what he believes is, or will be, the Brazilian position in that conference. This preparation for participating in conferences to present the Brazilian position is known in Itamaraty as 'homework'. The diplomat approaches his immediate superior in the Itamaraty hierarchy and discusses the proposed positions. The superior then analyzes the proposals and may modify them.[130]

Each person in the hierarchy will try to impose their views on the process. On the other hand, the person in charge of elaborating proposals will also take into account the prevailing perceptions and attitudes in the Ministry. After the coup in 1964, no diplomat would propose close relations with ex-USSR because he would be accused of being communist. Ten years later, when Itamaraty adopted pro-LDC policies[131], under the military regime, diplomats were expected to support such policies or they could damage their career prospects. This shows the importance of the model of shared perceptions to explain attitudes in Itamaraty.[132] After the immediate superior adds his views on Brazil's position in the conference, he consults his superior. Thus, a process of consultation is started which goes from the bottom of the Itamaraty diplomatic ladder, the third-secretaryship, until it reaches the top of the pyramid. Here the peculiarities of Itamaraty start to appear. The top of the pyramid is not, as one could expect, the Minister of State, but the General Secretary.[133]

The General Secretary, traditionally a career diplomat, will assure the continuity in the foreign policy despite Ministerial changes. The participation of the General Secretary is particularly important before any international events because he ensures that the official position of Itamaraty is 'understood'. The Minister, in most cases, is marginalized in this process. As a result, it is the General Secretary who will give the final approval for the initial directives which will guide the position of Brazilian diplomats abroad.[134] The culture of Itamaraty is of a highly hierarchical and disciplined structure. Some Brazilian diplomats compare Itamaraty to the Army or to the Church in terms of hierarchy and discipline. The General Secretary assures that the hierarchy and discipline will prevail, and it does prevail in most cases.[135] When a Brazilian delegate leaves the country he takes with him directives that he has to follow, or his career may suffer on his return. The most obvious penalty for a junior diplomat is to lose a promotion. In Itamaraty, this may affect the prospective career of a diplomat, including the possibility of achieving the much sought after Ambassadorial rank. This explains why few diplomats are ready to defy the instructions of the General Secretary as soon as they arrive at a conference or in any international event. However, during the negotiations, the margin for manoeuvre of the delegate grows, as the distance from the Ministry increases. Moreover, if the subject of the conference is technical, as in the GATT, the General Secretary may delegate decisions to the head of the Department in charge of the issue.[136]

The model mentioned above is a simplified version of a real DMP because it only includes the DMP within Itamaraty in Brasilia. It is useful to understand the way the DMP works for conferences when there is no structure outside Brazil involved. The real DMP, however, is much more complex because in most cases it involves an existing structure outside the country as well. The policy of Itamaraty is to always keep permanent delegations within any of the organizations of which Brazil is a member. Thus, Brazilian Missions abroad have to be considered an essential part of the DMP.[137]

There are two circumstances in which decisions are taken outside the country: an international event of limited duration, such as ECO-RIO (1992) where there is no permanent structure; or in an international organization of which Brazil is a member and maintains a permanent delegation, as in the case of Brazilian Mission to the GATT. The delegates are free to try to meet the directives and objectives set in Brasilia using all their skills. There is no method of negotiations recommended or preferred by Itamaraty. The personality of the negotiators, their ability to negotiate, their previous knowledge of the subject being discussed and their techniques (tough or subtle, cooperative or abrasive) will play an important role in the negotiations. Itamaraty leaves the way in which the stipulated results will be achieved to their discretion. Itamaraty is interested in results.[138]

When Brazilian diplomats are already at an international event it may be that the directives that they received from Brasilia before departing are no longer valid or have to be updated. This may occur for several reasons; perhaps because other delegations have presented proposals to discuss topics which were not expected or included in the original agenda. Another reason is that other delegations may present declarations and the Brazilian delegates will have to respond with Itamaraty's position either supporting or rejecting the declarations during the negotiations. It is possible that a Brazilian diplomat would want to communicate the attitude of other delegations to Brazil's positions or proposals.[139]

In all cases, the personal views of the Brazilian diplomats will start to acquire their own dynamism and the individual position of Brazilian negotiators will begin to prevail. In their telegram /telex to Itamaraty, Brazilian delegates may interpret or emphasize some aspects of the negotiations according to their own view of the process. Delegates then suggest to Itamaraty what would be the best position in certain committees. Diplomats can also increase or decrease the possibility of a proposal being accepted in a meeting according to their own views about the Brazilian position. However, this is a dangerous game, because the delegate may involve himself in a three way dialogue between experts on both sides of the DMP: in the conference and at home, with experts from Itamaraty.[140]

This may happen because when the General Secretary receives a telex from a Brazilian representative at a conference it triggers the hierarchical mechanism of Itamaraty, but in the opposite way to which it had done before. It goes from the General Secretary to the Under Secretary in charge of the issue being negotiated until it reaches the appropriate division in charge of that topic. In other words, a conference abroad is followed internally by the sector which deals with that matter. If there is a Conference about the Ozone Layer, it will be followed by the Division of Itamaraty in charge of the environment or a division in charge of accompanying an equivalent international organization such as the United Nations Environment Programme (UNEP). The General Secretary also receives inputs from other sources, such as the Brazilian Embassy where the conference is taking place. This ensures that the General Secretary receives information from at least two different sources besides the Brazilian delegates about the conference, as well as its repercussions.[141]

A main feature of Itamaraty is its will not to be isolated.[142] Hence, when a Brazilian delegate notes that his proposal has no chance of being approved or he is left out on a limb on an issue, he communicates this to Itamaraty in order that a new position be elaborated. There is an intense dialogue and consultations between Brazilian delegates and Itamaraty.[143] However, this is just part of the story. Under the title General Secretariat a structure is hidden within which individuals fight for influence. It fails to identify which groups are formulating policy or the place of the General Secretary within this process.

When there is a Permanent Brazilian Mission abroad, as in the case of GATT, there will not be one but two DMPs. This happens because the Permanent Mission abroad will have its own structure, similar to the structure of an Embassy. In the case of the GATT, the Brazilian Mission in Geneva has one Ambassador, one Minister in charge of economic affairs, which includes GATT and UNCTAD and one Minister in charge of political and legal affairs, which includes the United Nations and all conferences which take place in Geneva. The 'Economic Department' of the Brazilian Mission in Geneva includes diplomats who are in charge of negotiating Brazil's position in many fields in the GATT and in the Uruguay Round.[144]

The Heads of Brazilian Permanent Missions have to contact the General Secretary in order to inform him what is being discussed in an international organization. In this context, the hierarchical system works in the same way as for Brazilian representatives at an international conference. The Ambassador has to present a draft-proposal of Brazil's position in that organization. When the General Secretary receives the telegram with the proposals, it is addressed to the respective Under Secretariat in charge of that issue, reaching down the hierarchical ladder until it arrives at the specific division that deals with the topic. Once the proposal has been analyzed by the different levels in the hierarchy in charge of the issue, the draft proposal comes back, going up the hierarchical ladder again, but no longer in the form of a draft proposal, but of the official position.[145]

The Brazilian Representative abroad then receives his former draft proposal modified (or not) which is now called "directive" for the negotiations. This process will be repeated each time that a new proposal is presented during the negotiations, or when a new fact changes the course of the negotiations. However, it may happen that during the negotiations a new proposal is presented and an answer is expected the same day. Thus, there will not be time to dispatch a telex to Itamaraty requesting further directives. In this case, the Head of the Brazilian Mission will have to make his own decisions. He will base his position on previous similar circumstances. Inertia then plays an important role in dictating future action. In this respect, the shared values and prevailing perceptions, allied with the personal views of the representative, will be the main explanation for the position adopted.[146]

Apart from that, it is important to note that Brazilian Permanent Missions almost duplicate the structure of an Embassy, with many advisors and specialists. If there is no available time to consult the General Secretariat, the Brazilian diplomats who work in the Brazilian Permanent Missions will be consulted instead. Thus, the Brazilian representative abroad instead of being a complementary tool to the official structure, replaces the DMP in Brasilia, as happened in the case of the GATT.[147]

When such a situation arises, instead of one, there will be two DMPs proceeding simultaneously, which may or may not arrive at the same conclusions. If both come to the same conclusions there is no problem at all. But if there is at least one component of the DMP at home that is at odds with the line that is being taken abroad, a dispute will occur. In this case, it may take some time for this process to come to an end. It is not possible to say beforehand which process will prevail. In most cases, the General Secretariat prevails over one of its branches abroad due to its supremacy in human, organizational, and administrative resources. But there is no guarantee that this will happen. It will also depend on several factors which impinge on the DMP.[148]

In some cases, the support that the head of the mission abroad has at home is important. This support can be basically of three kinds:

a) ideological: if the representative is defending a line which is considered to be, or was considered to be, the prevailing position it will be difficult for the group at General Secretariat to develop an alternative or innovative approach. Itamaraty is a conservative structure and shared values and old perceptions play an important role there. And in case of conflicts, tradition is always a safe bet;

b) organizational: if the representative abroad was supporting a position which was also contested at Itamaraty by an alternative group. Today, even on the question of ideology, the old guard has lost its power to convince the new generation that the old policy is wiser or better than the new. However, the old group still controls the key positions, although not necessarily all of them, in the official structure at home. In this case an alternative policy will have difficulties being implemented even if it is already partly influencing the DMP at home;

c) political support: it may happen that a new position has already been established, and a new group which wants to break with tradition may have taken control of the key positions in the DMP of the organization at the headquarters in Brasilia. However, the head of the Brazilian mission abroad may have political support outside Itamaraty, which strengthens his position. He can also threaten to resign which would cause deep embarrassment to the country.[149]

In this case, the imposition of a new group is unlikely because results of such action are uncertain. It is necessary first to be sure how much political support the representative has outside the agency (and from whom) before trying to implement a new policy. This process also takes time and has to be done by someone who believes that he can depend on at least an equivalent amount or greater political support than the representative abroad.

Second, the ability of the representative to influence the DMP depends on his knowledge of the subject. If the representative has, or is believed to have, a deep knowledge of the subject being discussed, the probability that he is going to be challenged decreases considerably. The representative can claim better knowledge of the negotiations and the international climate and positions which prevail in the negotiations than officials at home in charge of the DMP. The representative can only be challenged by a group which wants to implement a new policy if this group, aside of holding key positions, has the support of experts in the field with a coherent approach. Otherwise, the new group will be undermined by the arguments of the representative.[150]

Third, the personality of the representative abroad assumes an important role. If the representative is seen as a tough person and inflexible negotiator, and is feared or respected at home for his character, such as a strong personality, a potential lobby for a change in policy will have problems building a coalition group to challenge him, because of the fear of the consequences that might result. If the representative is feared and is believed to have either political support outside the agency or allies in the key positions inside the agency, the likelihood that a new group will challenge him will be at a minimum, except if the other group has a similar breadth of support, inside and outside the agency.

Fourth, the importance of such factors as political support outside the agency, and control of key positions inside the agency, knowledge/expertise of a specialized issue, the personality of the representative, and shared values and perceptions are increased in an agency which not only dominates the DMP, but is also under no external control, as is the case of Brazil's policy related to the GATT. Then the representative has no one who can supervise his actions, since the institutions which should exercise external control, the Congressional Committee on Foreign Affairs, Itamaraty, or presidential advisers on international relations are not working properly. The result is the complete autonomy of the representative and the inversion of the DMP: a branch abroad elaborates and formulates decisions and then becomes the main agent of the DMP.

The Decision-Making process related to the GATT
- Figure 4 -

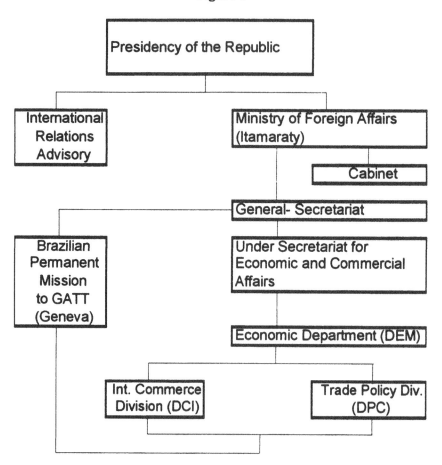

The table illustrates the DMP related to the GATT. One can note that nei-ther the President nor the Head of Itamaraty are part of the DMP although both have advisers at their disposal. Thus, formal communication is estab-lished between the Brazilian Mission and the General Secretariat. The DMP related to the GATT is quite simple and involves normally four offices: the General Secretariat, the Sub-Secretariat for Economic Affairs, the Economic Department and the Trade Policy Division.[151]

The main channel of communication between the General Secretariat and the Brazilian Mission to the GATT is still by telegram and telex. Although telephones and facsimile are used, they are not used as often as the telex. The first reason is to protect the delegate conducting the negotiations and to have a written record of their proposals and communications. What is more, not all officials of Itamaraty have access to international phone links, which also limits their use by key decision-makers. Thus, the availability of an authorized phone line is, in Itamaraty, an indicator of influence. The facsimile has the inconvenience of being accessible to any person near it, in a case where the head of a department does not have his own private number.[152]

All telegrams should pass, theoretically, through the General Secretariat, but the dynamic of the external negotiations, in particular those involving GATT, require some flexibility in the use of telegrams. As a result, direct communications developed between the Brazilian Mission to the GATT and the Division most interested in the process: in this case the Trade Policy Division.

The Trade Policy Division (DPC) is the place where all the Brazilian strategy related to the GATT was developed. This was always the place where the guidelines were determined as well as the orientation for Brazil's negotiations in the GATT. Technically the Head of the Trade Policy Division does not have administrative competence to send instructions to Brazilian representatives in Geneva. These have to be sent with the signature of the Head of the Economic Department. This strengthens the power of the Economic Department already alluded to. All directives for the Brazilian delegation needed, theoretically, to have the support of the Head of the Economic Department in order to become formal directives.

In spite of this administrative injunction, the Economic Department is not the only one to send telegrams directly to the Brazilian Mission at Geneva. All telegrams to Geneva must have the signature of the Head of the International Commerce Division (DCI). It does not mean that the telegrams had been written there. The telegrams could have been written in the Economic Department or in the General Secretariat, or by the Head of the Trade Policy Division. As may be seen from the diagram, the International Com. Division (DCI) was put beside the Trade Policy Division (DPC), although only DPC took part in the DMP.[153]

This illustrates another characteristic of Itamaraty, its decentralization. It is possible in Itamaraty for one of its Divisions to assume control of Brazilian policy without consulting other Divisions if it has the support, implicit or explicit, of the Head of the Economic Department (DEC). Thus, due to this delegation of functions, the Head of the DEC could transfer his administrative competence to send instructions to the GATT to the Head of the DPC. A sympathetic explanation says that as Itamaraty GATT's specialists were concentrated in this Division, the Brazilian Mission in Geneva needed to communicate with an office in Brasilia that could understand what was going on in Geneva. As a natural result, the DPC became the intermediary for the Brazilian Mission in Geneva in GATT affairs. A less sympathetic explanation is that Brazilian negotiators in the GATT used this expertise argument in order to exclude other actors of the DMP. Indeed, the DPC became very influential, in particular during the terms when Maciel and Batista were the Brazilian representative to the GATT.

Another important aspect of the DMP related to the GATT is that Heads of the Brazilian Permanent Mission in Geneva, which covers GATT, were always Ambassadors of great technical expertise and prestige (influence) at Itamaraty. For this reason, it would be very difficult for a Head of a Division or a Department Head to dictate the directives to the Representative in Geneva.

Brazil's position on the discussion of service issues

The strategic role of services for economic development

Traditional economic theory says that the growth of the service industry in domestic production is a consequence of economic development.[154] According to this view, development starts with the production of primary products until the appearance of manufacturing which then assumes dominance in the economy. Later on, the service sector develops and overtakes the industrial sector. This period corresponds to a post-industrial society. According to this theory, the importance of services to domestic industry increases as a result of development. Thus, it is not necessary to adopt a policy to stimulate the service sector, since its growth accompanies the increase of income. On the international level there is a natural division of labour, with Developed Countries (DCs) specialising in services, which require a high degree of technology and capital, and Less Developed Countries (LDCs) specialising in primary products and manufacturing.[155]

However, this theory has been challenged on several grounds. First, due to technological changes and the growth in the use of IT, service industries have undergone internal adjustment. Services which were available from inside some firms, such as advertising, started to be bought in from specialized agencies. On the other hand, due to the almost automatic availability of information, some firms, like supermarkets, started to enter other fields, such as the field of financing. Second, changes due to increased demand caused by higher personal incomes have played a minor role in the growth of the service sector. The main changes in the distribution of employment have resulted predominantly from changes in occupational structures within economic sectors.[156] Third, the introduction of services in the production of goods may reduce the labour costs per unit which means that comparative advantage cannot be based on low wages, even if it is for a labour intensive product.[157] Fourth, in the current environment, services are not a consequence of the development process, but a condition *sine qua non* for its existence. Indeed, the development of a modern service industry has created the complex-inter-linkage network which plays a multiple role in development. These inter-linkages happen in almost all service sectors such as banking and Information Technology (IT).[158]

Moreover, the service economy does not exist in isolation from the world economy.[159] The effect of this is that the service sector has a deep impact on the competitiveness of a country's foreign trade. As there is a linkage between rates of export growth and rates of economic growth, the conclusion is that the successful participation of a country in world trade today depends on an efficient service industry. For this reason, the service sector can be considered strategic to the process of development. Indeed, if a service is not provided efficiently, it has a negative impact on the export costs of a country.[160]

UNCTAD[161] has also noted that the existence of a well-structured shipping industry with adequate shipping services can mean the difference between a successful increase in exports and a setback in foreign trade. Not only can regular shipping services increase the reliability of a country's exports but, in addition, a competitive cost structure can stimulate the entry of other producers into the export sector. This would be unthinkable if the costs of port and shipping services were not in line with international standards.[162]

This analysis explains why the service sector was considered by Itamaraty to be a strategic one. Brazil considered this sector so strategic that it did not want to encourage the publication of studies about it. Indeed, even UNCTAD was not saved from this information boycott, and in the study carried out by that organization in 1985, Itamaraty refused to send information about the Brazilian service industry. Itamaraty's action in the service sector did not imply a refusal to recognize the importance of services. The best explanation for Itamaraty's stance on services is that Brazil favoured a multilateral approach to services, but only if it was carried out by an international organization which it considered reliable, such as UNCTAD. Moreover, Brazil was trying to develop its service industries, such as telecommunications and IT.

However, Brazil did not want to adopt the same kind of approach that it had in the 1950s when an automobile industry was created in Brazil but was controlled by Transnational Corporations (TNCs). Brazil wanted to create a service industry where the ownership of the companies would be in the hands of the State or of Brazilians. This became apparent in the case of the IT industry.[163]

Brazil's exports of services in the context of the service discussions

The export of services by LDCs was not as important as the export of other items, such as manufactured goods and food.[164] Thus, the arguments used by other LDCs[165] for not being interested in the service discussions were valid to Brazil. Among these arguments, it could be mentioned that the LDCs were mainly exporters of manufactured goods (for example, textiles) and of commodities, and not services. As a result, LDCs did not want to discuss services, but manufactured goods, textiles, food and commodities. Now, the importance of the exports of manufactured goods and food to Brazil will be illustrated.[166]

Although Brazil's exports of food were declining by an average of 4.5% per year in the 1980s, they still represented about 45% of Brazil's exports in 1980, at $9.3 bn.[167] In 1987, exports of food still accounted for more than 30% of Brazilian exports, or $8.5 bn.[168] This demonstrates the importance of this sector during the period considered.

On the other hand, Brazil's exports of manufactured goods showed a clear upward trend in the 1980s. Indeed, according to the World Bank, Brazilian manufactured exports rose from $7.7 billion in 1980 to $11.5 billion in 1984 and $11.7 billion in 1987, an increase of almost 50% in four years.[169] Using GATT's methodology the increase would have been even greater, from $7.5 billion in 1980 to $15.0 billion in 1987.[170] This represents an increase from around 35% in 1980 to almost 60% of Brazil's exports in 1987.[171] Certainly these data explain why Brazil wanted to discuss food and manufactured goods and not services. Moreover, the fear among LDCs that they would lose from an opening of the service sector to TNCs was shared by Brazil.

Brazil's exports of services were not negligible. Between 1980 and 1987 they were, on average, $1.9 billion per year.[172] This represented around 9% of Brazil's total exports. However, Brazil's imports of services were quite high: around $4.5 billion per year, on average, between 1980 and 1986.[173] This was the equivalent of around 25% of Brazil's imports. As a result of such imports of services, Brazil had a deficit in its service account of around $2.7 billion, on average, between 1980 and 1986.[174]

Brazil did not believe that this situation would change with an opening of its service market. In fact, Brazil feared it would get worse. Thus, Brazil felt that it was not competitive enough to liberalize its service sector. Moreover, Brazil had a domestic service sector which represented about 50% of its GDP.[175] It feared that this sector could either be destroyed by foreign competition, or fall into foreign ownership.

Some political implications of the discussions on services

Brazil also feared that the discussion on issues associated with services, such as FDI, would revive old debates over the role of private FDI that had been forgotten, but were not dead. In particular, Brazil had strict legislation concerning FDI in the field of energy, especially oil. If the new Round of negotiations under the aegis of the GATT determined that all service sectors should be opened to FDI, Brazil feared that there could be demonstrations to maintain the State monopoly.

Brazil argued that the interests of the LDCs were not being addressed in spite of promises by the DCs. The Multi Fibre Arrangement (MFA) and Voluntary Exports Restraints (VERs) continued to exist in spite of the fact that they were contrary to the spirit and the rules of the GATT.[176] Brazil argued that if the spirit of the GATT was violated in such old areas it could not extend its power to new ones, such as services.[177] Brazil mentioned as examples of protectionist measures penalty duties imposed on Brazilian steel pipe as well as quotas.

Brazil agreed in 1984 to a five year pact to voluntarily restrain its exports of steel to the US. Another sector in which Brazil felt that it had a comparative advantage was textiles. Thus, Brazil considered the MFA prejudicial to its interests. Moreover, other Brazilian products such as ethanol faced high US tariff barriers applied to alcohol imports.[178]

On the other hand, the US accused Brazil of unfair trade practices. The main complaint of the US was that the Brazilian Export Programme (BEFIEX) constituted a subsidy.[179] Moreover, the US was fighting against the Brazilian Law on IT, which prevented foreign companies from producing microcomputers in Brazil. The US government argued that the suspension of tariff concessions to Brazilian imports was a compensation for the loss in US sales due to Brazil's informatics policy.[180]

Brazil was aware of the strategic importance of the service sectors, in particular IT.[181] It also knew that IT was going to be the main factor in competitiveness. This is the reason why successive governments wanted to encourage Brazilian firms in the IT sector. This strategy became clear when the Law on IT was approved by parliament in 1985, with the open support of the government. Although the Law was restricted initially to hardware, it had provisions for software.[182] This case illustrated that there was a desire within the government not only to supply a domestic market estimated at $1.6 billion per annum, but also to ensure that the main decisions would be taken in Brazil, that is, that they would ensure national control of decisions. This explains why the protected market for microcomputers was expanded to include data processing. Brazil already had some firms in some service sectors, such as in telecommunications, in satellites and in IT.

The Brazilian government believed that these firms had an important role to play in Brazil's development. It was convinced that an opening of the service market in telephony, for instance to TNCs such as AT&T would cause the collapse of national firms in this sector and affect the process of development as a whole.[183]

Brazil maintained that all gains from a liberalization in services would go to DCs, since the most efficient service providers were TNCs from DCs. Itamaraty believed that Brazil could not compete in services. This was a misconception of comparative advantages, since some service sectors are very labour intensive, and Brazil has labour in abundance.[184] A clear example is the construction sector, where Brazil had an obvious comparative advantage. However, this was not properly explored. Indeed, Brazil's share in works abroad is not as important as it might be, when it is considered that Brazilian firms have significant experience with mega-constructions in Brazil.[185]

However, in the case of services, the perception by Itamaraty that Brazilian firms could not compete with DCs became more important than the fact that Brazilian firms had clear comparative advantages due to the lower salaries in Brazil.[186]

Reasons that explain Brazil's refusal to discuss services

Many reasons were put forward to explain Brazil's refusal to present technical studies in services, but the most important were:

1) Human resources: it was argued that there was no one in Brazil with sufficient expertise to prepare technical studies on services, in Itamaraty or in the Universities.

2) High costs: Even if there were professionals to undertake these studies, Itamaraty did not have enough money to pay them.

3) Lack of interest: Itamaraty was not interested in services. Batista considered that Brazil's objective in the GATT was to discuss products of national interest, for instance, manufactured goods, and not services. Thus, Itamaraty should concentrate its studies on these products.

4) Capitulation: If Brazil circulated studies in the GATT according to the 1982 Declaration, it would be implicitly accepting that services should be included in the GATT.

All these arguments can be challenged on different grounds.

1) Human resources: Itamaraty officials had previously negotiated sectorial service agreements in the UNCTAD and in other organizations. Thus, Brazilian diplomats had taken part in service negotiations before and could be employed to direct studies together with economists and technical staff from Brazil or from international organizations and could thereby prepare at least some sectorial studies. In fact, Itamaraty does have a staff of

economists, posted in different Departments, in Brazil and abroad, who could be employed for these studies. If this staff was insufficient, or if they were insufficiently prepared, Itamaraty could request additional staff from other Ministries to fill the gap. Moreover, it is hard to believe that there was no academic able to coordinate a study on services in all Brazilian academia. Finally, if there were no academic able to study services, Brazil certainly could send economists or diplomats to be trained in an international organization dealing with services, such as OECD, UNCTAD, the World Bank (IBRD) or IMF. Brazil already sends thousands of students to carry out MA and PhD programmes at universities in the US and in Europe. Certainly Brazil could have reserved some scholarships for students who wanted to research services, if Itamaraty had been interested in doing so. In fact, Itamaraty receives funds from the Organization of American States (OAS) to send students to carry out research abroad. Itamaraty could have directed these resources towards training experts in services.

2) High costs: Apart from the existence of resources mentioned above, Itamaraty wastes money. Itamaraty has many Ambassadors in the same country (seven in the US), representing Brazil in different fora. With creativity and reallocation of Ambassadors, enough money could be saved to spend on a technical study. Itamaraty could also train some diplomats in services, whether by way of intensive training at the OECD or any institution dealing with services in order to reduce costs.[187] Moreover, if Brazil was without funds, and its diplomats unavailable, Itamaraty could ask international organizations to prepare technical studies: OECD, IMF, IBRD, the United Nations Economic Commission for Latin America (ECLA), the Inter-American Development Bank (IDB), and UNCTAD. Itamaraty could ask sectorial associations to pay for a study on the role of their respective sectors in the Brazilian economy. Itamaraty could also request funds from the IBRD, IDB or IMF to train economists in services. Brazil could also make use of exchange programmes with foreign Universities in order to offer scholarships to lecturers from DCs to stay in Brazil and to teach fundamental aspects of internal trade in services. In DCs there are hundreds of PhD. students and lectures who would like to live abroad. The costs of this programme would not be high, since most Brazilian universities already have accommodation and the gains would overcome its costs.

3) Lack of interest: One cannot be interested in something if one does not know anything about it. Diplomats emphasized that Brazil was not a *demandeur* of services, which in diplomatic code means that Brazil did not

want to discuss services.[188] If Itamaraty thought that services were not of interest to Brazil it should have prepared studies to prove this lack of interest. If Itamaraty could have done that, it would have been really surprising, because modern development theory emphasizes the need for services to allow economic development.[189] In fact, Brazil was interested in developing its service industry, and Batista accepted the need for an agreement on services but, for ideological reasons, he refused to accept the GATT as such a forum.

4) Capitulation. It is a mistake to believe that Brazil preparing and circulating studies on services would be a way of admitting that GATT was the right place to negotiate services. Brazil could have prepared its studies and then presented them in other fora, such as UNCTAD, IMF, the IBRD, or IDB. In that case Brazil could have stated that it was circulating studies without prejudice to its stance which at that time opposed the negotiations of service within the GATT.

Brazil's arguments against the circulation of studies at the GATT became weaker and weaker as time went on although Itamaraty was refusing to prepare the studies. As a result, Brazil's position became vulnerable in the negotiations preliminary to the launching of the Round. When the preparations for the new Round began, Brazil still knew nothing about the impact of liberalization of services on its economy, and what the possible consequence resulting from the creation of an international framework in this field would be.

Brazil went to the meetings on the preparation for the new Round without a proper knowledge of its service sector and the impact of liberalization.[190] So Itamaraty, which is extremely strict about the preparation of its diplomats going to negotiations, was caught in its own trap. Batista could not discuss something he did not know about without invoking old values, prejudices, ideologies and perceptions. The best alternative to a country in this situation is therefore to try to block things as much as it can in the hope that some day the subject will be forgotten. As this eventuality did not arise Brazil continued to maintain its blocking policy. Later, some secret studies were carried out by the Economic Department of Itamaraty, based on questionnaires sent to private companies which might be interested in an agreement on services. Without any knowledge of the possible impact of the subject being discussed, Brazilian firms affirmed that they did not have any interest in the changing of the rules or in opening the Brazilian market. The questionnaires lacked any objectivity or depth. It is hard to imagine that a decision-maker could take a position based on them.[191]

It is very difficult to explain why Brazil did not ask an organization such as UNCTAD, with which Brazil sympathized, for a study to be prepared of its service sector. Human resources and high costs can be dismissed since it would be UNCTAD's concern. The main explanation is that Batista believed that Brazil could successfully exclude services from the GATT negotiations and bring them to UNCTAD or to a neutral new forum. Even if services were included in a multilateral negotiation, Batista could argue that trade in services was a new issue and Brazil knew nothing about it. Thus, Batista probably believed that the non-existence of previous studies carried out by Brazil would work in his favour. He could use Brazil's ignorance on services to slow down the negotiations, as he did during the Uruguay Round.[192]

Brazil's participation in coalitions before the launching and during the Uruguay Round[193]

One of the features of world politics in the post-war era is the existence of international institutions which affect everyday life in the field of trade, telecommunications, etc. Aware of this fact, Brazil participates in these world regimes together with other nations, forming alliances or coalitions. The main reasons for this are probably Itamaraty's perception that it has no bargaining power in the international system, which is not the case.

An important aspect of this section and those which follow it are to demonstrate that Brazil's participation in coalitions before and during the Uruguay Round was a direct result of the personal view of the Brazilian negotiator himself of the negotiating process. The positions assumed by the Brazilians do not necessarily reflect the official position of Itamaraty. Although this seems a contradiction, since by definition the Brazilian representative has to follow instructions, it is possible that a representative influences the Decision-Making Process (DMP) in Brasilia to such a point that he becomes the main decision-maker and headquarters of Itamaraty in Brasilia just receive news of the outcome of the process. The way that this may occur has been demonstrated in the last chapter. The two most important individual reasons why this occurs are the decentralized system of Itamaraty, which expects the diplomats abroad to take decisions, and the impossibility of controlling the decisions to be taken by the representative, except by his immediate removal, which is not a common practice in Brazilian diplomacy. In order to illustrate this point, two coalitions are going to be analyzed in more depth: the Group of 10 (G-10), which represents a typical coalition of Less Developed Countries (LDCs), and the Cairns Group, a sectorial coalition which includes LDCs and Developed Countries (DCs).

The Latin American group

Initially, the Brazilian position regarding international trade issues was co-ordinated at a regional level. This was already the case in UNCTAD, because this institution based its works on geographical criteria. Naturally, Brazil brought this pattern to GATT, where it intended to represent not only Latin American countries, but other LDCs as well. Thus, when the discussions on the launching of a new Round started, Brazil tried to repeat the pattern. Indeed, Brazil had been trying to develop a common stance among Latin American countries in regional meetings to 'prepare' them for the 1982 Ministerial Meeting in November. These regional meetings were called Latin American Coordination Meetings, and took place throughout 1982.[194]

The main conclusion of these Meetings was that trade in services required the presence of the provider of the service, which required Foreign Direct Investment (FDI). Thus, the discussion on services included the issue of FDI by way of the right of establishment. It was felt that as the discussions would centre on the right of establishment and on FDI, a suitable forum would be needed to discuss this. In the minds of Latin American countries the issue of services effectively assumed a higher legal competence and technical expertise of GATT, which should only discuss trade. For these countries, the GATT was not even a proper forum to discuss the issue of trade in services, let alone FDI. The Latin American position was expressed in regional fora such as the Latin American Economic System (SELA), which had 26 members, of which 16 were members of GATT. SELA included countries from South America, Central America and the Caribbean.

Certainly, Brazil's capacity for mobilization was reflected in the negotiations, where Itamaraty could always argue that it was speaking not only on its own behalf, but also on the behalf of Latin American countries and LDCs in general. In these Meetings, Brazil always emphasized that services were, or should be, an instrument for stimulating development. Therefore, any discussion on services should take into account the development interests of LDCs. The second aspect of the Brazilian position was to question the GATT as the proper place to discuss services, since the GATT had no legal competence to do so. If multilateral action should be taken, Brazil maintained that the UNCTAD would be the proper place to do so, since it already had some expertise in the subject. Third, Brazil maintained that it was out of the question that LDCs make concessions on services in order to receive concessions on goods, under the form of the General System of Preferences (GSP), for instance.[195]

With the aim of obtaining a united Latin American position, two High Level Coordination Meetings were convened, one in Caracas (22-24 August), and one in Brasilia (26-27 May). At these Meetings, several recommendations were approved. The main aspects of these were to emphasize the lack of priority of the issue of services to Latin American countries, and to coordinate the opposition of these countries to the inclusion of services in the GATT. The results of these meetings demonstrated that the Latin American countries intended to create their own service industries before discussing opening their markets to FDI.[196] Moreover, one should not forget that Brazil was giving subsidies, and financial support towards the creation of a national Information Technology (IT) industry, which should be able to develop an endogenous technology. However, in spite of the official support of Latin American countries for Brazil's opposition to the introduction of services in the GATT, the stance of these countries in the GATT was far from clear. Brazil learnt that although Latin American countries were ready, in regional forums, to subscribe to rigorous rhetorical opposition to FDI, they were not ready to maintain a position of open confrontation with the US. Some countries, such as Barbados, and Jamaica had hopes of exporting of specific services, such as transborder data flows.[197] Other countries, such as Mexico, which only joined the GATT in 1987, had the objective of increasing its trade with the US through free-trade agreements, and would not create a conflict with that country on the issue of services. Finally, other countries, such as Colombia and Venezuela, had other specific interests in their relationship with the US (for example, fight against drugs). For this reason, they wanted to maintain a special relationship with the US, and would not allow the service issue to interfere, even if they were in principle against the introduction of services in the GATT.

Moreover, it seems that Brazil did not realize that the SELA was basically a rhetorical forum, meaning that any country could attend and make any statement but this statement would not necessarily be reflected in any official position. In GATT, on the contrary, the positions would have a direct effect on the trade negotiations. That is why countries in Latin America felt free to say what they wanted in the SELA, looking to their domestic constituencies, but would not maintain the same position in GATT, where it was necessary to take part in technical discussions. In the end, Brazil could only depend on the full support of four countries in the region: Argentina, Cuba, Nicaragua and Peru. Unfortunately, Brazil was not in good company. Except Argentina, the other three countries could be considered as marginalized in international affairs, and had no influence on GATT.[198]

Only Argentina could be considered influential on GATT issues, but agricultural issues, not services. However, it tried to maintain a more flexible position than Brazil on the issue of services. As a consequence of this lack of support, Brazilian strategy had to be reformulated. Brazil had to seek not only partners in Latin America, but also from other regions. Moreover, Brazil's future partners were not only required to be against the inclusion of services in the GATT, but also to be able to keep a firm position on the subject. They had to be influential, preferably key-countries in their regions and less dependent on the US than Latin American countries in order to resist the bilateral pressures that would inevitably appear. Finally, Brazil had to try to attract support from countries with a historical role in foreign affairs. These countries needed to be principled, demonstrate leadership and the capacity for mobilization, but also flexibility to negotiate if the situation so required. These characteristics were to be found in the G-10, though to different degrees.

Was there a secret Brazil-India alliance?

Before starting to discuss the G-10, it should be considered whether the Group really existed. Some authors suggest that the G-10 might only be a smoke-screen to disguise the interests (self-perceived) of its two main members, Brazil and India. According to this view, the alliance of Brazil and India was a marriage of convenience and interests, based on the perception (true or false) that these two countries had different interests from other LDCs in general, and from the Group of 77 (G-77) in particular. Brazil would be a 'NIC with a foreign policy'.[199] As a result, the alliance wanted to exploit the contradictions among DCs to their own benefit. This would explain, for instance, the reticence of Brazil to joining the Cairns Group, since it would be difficult to maintain an active Brazilian presence in both coalitions.

This approach has the merit of underlining the fact the two most influential members of the G-10 coalition were Brazil and India. However, it fails to answer other questions. If the G-10 was only an alliance of Brazil and India, why was the G-10 created in the first place? The argument of the smoke-screen is superficial, because it does not justify the creation of a coalition which had been in place since 1982. Moreover, it is incorrect to say that Brazil only perceived that it had different interests from other LDCs in the middle of the 1980s, when the G-10 was already working. Since the end of the 1970s, when UNCTAD was discussing the Common Fund, Brazil had perceived that not all LDC interests were identical. This helps to explain why Brazil was one the last LDC to sign and ratify the Common Fund. Furthermore, one should not confuse tactics with strategy. Certainly, the alliance of Brazil and India did exist, but the G-10 cannot be reduced to this alone. The alliance was the most dynamic aspect of the G-10, but this group was much more complex than just that alliance. Indeed, the G-10 included Yugoslavia, one of the most respected leaders of the Non-Aligned Movement; Egypt, Tanzania and Nigeria, the most influential countries from Africa; Brazil and Argentina, the most influential countries from Latin America; and India, the most influential LDC in Asia. Thus, the countries which were part of the G-10 were, in most cases, key-countries or middle powers with strong regional influence. With the inclusion of Argentina, Yugoslavia and Nigeria (not to mention Brazil and India) it was assured that the G-10 would also keep a high profile, and could transform the service issue into a North-South battle, as Brazil and India wanted.[200]

It is interesting to note that in the construction of this coalition, Brazil reproduced the existing pattern of UNCTAD, based on geographical criteria. The answer to two questions, however, helps to explain the G-10. First, did the G-10 coalition represent the opinion of all, or at least the majority of the LDCs? And second, if it did represent them, would it work? These questions will be answered very shortly. But before that, we will examine briefly the membership and the aims of the G-10.[201]

The group of ten developing countries (G-10)

Members and aims

The G-10 was officially created in 1984, following the Work Programme negotiations,[202] when some countries noted that 'new issues', such as services, were given full consideration, while some provisions proposed in the Tokyo Round and in the 1982 Ministerial Declaration had not been fully implemented.[203]

It is interesting to note that although Brazil and India were the spokesmen of the LDCs in the GATT,[204] the G-10 never managed to become a 'popular' coalition among LDCs. According to Hamilton & Whalley (1989), it had only five 'firm' members.[205] They were: Argentina, Brazil, India, Egypt and Yugoslavia, the so called 'Gang of Five'.

Eventually, the Group evolved and included another five members: Cuba, Nicaragua, Nigeria, Peru and Tanzania. Except Nigeria, the other countries were less influential in the G-10.

According to Hamilton & Whalley, the G-10 can be defined as a blocking coalition, since it blocked the launch of the Uruguay Round for some time.[206] It could also be defined as an agenda-moving coalition, since it wanted to include (and exclude) some issues of the negotiations.[207]

In short, we could say that the main objectives of the G-10 towards the new Round were:

1) To assure that all the negotiations agreed during the Tokyo Round, including tariff reductions, would be put in place before the launch of a new Round.

2) Not to start the discussions of a new Round without concluding the inclusion of the 'old issues' in the GATT. These 'old issues' included agriculture, textiles and clothing. Agriculture had not been discussed in the GATT since 1955 when the US asked for a waiver.[208] Textiles and clothing were regulated in a special regime, technically outside GATT rules, the Multi Fibre Arrangement (MFA).

3) To obtain a commitment from DCs that they would not increase their tariffs during the negotiations for a new Round. This commitment became known, in GATT jargon, 'standstill'.

4) To achieve an abolition of all trade practices of DCs which were against the GATT rules, or in the gray area, before the launch of the new Round. This request became known as 'rollback'.

5) Not to discuss 'new issues' in the new Round. If this was not possible, the G-10 wanted to discuss services outside the GATT, preferably in UNCTAD.

An interesting question is to know if this programme of the G-10 represented the aims of all, or at least, the majority of LDCs. This is the topic of the next section.

Did the G-10 coalition represent the majority of LDCs?

To answer this question it is necessary to know if there were mechanisms for assessing and evaluating the point of view of other LDCs. Some authors have suggested that although the number of countries which took part in that coalition was relatively small, there was wider support for that group.[209] According to this view, tacit support for the G-10 was widespread among LDCs. However, there is no concrete evidence to support this view. This book does not take into consideration tacit support, only that which is open and vocal. In order to determine if there was support, this would have to be translated into declarations of support or a nominal vote. Furthermore, it is important to note that silent support cannot be measured.

It should also be emphasized that part of Brazil's influence in the GATT was based on the assumption that it represented the interest of LDCs, and that, as a result, when Brazil expressed its position in the GATT it was speaking on behalf of the LDCs as well. In this case, Brazil and India were the spokesmen of LDCs, as Golt noted. However, one cannot accept this assumption if there is no instance of other countries supporting this bilateral alliance. Thus, the question that can be put is: Does the assumption that Brazil and India were the main spokesmen of LDCs in the GATT system apply to the G-10 in the case of services as well? In this regard it is important to note that when Brazil reproduced the method of the UNCTAD (geographical criteria) in the GATT, Brazil was repeating one of the main defects of UNCTAD, and none of its qualities. That is if one accepts what is said about this criteria by a former member of its staff, Thomas Weiss.[210] Furthermore, it seems that when Brazil and India decided to create the coalition, they thought the support of other LDCs would be automatic, since those two countries were still considered to be the leaders of the Group of 77 in UNCTAD, which comprised almost all LDCs. However, the G-10 became, at best, a poor imitation of UNCTAD in the GATT. This happened because, as Weissman noted, the geographical criterion does not ensure broad representation, as is its intent. In fact, it only reinforces the idea of middle powers and regional influence, against which UNCTAD fought. The countries which have a stronger interest in a subject are not guaranteed that their voice will be heard. Quite the opposite, the geographical criterion assures the regional powers automatic representation - even if they are not interested in a particular subject. Certainly this process jeopardizes the interests of less influential countries which do not have any alternative channel to make themselves heard. Moreover, when the G-10 was created, neither Brazil nor India could say that they represented all LDCs. They were only defending what they believed were their own interests. The latter can be confirmed because since 1984 it became apparent that Brazil no longer even represented the Latin American countries.

As was mentioned, of the 16 member States of the SELA which were simultaneously members of GATT, only 5 adhered to the G-10, or less than one third.[211] As Sciamma noted, there was a defection of countries from SELA. The most surprising aspect of this episode is not the defections themselves, but the fact that Brazil continued to pretend that this had not happened. This was the first sign that Brazil was becoming isolated in the GATT. The second was when the US had proposed and obtained in 1985, by way of a vote of the GATT membership, the convention of a Special Session to decide over the launching of the new Round in September. Brazil and India were convinced that they could behave as leaders of the G-77 and create a mini-coalition in services, since they considered that there was no contradiction in principle between being part of both groups.

However, it seems that Brazil did not realize that its interests did not coincide with the interests of other LDCs at least on the issue of services. As Brazil had a deficit of US$12,9 bi in 1984[212] due to the payment of foreign debt, and some LDCs were in a similar situation, Batista imagined that other LDCs would support Brazil's position as they had done so many times before in the GATT. In this instance, Batista made three mistakes simultaneously. First, discussions on the GATT did not cover factor services (viz. income of capital), which would have included the issue of foreign debt. Second, even if negotiations included factor services, many LDCs which had a lower foreign debt than Brazil, such as the Asian NICs, had no reason to be worried about the impact of trade liberalization on their current account.[213] Third, with regard to the aspects of services which were being discussed in the GATT meetings many countries, such as Mexico, Singapore and South Korea, had a surplus and not a deficit as Brazil had. Whilst Brazil thought that its own situation as an indebted country could be extrapolated to all LDCs. Batista did not consider that LDCs had comparative advantages in some service sectors, such as South Korea in construction services and Singapore in air transport and financial services.[214]

The answer to the question posed at the beginning of this section is that not only did Brazil not represent most LDCs, but it also had a misconception of their interests. There was no mechanism for consultation between the G-10 and other LDCs. One can propose two hypotheses to explain the lack of coordination between the G-10 and other LDCs. The first of these is the assumption that as Brazil and India were the voice of LDCs, they did not need to consult them, since their position would represent the LDCs' position. Another hypothesis is that Brazil was so determined to block any effort to introduce services in the GATT, that it believed that its own influence, together with that of India and the G-10, was enough to prevent a discussion on services.

This could be explained by the personality and style of the first Brazilian Ambassador to the GATT, Batista, during the period under review, too centralizing and a poor coordinator.[215] In any case the result was the same. The G-10 did not consult LDCs which isolated its members from other LDCs. LDCs were divided into two groups: those who did not want to see services in the GATT - the hard-liners, the G-10, and those who were ready to accept them if some safeguards were taken - the moderates or the Group of 20.

The Group of 20 moderate LDCs (the G-20) represented the first open challenge to the role of Brazil and India as the spokesmen of LDCs in the GATT system. Although the hand of the G-20 was weaker than it would have been if it had included Brazil and India, as Australian Ambassador Oxley noted, it did indicate that the role of Brazil and India was openly put into question.[216]

Could the G-10 work? In order to answer this question it is necessary to know what the G-10 wanted. The 'programme' of the G-10 was based on its draft proposal for the launching of the Uruguay Round to the Preparatory

Committee (PrepCom). Although it seems clear that the presentation of the G-10 proposal had as its main objective to obstruct the work of PrepCom, it is assumed that it reflected the interests of the G-10, as no group could be expected to submit a proposal against its own goals. Thus, even though in the case of the G-10, Brazil and India created what can be called a negative coalition whose main goal was to block the inclusion of services in the prospective new Round, this does not mean that nothing positive could be derived from the Brazil-India alliance. We examine now the positive and negative aspects of the G-10 proposal, whose main architect was Batista.

On the positive side, Brazil wanted a ban (a roll-back) on all existing protectionist measures - such as Voluntary Export Restraints (VERs), quotas, etc. Brazil also wanted a commitment from DCs that they would not adopt other protectionist measures after the launching of the Round. There was also a trade-off within the G-10 between the interests of its members. The liberalization of trade in agricultural products and in particular trade in tropical products was another important goal of Batista, though it was not important to India. India supported Brazil in this matter and in exchange Brazil supported India on the issue of the liberalization of international trade in textiles (ending the MFA). The former was not so important to Brazil's demands, but it was vital to India since her main manufactured exports were textiles. The G-10 also wanted better access to the DC markets and a control on the use of safeguards.

On the negative side the LDCs wanted a wider integration in the GATT system through the use of Special and Differential (S&D) treatment and an expansion of the GSP. However, as Koekkoek noted, the integration of LDCs into the GATT system requires the progressive application of GATT rules and procedures to them in the same way as they apply, in principle, to DCs.[217] The S&D treatment does not ensure this, on the contrary, it constitutes an exception to it.

Moreover, S&D treatment became valueless property,[218] or something useless. In spite of this, both demands were a permanent part of the G-10 programme. Thus, the main substantive aspect of the G-10 coalition was to try to prevent the discussion of services in the Uruguay Round. When analyzing the positive and negative aspects of the G-10 demands, one should not forget that the G-10 was formed to deal with the issue of services. Therefore, the fact that there were many positive contributions from the G-10 does not mean that the group was willing to exchange these positive demands for an inclusion of services in the GATT framework. On the contrary, they were considered a necessary condition, but not sufficient to launch the Uruguay Round.

The realization of these demands did not guarantee that the issue of services could be included in the Punta Declaration. Therefore, services should be seen as the cornerstone of the coalition and it is for this reason that the G-10 has been referred to as a negative coalition. Indeed India's main objective was to exclude services from the Uruguay Round.[219] If this was not possible, the second option was not to prevent any link being made with the GATT framework. This was to avoid the DC seeking concessions on services as a price for concessions goods to LDCs.

However, concessions on goods were only one way of getting LDCs to make concessions on services. A second alternative was to make an international agreement on services which would exclude LDCs from its benefits. This would prevent the appearance of the free-riding problem. Desai's conclusion is that the main goal of the G-10 coalition - preventing foreign competition in services - was unworkable due to the vulnerability of the position of its main members. This was because these two countries adopted a hard line position which would be difficult to maintain. This is not without considering the fact that both Brazilian and Indian markets for services would be opened by bilateral pressure from the US, as the South Korean insurance market had been.[220] However, this does not mean that Brazil and India could not contribute to constructive solutions if they wanted.[221]

Bhagwati came to the same conclusion as Desai.[222] In 1987 he had declared that the position of the G-10 was unsustainable and would, in its extreme form, lead to the adoption of a code regulating services against their interests as the subsidies code adopted during the Tokyo Round had. If the LDCs had wanted to influence the outcome of a prospective agreement on services or at least its safeguards, the LDCs would have had to argue for them. However, they could not do so unless they actively participated in the rule making. This is what happened.

The Cairns Group[223]

General aspects

The situation in agriculture was very complex due to the wide variety of proposals. While the US initially sought the abolition of all trade distortions in agriculture, the EC only agreed to short-term adjustments in the Common Agricultural Policy (CAP).[224] The Cairns Group was in an awkward position. It aimed to liberalize agricultural trade in the long run, as the US did, but it would consider short run proposals, such as those presented by the EC.[225] Thus, the Cairns Group's room for manouevre was limited by the respective US and EC positions. However, the changing configuration of power in the global political economy diminished the ability of these two major actors to set the agenda and to direct the negotiations themselves.[226] The Cairns Group worked as a bridge builder and consensus seeker between the major actors, and between the major actors and antagonistic LDCs.[227] Within this context, Brazil's position was essentially contradictory. On one hand Brazil, as a food exporter, was interested, in principle, in the liberalization of the agricultural sector by the EC. On the other hand, ideological constraints, represented by the Brazilian representative in the GATT, Batista, prevented Brazil from a full participation in coalition between LDCs and DCs. This is the argument which will be developed in this section. It should be no surprise that Brazil's participation in the Cairns Group will essentially be contradictory.

Indeed, the Cairns Group was made up of countries which vary widely (for example, Canada, Hungary, Argentina, Brazil and Australia). Nonetheless, it was characterized for its relative cohesion.[228] It has been suggested that this can be explained by the fact that the Cairns Group shared common interests and was a natural ally of the US. In fact, interests within the Cairns Group[229] varied and continuous work was needed to coordinate positions.

Origins

The Cairns Group stirred to life at the end of 1985. The then Australian Ambassador to the GATT, Alan Oxley, noted that a new round of negotiations could be launched at any moment. He warned that if agricultural exporters wanted this issue to be included in the new Round they could not leave it in the hands of the US and EC.[230] It would be necessary to build a coalition of interests. Oxley then contacted his Uruguayan and New Zealand counterparts. Uruguay was charged with contacting Brazil and Argentina, while the Australian delegation approached Thailand. By March 1986, the first meeting to discuss agricultural trade took place at Montevideo. The participants would constitute the core of the Cairns Group. In July 1986, it was the turn of Thailand to organize a broader, preliminary, meeting at Pattaya.

Finally, in August 1986 the Group met at Cairns, in Australia, which would lend its name to the coalition.[231] It was the first time a group was built around a common interest, that is, agricultural exports, by a coalition of LDCs, DCs and Asian countries.[232] The Group accounted for around 25% of world exports of agricultural products, more than 50% of world exports of beef, more than 35% of world exports of wheat and more than 35% of rice exports.[233]

Aims of the Cairns Group

Oxley believes that the reasons for the success of the Group were fourfold. First, the Group's common interests were strong.[234] All countries in the group would benefit from an opening in the market for agricultural products. Second, the initial commitment of the Group was at Ministerial Level. Third, the Group attended to the domestic political interests of its members. Fourth, there was a significant dispute between the US and the EC on this issue. The Cairns Group could, therefore, play down this dispute.[235] The final objective of the Group was complete world trade liberalization in agriculture.

Brazil's position

Agricultural Trade liberalization was exactly what Brazil wanted. But Brazil's belief in protectionism, and its commitment to other LDCs in the G-10, prevented it from enjoying full membership in the Cairns Group. This was despite Brazil's strong interest in the export of agricultural products: around 50% of Brazil's exports are agricultural, or food products.[236] Thus, it was in

Brazil's best interests to take an active part in the Cairns Group. However, Brazil's insistence that the Cairns Group should only be an informal group for coordinating positions obviously weakened the position of the Group in negotiations. How does one explain this contradiction?

One explanation has ideological roots. Brazil was a member of the G-77 at UNCTAD, which was made up solely of LDCs, where Brazil was very active.[237] Thus, Itamaraty felt that it could not join a group which linked LDCs and DCs because it would be a contradiction for Brazil to join other DCs in a common cause. Indeed, while Brazil was very much involved in the struggle for a New International Economic Order (NIEO), this kind of position made some sense. But how does one explain this attitude if there was no prospect of a change for a NIEO?

Another line of explanation, similar to the first but with a subtle difference, is based on power. In this view, Brazil was not interested in LDCs' development, but wanted only to be their leader in other fora, such as UNCTAD. The weak point of this explanation is that power would be an end in itself. This does not explain Brazil's refusal to participate effectively in the Cairns Group, where it could also have tried to exercise influence.

An alternative line of explanation is based on the Brazilian Decision-Making Process (DMP). As was mentioned before, Itamaraty is decentralized. This gives autonomy to its delegates and representatives. As a result, Itamaraty's position will depend on its negotiator's understanding of what is, and what is not, the national interest. In the case of the GATT, Brazil's negotiator, Batista, was extremely nationalistic and had a very negative view of the US. He was convinced that the Cairns Group only represented the interests of the US.[238] During the period that Batista was leading the Brazilian negotiating team, he managed to prevent the Cairns Group from working on a formal basis. This ended after 1987 when Tarso became *de facto* Minister of Foreign Affairs, and recalled Batista from his position in Geneva at the end of 1987.[239]

Another explanation of Brazil's attitude, on a more profound level, is related to the self-image of the country. In spite of the fact that 50% of Brazil's exports are agricultural products or food, Brazil did not see itself as an agricultural exporter.[240] It is amazing that a country whose exports are more than 50% accounted for by either agricultural products or food does not perceive itself as an agricultural exporter. Itamaraty had stated that it was not clear whether Brazil would benefit from agricultural trade liberalization.

These perceptions do not change the fact that Brazil was a food exporter and could benefit from agricultural trade liberalization.

However, the under-estimation of the agriculture sector demonstrated the importance of the impact which UNCTAD had in Brazil. Since Brazil's main goal was to export manufactured goods, Brazil wanted to be seen as an exporter of manufactured products, or, perhaps as a NIC, but not as an agricultural exporter. As a result, if Brazil had accepted the fact that it was an agricultural exporter it would have implied that all the effort it had expended on industrialization was in vain. The UNCTAD heritage was so strong that when Australia started to put pressure on Brazil to agree that the Cairns Group present a comprehensive trade liberalization proposal in agriculture it received a very strange answer from Brazil. Tarso said he could accept it if the Cairns Group recognized the special interest of LDCs. This was accepted by Australia.[241]

Needless to say the acceptance of the proposal meant that Brazil was not only coordinating positions in the Cairns Group, but was agreeing to a joint position. In other words, Brazil was collaborating in a group which involved DCs. In practice, Brazil was rejecting the principle of solidarity among LDCs, which was the *leitmotif* of UNCTAD. Therefore, it is correct to argue that the Cairns group represents a U-turn in Brazil's political strategy of solidarity with LDCs, which prevailed at UNCTAD (the G-77). This occurred in spite of the fact that Brazil argued in the Cairns Group that S&D treatment for LDCs should prevail over its interests in agriculture.[242] This represents a contradiction, since there was no unity among LDCs on agricultural issues.[243] And as Don (1989) noted, the insistence on S&D treatment might reduce the opportunity of LDCs to reap the benefits from liberalization.[244]

Divisions within Cairns Group

In general, a condition for the success of a coalition is its capacity to overcome internal differences in order to achieve a common goal. However, it seems that the Cairns Group was more heteregeneous than was thought. It was divided into two sub-groups. The hard-line sub-group, made up of Argentina and Brazil, wanted deep reforms in order to bring *de facto* agriculture into the GATT regime. Canada led the conservative sub-group and wanted more moderate changes. On at least two issues the difference of approach in the Cairns Group became very clear: internal support for farmers and market access. Hard-liners wanted a cut of at least 50% in internal support to farmers.[245] Canada did not subscribe to this position. On market access, the Cairns Group wanted a 75% reduction of tariff equivalents. Canada, however, proposed that quantitative import restrictions be permitted in products under supply control, that is, dairy and poultry products.[246] It was easier for Itamaraty than for Canada to call for cuts in internal support for farmers in the EC and in the US because Brazil's agriculture programme is based on price support and not on support for farmers, as in Canada. It seems that programmes based on support for farmers are more susceptible to influence from special interests than programmes based on price support to commodities.

Eventually, this started to cause concern, since there was a gap between Canadian rhetoric and practice.[247] Indeed, Canada was later perceived as a free-rider within the Cairns Group. In fact, Canada did not respect the principles of the Cairns Group of "rollback and standstill" and increased the subsidies of the domestic grain and oilseeds industry.

The Australian position in the Group was quite interesting. It badly needed agricultural trade liberalization since it depended on the export of some agricultural products (beef, dairy products, etc.). Thus, it supported the US efforts to liberalize agricultural trade, but it clashed with the US on competition for markets.[248] But it is beyond dispute that the similarities of views between Australia and the US on many trade related agricultural issues eased relation between the US and the Cairns Group. Australia became the main mediator and stabiliser of the coalition.

These different views within the Cairns Group instead of becoming an obstacle to negotiations became a useful weapon. When the Cairns Group wanted to radicalize its position, it would use Brazil or preferably Argentina. This was what happened in 1988. During the Montreal negotiations, Argentina refused to accept a compromise between the US and the EC in agriculture and put on hold all negotiations in the Uruguay Round in the name of freer trade.

The fact that an LDC was arguing and halting the trade negotiations in the name of freer trade was very embarrasing to the US, which was accepting a less than optimal situation. Afterwards, the US and EC started to negotiate again and a solution more acceptable to the Cairns Group was found.

The importance of the Cairns Group was that it had something very concrete to offer to all its members: agricultural trade liberalization. This was enough to mobilize the Group, since all its members stood to gain in different degrees from it. The only country which was not very sure about what it could gain from agricultural liberalization was Brazil.[249]

Conclusions

Although parliament did not have a direct impact in the DMP related to the GATT, some MPS, such as Roberto Campos had an indirect influence. Basically, this happened through the attack of the ISI model which contributed to the strengthening of the moderate group in Itamaraty, where the Decision-Making Process (DMP) takes place. This agency has a monopoly in the formation of Brazil's policy to the GATT and also in the representation of Brazil abroad.

This fact is unique in world diplomacy. All countries rely on their Ministry of Finance or Trade to take part in international economic agreements. Brazil is the only one to rely on its Ministry of Foreign Affairs (Itamaraty). This fact has clear consequences for Brazil's foreign affairs and for its position in the GATT. First, decisions about GATT were taken by a very small number of individuals of Itamaraty. Second, this group does not have to explain its decisions to the President, to Parliament, or to other Ministries. Third, as the DMP is concentrated in the hands of few individuals, the result may be an inversion of the process. Instead of following instructions from Itamaraty, some representatives in the GATT interpret the instructions, and send back the positions taken in the GATT. Fourth, Itamaraty held information about what was happening in the GATT. An example of this fact occurred when individuals representing Brazil in the GATT refused to carry out any studies on services and prevented other groups or departments from doing so. The pretexts used for not preparing the studies were the most diverse but all of them had the same effect: they left Brazilian negotiators in a difficult situation, because they lacked information. The discussions at the GATT were political, since there were no technical studies. The country was unaware of possible benefits which could result from service liberalization.

Concerning DMP theories, this chapter concluded that the DMP in Brazil vis-à-vis the GATT is dominated by an agency (Itamaraty) vulnerable to the influence of personalities and in which the outcome was dependent on old values and assumptions. In Itamaraty, the main principle motivating Brazilian negotiators abroad is the mercantilism one. Mercantilism here means a belief that national interest should prevail in international trade, a consensus that imports are prejudicial to the country and to the search for self-sufficiency in most, if not all, sectors.

As a result, due to the substantial autonomy of Itamaraty, there are two ways in which Brazil's position in the GATT may be changed or in which to modify this mercantilism perspective. The first is the assumption to power of a President of Republic or an individual in Itamaraty with strong views on foreign policy or international trade policy in particular. This is rare in Brazil, where most Presidents are not very interested in foreign affairs and even when they are, they leave the decisions to Itamaraty. An exception was Collor. However, when he took power in 1990, Brazil's position had already changed in the GATT and he maintained it. For this reason, he was not included here.

There is however a mechanism for changing Brazil's position in the GATT. It is by way of a power struggle inside Itamaraty, where groups with different perspectives fight for influence and for the control of the DMP inside the agency. The outcome will be decided not only by the existence of strong arguments from each side, but by the existence of leaders in each group, capable of carrying enough political support from outside the agency in order to take control of the key-positions in the agency responsible for the final decisions.

In Brazil, the most important position is the job of General Secretary of Itamaraty, followed by the Under-General Secretary of Administration.[250] Tarso took *de facto* control of the apparatus of Itamaraty after the departure of the Minister Setúbal and the entry of Abreu Sodré in 1986. But it took a while until the new position of Itamaraty was 'understood' in Geneva. Only after the removal of Batista in 1987 was it possible to express the new thinking in GATT negotiations, since Brazil changed its position in the Uruguay Round of GATT only in 1988. It is worth noting that, in Brazil, ideology and values are very important factors in explaining the maintenance of a position, even if it is considered that this position no longer reflects the country's interests.

This chapter has described Brazil's view on the service sector and its role in the development of this sector. Basically, as discussed in the Introduction and in Chapter 1, the values which prevailed in Brazil were based on economic nationalism and ISI policies. This explains the reluctance of Brazil's negotiator to accept a liberalization of the service sector. The idea of economic power and the objective of building a service industry, through the use of infant industry argument, were tantamount. Brazil's behaviour was based on preserving its own interests, as perceived by its main decision-makers, such as Batista, as the Neo-realist Theory suggests. The values of Itamaraty are the main guide to explain Batista's behaviour.

This chapter also summarized Brazil's position on services in the GATT at the beginning of the 1980s. Brazil then refused to submit studies on its service sector. Brazil's Ambassador to the GATT, Batista, gave many reasons for this refusal. However, most of the reasons presented were only a smoke-screen for the real ones, which had an ideological nature: Brazil's strong bias against free-trade. Indeed, Brazil agreed to discuss services in all other fora, except the GATT. The best explanation for this bias is that GATT principles, which included *inter alia*, trade liberalization, were alien to the model adopted by Brazil since the 1930s (or even before) which was based on ISI.

However, a closer analysis of some service sectors, such as financial services and insurance, demonstrates that Brazil could gain by liberalizing its trade in services. Thus, Brazil's fear that a sudden liberalization of trade in services could lead to a destruction of Brazil's service sector by foreign competitors is unfounded. There is room for both foreign and national firms.

As a result, Batista's refusal to carry out studies for the GATT was against Brazil's self-interests and jeopardized the development of other economic sectors. Batista believed that by refusing to carry out studies he was helping Brazilian firms. In fact, Brazilian consumers lost in income and Brazil's economy lost in efficiency and competitiveness, due to the perception at Itamaraty, shared by its elite, that liberalizing services was against the national interest. This illustrates how the perception of individuals in key positions can influence the Decision-Making Process. It confirms the importance of shared beliefs and ideologies.

In fact, the importance of shared beliefs and ideologies show that the behaviour of a State, or the behaviour of its representatives is not a rational process, at least in the Brazilian case. The issue of trade in services has been proposed since at least 1982, during the GATT Ministerial Meeting. Batista, as part of the ruling elite at Itamaraty, decided that an agreement on trade in services was against Brazil's interests, based on his values and perceptions, and started to fight against any agreement on that issue in the GATT. The most interesting point is that Batista took this decision not based on technical arguments or studies, but on his own personal values and perceptions. His ideology was part of the shared beliefs and values which prevailed at Itamaraty. This emphasizes the role of the personality of the decision-makers when they lead an agency which gives them autonomy to speak on its behalf.

This is the opposite of what rational choice theory proposes. This theory also assumes that States have full information about the issues over which they have to take their decisions. No argument can justify such lack of knowledge, since there were international organizations that could provide it. Only ideology and values can explain Brazil's behaviour against an agreement on services. Indeed, the values of the decision-makers and the Institutions to which they belong override the search cooperation. Contrary to what Keohane suggests, expectations may not meet in regimes. This will be illustrated in the next chapter, which will discuss Brazil's behaviour at the 1982 Ministerial Meeting.

Brazil's participation in coalitions before and during the Uruguay Round varied according to the representative in charge of the negotiating process. When it was Batista, the first Brazilian negotiator at the Uruguay Round, he emphasized the Group of 10 as the main forum to coordinate Brazil's positions. The reason for this is that the G-10 emphasized more the issues that Batista believed in. Among them, his deep suspicions about the service sector in the Uruguay Round, and its emphasis on the negotiations for manufactured goods. This position was consistent with Batista's personal belief in the UNCTAD and United Nations Commission for Latin America (ECLA) doctrine of Import Substitution Industrialization (ISI) policies and priority to industrialization and full support to the export of manufactured goods. In the period that Batista was Brazil's representative in Geneva, the Cairns Group had only secondary importance in Brazil's political strategy at the Uruguay Round. This can be put down to the fact that the Cairns Group emphasized agricultural products, which were not a priority to Batista, since he believed that Brazil had a natural industrial vocation.[251]

When Batista was replaced by Ricupero in 1987, there was a complete change in the orientation of Brazil's participation in coalitions at the Uruguay Round. One should bear in mind that Ricupero belonged to the same school of thinking as Tarso. This meant that Ricupero had a more pragmatic style than his predecessor. In agriculture, Ricupero also shared

Tarso's view and considered that although Brazil might have an industrial vocation this did not mean that Brazil should have to sacrifice its agricultural interests in trade liberalization in favour of such industrial vocation. As a result, for Ricupero, as for Tarso, agriculture should have at least the same importance given to it as manufactured goods.

This new position immediately reflected in the coalitions and in Brazil's attitude in the new Round. In the same way that the level of acceptance of a service agreement in the Uruguay Round of the GATT by Brazil increased, the level of interest of Brazil in the G-10 decreased. This reinforces our previous hypothesis that in spite of the fact that the G-10 had a work programme which involved different issues (rollback, standstill, end of MFA, liberalization of agricultural trade, etc.), it was in its essence a negative coalition against negotiations on services.

Indeed, after the arrival of Ricupero, when Brazil decided to work positively in a service agreement in the Uruguay Round, the G-10 lost its *raison d'être*, Brazil became a strong supporter of the Cairns Group and the G-10 eventually disbanded. The Cairns Group became a kind of balance in the Round, and was probably the most influential. This proves the point that this chapter raised initially that the personality and values of Brazil's representative in the GATT is very important in Brazil's DMP.

End Notes

1.   See: Kennedy & Fonseca, *op.cit.*, p.30-40.
2.   See: Kennedy & Fonseca, 1989, *op.cit.*, p.30.
3.   Ezran et al. (1986) notes that Brazil had the second highest level of tariffs among the 50 LDCs studied by him. See: Ezran et al., 1986, *op.cit.*, p.22.
4.   Kennedy & Fonseca, 1987, *op.cit.*, p.36.
5.   Kennedy & Fonseca, 1989, *op.cit.*, p.40.
6.   Batista was Brazil's Ambassador to GATT from 1983 to 1987. He will be discusssed later on.
7.   See: Batista, 1987, Trade in Services: Brazil's Perspective on the Negotiating Process. In *SELA Capitulos* (16): pp. 61-66.
8.   Diplomats argued that there was no definition of national interests with regard to services from the government. Thus, Batista defined it, according to his own perceptions.
9.   This lack of interest by politicians in foreign affairs also applies to the position

of Minister of Foreign Affairs. They do not wish to head Itamaraty because the Ministry has no money and does not offer many opportunities for favouritism, which still plays an important role in Brazil.

10. This situation changed in 1991, when there was the first open competition to advise the Congress in International Relations.

11. Until the end of the 1980s there were no Ph.D courses of IR in Brazil. Most experts in IR in Brazil either come from other areas (viz, political science) or have studied abroad.

12. Except in the case of Intellectual Property Rights (IPRs).

13. Tarso was General Secretary of Itamaraty (1985-1990) and became *de facto* Minister of Foreign Affairs after 1987. We will discuss his policies related to GATT later on.

14. Roett, 1992, *op.cit.*, p.27.

15. See: Cleary, 1987, *op.cit.*

16. Ibid.

17. Confidential interview with a Brazilian diplomat.

18. Just the fact that Setúbal was not a career diplomat implied a break in the tradition, maintained in its essence by the military regime, of nominating only diplomats to head Itamaraty.

19. Gibson Barboza received no guidelines from the President before taking office as Foreign Minister. Barboza, 1992, *Na Diplomacia, o Traço Todo da Vida.* Rio de Janeiro, Record. p.132.

20. Barboza said that he always had absolute autonomy to plan and to execute Brazil's foreign policy (Barboza, 1992, *op.cit.*, p.128). Minister Guerreiro was told by the President to follow the principles of the former Minister. Guerreiro, 1992, *Lembranças de um Empregado do Itamaraty.* São Paulo, Siciliano. p.27.

21. The President may dictate the guidelines, but will hardly be able to discuss technicalities.

22. Roett said that Sarney was unprepared for the Presidency and had little interested in it. Roett, 1992, *op.cit.*, p.27.

23. Barboza, 1992, *op.cit.*, p.132.

24. Sodré and Setúbal are examples of non-technical nominations.

25. Ex-President Quadros used to complain that his guidelines were not 'understood' at Itamaraty.

26. In Brazil who gives the instructions to the negotiators is not the Minister of State, but Itamaraty's General Secretary or a Head of one of its Departments.

27. Barboza said that he could hardly leave his position as Minister to travel because each absence from the headquarters of Itamaraty required significant effort from him to regain effective control over it. Barboza, 1992, *op.cit.*, p.134.

28. Sarney was very interested in the Brazil-US dispute in IT.

29. The exceptions are Quadros (1961) and Geisel (1974-1979).

30. Confidential Interviews with Brazilian diplomats.

31. Tarso said that: "a sub-product of our attitude in the GATT was that I expanded

with credibility the area of decisions in trade policy, with proper domestic consultations and making the matter exclusive of Itamaraty". Tachinardi, 1993, *op.cit.*, pp.232-233.

32.   It should be noted that periodically the structure of the Ministries of Economy, Finance might change with the arrival of a new President.

33.   Kennedy & Fonseca, 1989, *op.cit.*, p.37.

34.   According to the Minister chosen, it was possible to say if the President would emphasize growth or fight against inflation.

35.   Kennedy and Fonseca, 1989, *op.cit.*, p.42.

36.   *Ibid.*

37.   *Folha de São Paulo* 20/09/78. Officials from the Ministry of Agriculture complained that they were not invited for discussions about the Brazilian position in the GATT.

38.   The IBC was the influential Brazilian agency for coffee.

39.   In the middle of the Brazil-US dispute in IT, MIC declared its intention to ask for market protection for pharmaceutical products. This triggered the opening of another case against Brazil based on the lack of IPRs. Bastos, 1992, *op.cit.*, pp.14-15.

40.   Kennedy & Fonseca, 1989, *op.cit.*, p.37.

41.   Kennedy & Fonseca, 1989, *op.cit.*, p.40.

42.   Ministries which are part of CONCEX: Itamaraty, Finance, MIC, Science and Technology, SEPLAN, Agriculture, Banco do Brasil, Central Bank, CACEX and eight representatives of private sector.

43.   However, CACEX the most powerful agency in charge of controlling import licences was linked to Banco do Brasil, and, indirectly to Ministry of Finance.

44.   Lima, 1986, *op.cit.*, p.330.

45.   In this case the President supported the Finance Ministry.

46.   During the 1982 Ministerial Meeting, the Finance Ministry obtained Presidential support to oblige Itamaraty to accept studies of services in the 1982 Ministerial Declaration in exchange for US loans and an extension of Brazil's subsidies to its exports. Lima, 1986, *op.cit.*, pp.332-337.

47.   See: Tachinardi, 1993, *op.cit.*, p.226 and p.236.

48.   Confidential interview with a Brazilian Ambassador.

49.   Confidential interview with a Brazilian diplomat.

50.   See: Batista, 1987, *op.cit.* and Brazil.GIS, 1986, *Relatório*. Brasilia, MRE.

51.   Brazil had some influence in the developments, as the creation of the dual-track procedure shows, but not on the agenda.

52.   An official from Itamaraty stated that it was not the function of Itamaraty to explain the character of the decisions taken at international fora. Confidential interview with a Brazilian diplomat.

53.   Details of the process will remain unknown even to the government. Officials will hide the true reasons behind decisions.

54.   Nau, 1989, *op.cit.*, p.12.

55. This division was made for analytical purposes only. The third group ('others') was created in order to include approaches that could not find a place in one of the two former groups.

56. From now on, Batista. The group includes also, *inter alia*, Correa Costa, Guerreiro, Huguenet, Rego Barros, Barbosa and Proença Rosa.

57. See Batista in Tachinardi, 1993, *op.cit.*, p.244.

58. See Williams, 1991, *op.cit.*, pp.41-45.

59. See Lima, 1986, *op.cit.*, pp.246-247.

60. See end note 7. The history of Brazil in the GATT is out of the scope of this book.

61. See: *Financial Times* 16/12/94.

62. Batista statements in Tachinardi, 1993, *op.cit.*, p.246.

63. GATT, 1987, *GATT Activities 1986*. Geneva, GATT. pp.26-27.

64. Tachinardi, 1993, *op.cit.*, p.245.

65. See Introduction.

66. Tachinardi, 1993, *op.cit.*, p.240.

67. Nau, 1989, *op.cit.*, p.21.

68. From now on Tarso. His group included also Thompson Flôres, Ricupero, Gelson Fonseca, Graça Lima and Soares Neves.

69. Confidential interview with a Brazilian diplomat.

70. Ibid.

71. Interview with Tarso.

72. Ibid.

73. Ibid.

74. See: Cohen, S., 1988, *The Making of United States International Economic Policy. Principles, Problems and Proposals for Reform*. New York, Praeger.

75. Confidential interview with a Brazilian Ambassador.

76. The references are to the structure of Itamaraty in 1985.

77. Itamaraty, 1988, *Relatório 1987*. Brasilia, MRE. p.275.

78. Confidential interview with a Brazilian diplomat.

79. Confidential interview with a Brazilian diplomat.

80. Barboza, 1992, *op.cit.*, p.132.

81. Barboza, 1992, *op.cit.*, p.132.

82. Confidential interview with a Brazilian diplomat.

83. Confidential interview with an official from Itamaraty.

84. Confidential interview with an official from Itamaraty.

85. See Rego Barros, 1987, *op.cit.*

86. See Brazil. Itamaraty. *Lista do Corpo Diplomatico*. Setembro 1984, Abril 1986 and Outubro 1988.

87. ALADI was the Latin American group for regional integration.

88. See Brazil Itamaraty *Relatório. 1987*. pp. 275-280.

89. See Kennedy & Fonseca, 1987, p.30.

90. Confidential interview with a Brazilian Ambassador.

91.   Confidential interview with a Brazilian Ambassador.
92.   Confidential interviews with a Brazilian Amassador and Brazilian Professors.
93.   See Maciel (1986).
94.   Confidential interview with a Brazilian Ambassador.
95.   Some claim that Batista tried to hide Brazil's problems behind services, while others argued that, in the lack of a policy for services, Batista radicalized. Confidential interviews with Brazilian diplomats.
96.   See GATT. *GATT Activities 1982.* Gatt, Geneva, 1983.
97.   In 1986, an Inter-Ministerial Group of Services (GIS) made a research about the service sector, but it was a compilation of laws and reports of state agencies. See Brazil. GIS (1986).
98.   This will be the topic of Chapter 3.
99.   Confidential interview with a Brazilian Ambassador.
100. Confidential interview with a Brazilian Ambassador.
101. Confidential interview with a Brazilian Ambassador.
102. Confidential interview with an Itamaraty official.
103. See Odell, 1992, op.cit.
104. See Odell (1992) and Bastos (1992). More on this later.
105. The results of the Special Session is in GATT. *BISD. 32nd Supp. Protocols 1984-1985.* GATT, Geneva, 1986. p.9. and see also GATT. *BISD 32nd Suppl. 1984-1985.* op.cit. pp.70-84.
106. Even if Tarso and Batista were not the minds behind each group, this is not relevant, since the positions they held were more important than the intellectual leadership of the group.
107. Tarso notes that the only product that could be used to retaliate against the US was coal. See Tachinardi (1993) p.234.
108. Between 1979 and 1984 Brazil's exports increased 80% from US$ 15,2 to US$ 27 bi. See IMF, 1994, *IFS 1993.* p.242.
109. Confidential interview with a Brazilian Ambassador.
110. Confidential interview with an official from Itamaraty.
111. The reasons why Setúbal left the government are unclear. It is likely is that he wanted to return to his Itaú Bank.
112. Confidential interview with an official from Itamaraty.
113. More on this issue later on.
114. Confidential interview with a Brazilian Ambassador.
115. Ibid. The ISI model is a good example of this.
116. Confidential interview with a Brazilian Ambassador.
117. Economic development became an explicit objective of Itamaraty only in the 1950s. See Caldas, R. *A Política Externa do Governo Kubistchek.* Brasilia, Thesaurus, 1996.
118. Rego Barros, S., 1987, O GATT de Havana a Punta del Este. *Revista Brasileira de Comércio Exterior n.9. Janeiro 1987.*
119. Brazil, Itamaraty, 1989, *op.cit.*, p.238.

120. The Head of a Division can send instructions with the support of the Head of a Department as was the case of Huguenet.
121. Confidential interview with a Brazilian Diplomat.
122. See *Construção Hoje*, 30/04/86. pp.28-30.
123. *Ibid*, p.30.
124. Brazil, Group Inter-ministerial de Serviços, 1986, *Relatório*. Brasilia, MRE.
125. For the Declaration which launched the Round, see: GATT, 1987, *BISD* 1985-1986 session. Geneva, GATT.
126. Confidential interview with a Brazilian Ambassador. I thank this person for having called my attention to this fact.
127. Confidential interview with a Brazilian Ambassador.
128. Interview given in 1993. His opinion is based on these three reasons: The excellence of the Institute Rio Branco, which prepares Brazilian Diplomats; The work prepared before the conferences; and the ability of Brazilian diplomats to speak foreign languages (they must speak at least three languages).
129. Confidential interviews with GATT officials.
130. Confidential interview with a Brazilian diplomat.
131. Especially in support of African countries. See: Roett, 1992, *op.cit.*, p.191.
132. On shared perception, see: Cohen, S. & Meltzer, R., 1982, *Unites States International Economic Policy in Action. Diversity of Decision Making*. New York, Praeger.
133. Confidential interview with a GATT official.
134. Confidential interview with a Brazilian diplomat.
135. Confidential interview with a Brazilian Ambassador.
136. Confidential interview with a Brazilian diplomat.
137. Although technically they should only follow instructions. Confidential interview n.33.
138. Confidential interview with a Brazilian Ambassador.
139. This increases the importance of the position of Brazilian representative. In fact, Brazilian diplomats are expected to assume positions. Confidential interview with a Brazilian diplomat.
140. Sometimes with their superiors.
141. If the conference is very important, such as the Uruguay Round, they may receive inputs from Brazilian Embassies abroad. Confidential interview with a Brazilian diplomat.
142. Confidential interview with a Brazilian Ambassador.
143. Confidential interview with a Brazilian Ambassador.
144. See: Martone, C. & Braga, C., 1988, *Brazil and the Uruguay Round*. São Paulo, USP.
145. Confidential interview with a Brazilian Ambassador.
146. Confidential Interview with a Brazilian Ambassador.
147. Confidential Interview with a Brazilian diplomat.
148. About Itamaraty's DMP, see: Fontaine, R., 1970, op.cit.

149. This weapon was used by Maciel. Confidential interview with a Brazilian Ambassador.

150. The fact that Tarso had advisors specialized in GATT helped him in his fight against Batista. Confidential interview with Itamaraty official.

151. The Trade Policy Division (DPC), in charge of the GATT, has internal Committees which will not be considered here.

152. The same occurs with telegram/telex, but they are codified and received in rooms where only authorized officials enter.

153. Some Diplomats are convinced that there was an over-concentration of function in the DPC.

154. Clark, 1957. The condition of Economic Progress. London, Macmillan.

155. UNCTAD, 1985c. Services and the Development Process. Study by the UNCTAD Secretariat. Geneva, UNCTAD. p.11.

156. Ibid.

157. UNCTAD, 1985c, op.cit., p.11.

158. UNCTAD, 1985c, op.cit., p.12.

159. Ibid.

160. Ibid.

161. Ibid.

162. Some Brazilian firms export from Argentina, which has lower Port costs than Brazil.

163. For Brazil's perspective in technology issues, see: Brazil. Presidência da República, 1974, The II Basic Plan of Scientific and Technological Development (II PBCT). Brasilia, SEPLAN.

164 Koekkoek, 1988, Trade in Services, Developing Countries and the Uruguay Round. The World Economy (1):151-156. p.152.

165. Koekkoek, 1988, op.cit. p.151.

166. Koekkoek, 1988, op.cit. p.152.

167. GATT, 1993. *Brazil, 1992. Policy Trade Review*. Geneva, GATT.

168. Some food exports are in a grey area between manufactured goods and commodities exports, for example orange juice.

169. GATT, 1990, International Trade 1988-89. Geneva, GATT. p.42.

170. GATT, 1990, op.cit., p.42.

171. IBRD, 1988, World Tables - 1987, p.67 & IBRD, 1990, World Tables 1988-89, p.147. Washington, IBRD.

172. GATT, 1989, op.cit., Table AD1.

173. IMF, 1992, IFS Yearbook 1991. Washington, IMF. p.257.

174. IMF, 1992, op.cit., p.257.

175. World Bank, 1991, op.cit., p.145, data at factor costs.

176. GATT, 1983. BISD. 39th Supp. 1981-1982. Geneva, GATT, pp.164-164.

177. An article in The Times stated that:"Brazil and India pointed out that services are not within the GATT's present competence and contend they are being pressured to accept their inclusion in exchange for concessions in traditional trade

such as alleviation of recent restrictions imposed on their exports, in violation of GATT's rules". The Times, 30/09/85. See: GATT, 1985, Focus Newsletter 36, October-November, Geneva. p.8.

178. See Itamaraty, 1985, Relatorio 1984. Brasilia, MRE.

179. See Lima, 1986, op.cit.

180. GATT, 1987, GATT Activities 1986. Geneva, GATT, p.73.

181. See note 163.

182. See Law of Informatics of 1985.

183. The problem of the lack of non-existence of indigenous technology was a reason for serious concern to governments in the period 1960-1989. The annual reports from Itamaraty mentioned the issue of technology constantly in the period.

184. Jones, R. & Kierkowski, H. 1990, "The Role of Services in the Production and International Trade". In Jones, R. & Kruegman, A. The Political Economy of International Trade. Cambridge, Basil Blackwell. p.45.

185. Among the mega-construction in Brazil could be mentioned Itaipu.

186. A non-qualified worker in construction in Brazil can be hired at the minimum wage, which is little more than $100 per month. A qualified worker can be hired for no more than $1000 per month.

187. Brazil could, for example, send diplomats who live in Paris to attend courses at the OECD, those who live in Washington to attend courses at the IMF or at the IBRD and those who live in Geneva to attend seminars at UNCTAD and GATT. Diplomats could also attend Universities offering courses in the field of services.

188. Confidential interview with a Brazilian Diplomat.

189. See Bhagwatti, 1987b, "International Trade in Services and its Relevance for Economic Development". In Giani, O.(ed.). The Emergent Service Economy. London, Pergamon Press.

190. The only 'study' led by Itamaraty, the Inter-ministerial Group on Services (GIS) merely produced a compilation of existing legislation. See: Brazil.GIS, 1986, op.cit.

191. There were confidential 'papers' prepared by diplomats, but they were not technical studies. Interview with Brazilian Diplomats.

192. See Chapter 3.

193. For a question of space, we cannot analyze all the coalitions which influenced the Uruguay Round. We will concentrate on those in which Brazil took part. The Group 'De La Paix' has been chosen due to its importance in the elaboration of the Declaration which launched the Uruguay Round.

194. See the Final Report of the Latin American Coordinating Meeting 4-6 October 1982.

195. Sciamma, G., 1988, La Evoluzione de la Posizione del Brasile nell'Uruguay Round del GATT, con Particular Refirimiento al Commercio Internazionale di Servizi. Milan, Universita Comercialle Luigi Bocconi. p.110.

196. See Decision n.153 of the IX Meeting of the Latin American Council.

197. Sciamma, 1988, op.cit, p.112.

198. See Curzon & Curzon, 1974, op.cit.

199. Confidential interview with a Brazilian Ambassador.

200. Abreu, 1992, O Brasil e o GATT. Rio de Janeiro, PUC. (Discussion Paper).

201. It seems that these countries had political interests. Yugoslavia was very active in the Non-Aligned Movement, Nigeria wanted to prove that it was a regional leader and Argentina, under Alfonsin thought that it could put a New International Economic Order (NIEO) on the diplomatic agenda.

202. Hamilton & Whalley, 1989, op.cit., p.550.

203. See: Hamilton & Whalley, 1989, op.cit., p.550.

204. Ibid.

205. Hamilton & Whalley, 1989, op.cit., p.550.

206. Hamilton & Whalley, 1989, op.cit., p.554.

207. Hamilton & Whalley, 1989, op.cit., p.550.

208. See Wiener, J. 1994, Making rules for Agriculture in the Uruguay Round of the GATT: a Study in International Leadership. Canterbury, University of Kent.

209. Nayar, 1988, 'Some Reflection on the Uruguay Round and Trade in Services'. Journal of World Trade Law 22 (5):35-47. p.35.

210. Weiss, T., 1986, Multilateral Development Diplomacy in UNCTAD. The Lessons of Group Negotiations: 1964-1984. Basingstoke, Macmillan.

211. Argentina, Brazil, Cuba, Peru and Nicaragua.

212. See Banco Central do Brasil, 1985, Relatório. Brasilia, BCB.

213. IMF, 1986, Balance of Payment Statistics - 1985 vol.36 Part.1. Washington, IMF.

214. Schott, J. & Mazza, J., 1988, 'Trade in Services and Developing Countries'. Journal of World Trade Law 20 (3):255-273. p.260.

215. Confidential interview with a Brazilian Ambassador.

216. Oxley, A., 1990, The Challenge of Free Trade. London, Harvester Wheatsheaf. p.138.

217. Koekkoek, 1989, Developing Countries and the Uruguay Round. Some Aspects. Rotterdam, Universiteits Erasmus Drukkerij. p.42.

218. Desai, A., 1989, "India in the Uruguay Round". In Journal of World Trade 23 (6): 33-58; p.37.

219. Desai, 1989, op.cit., p.52.

220. Desai, 1989, op.cit., p.49.

221. Desai, 1989, op.cit., p.53.

222. Bhagwati, 1987b, "Services". In Finger, D. & Olechowski, A., 1987, op.cit., p.215.

223. A comprehensive review of the Cairns Group is beyond the scope of this thesis. See: Cooper, A.; Higgott, R.; Nossal, K., 1993, Relocating Middle Powers. Australia and Canada in A Changing World Order. Vancouver, UBC Press.

224. Denton, G. & Laite, J., 1990, The Uruguay Round: Freeing World Trade in Manufacturing, Agriculture, Services and Investment. London, H.M.S.O.. Wil-

ton Park Conference. p.15.
225. Guyomard, H.; Mahé, L.P.; Munk, K.; & Roe, T., 1993, "Agriculture in the Uruguay Round ambitions and realities". In Economic Papers, N.101, March. Brussels, CEC., p.16.
226. Higgott, R. & Cooper, A., 1990, "Middle Power Leadership and Coalition Building: Australia, the Group of Cairns and the Uruguay Round of Trade Negotiations". In International Organization 44 (4): 589-631 Autumn 1990, p.591.
227. Higgott, R. & Cooper, A., 1990, op.cit., pp. 591-592.
228. Denton, G. & Laie, J., 1990, op.cit,. p.16.
229. This issue will be discussed in more detail later on.
230. Oxley, 1990, op.cit., p.118.
231. The Group included Argentina, Australia, Brazil, Canada, Chile, Colombia, Hungary, Indonesia, Malaysia, New Zealand, the Philippines and Thailand and Uruguay. Fiji was also a member of the Group, but as it was not a member of the GATT, it just met when there was a GATT Ministerial Meeting.
232. Oxley, 1990, op.cit., p.119.
233. Oxley, pp.113-4. The Group accounted for more than 25% of total exports of dairy products and 25% of sugar exports. This is a pattern similar to US or EU agricultural trade.
234. This is disputed by Finlayson & Weston (1990 p.41). They are convinced that the Cairns member States have strong differences between them. These include: some countries which are food exporters, others are raw material exporters as well (such as Brazil). Some countries export temperate climate products, others tropical products. Finally, some countries have low intervention in agriculture and are in favour of free-trade in this sector. Other countries are characterized by a high degree of intervention in agricultural markets and want to keep it that way, such as Canada.
235. Oxley, 1990, op.cit., pp.119-121.
236. Oxley, 1990, op.cit., p.115.
237. Nye, 1974, op.cit.
238. See, for example, his statement quoted in Tachinardi, 1993, A Guerra das Patentes, São Paulo, Paz e Terra.
239. Confidential interview with a Brazilian Ambassador.
240. See Brazil, MRE 1988 p.26.
241. Oxley, 1990, op.cit., p.112.
242. Hamilton & Whalley, 1989, op.cit., p.553.
243. One could argue that Brazil's reasons for taking part in the Cairns Group had another significance. Brazil wanted to reap the advantages of being a member of the Cairns Group whilst at the same time trying to continue to be a spokesman for LDCs in order to maintain its influence in international fora. However, the problem is: a) In 1986/1987 Brazil was no longer a spokesman for all LDCs; b) most LDCs did not want to liberalize their agricultural trade because they had subsidized agricultural products and they also forbade agricultural imports.

Thus, sooner or later, Brazil would have to make a choice on this issue. The Cairns Group represents the interests of agricultural exporters and not importers, since the ending of subsidies implies an increase in international prices of agricultural products and not a decrease.

244. Don, H; Gunasekara, B., Parsons, D. & Kirby, M., 1989, Agricultural Policy, The GATT and Developing Countries. Canberra, AGPS.
245. Guyomard, H. et al., 1993, op.cit., p.21.
246. Guyomard et al., op.cit., 1993, p.20.
247. Higgott & Cooper, 1990, op.cit., p.618.
248. Guyomard et al., 1993, op.cit, p.20.
249. See Chapter 3.
250. Due to the possibility of transferring/promoting diplomats.
251. Batista, in Tachinardi, 1993, op.cit..

3. The Launching of the Uruguay Round at Punta del Este and Brazil's Initial Position

Introduction

The objective of this chapter is fourfold. The first section of this chapter aims to analyze Brazil's position during the launching of the Uruguay Round. It describes Brazil's alliance with India, and how the Group of 10 (G-10) radicalized its position. In spite of this radical position the section shows how the G-10 managed to have its main goals included in the Punta del Este Declaration.

The second section of this chapter gives an overview of the Uruguay Round and its objectives. The third part of this chapter deals with Brazil's position in two other selected sectors: tariffs and "old" issues. Through these two different areas it is possible to perceive the contradiction in Brazil's position in the Round. Batista refused to join an agreement in services in the Uruguay Round, because any agreement to liberalize under the aegis of, or under, GATT principles assumed free-trade, which Brazil's main negotiator, Batista, considered a naive assumption. On the other hand, it was exactly this naive assumption that Batista required the Developed Countries (DCs) to follow on the old issues, such as agriculture and textiles, aimed at ending the Multi Fibre Arrangement (MFA). But what is good for the DCs is not necessarily good for Brazil. As a result, Brazil supported trade liberalization for DCs, but not for itself. In Batista's proposal, DCs would eliminate almost all their tariffs, while Brazil would bind its tariff structure at the level it was for a period of ten years. In this period the influence of the Cairns Group was limited due to the reserves of Batista for this Group.

Finally, this chapter wants to discuss the reasons for Brazil's initial position in the Uruguay Round against services. Although the Uruguay

Round had already started, Batista maintained the essence of his positions against a service agreement. His arguments were divided into three groups according to their nature: legal, economic or political. However, it could be said that they were only a smoke-screen to hide Batista's concerns over a prospective agreement in the Uruguay Round of the GATT.

The launching of the Uruguay Round

Reconciling radical positions: US versus Brazil and India

Brazil started to discuss the proposed introduction of services at Punta del Este in its defensive fashion. At home, Brazil was adopting protectionist measures for its Information Technology (IT) industry and restricting the flow of data processing outside the country. As a result of the last US-Brazilian dispute at the GATT during 1985, when the US delegation called for a Special Session to be convened, Brazil decided to adopt a low-profile. However, Brazil maintained its opposition to the introduction of services in the GATT.[1]

Batista realized that it did not have a majority in the GATT Assembly, and tried to maximize the gains of any concessions for Brazil. Thus, in contradiction to his previous hard-line position, Brazil sought a trade-off for concessions in services.[2] However, this trade-off meant that Brazil agreed to discuss services in a multilateral forum, as the US wanted, if Brazilian requirements were met.[3] The main goal of this trade-off was to prevent bilateral pressures from the US, such as Section 301 and Super 301, which had already been used against Brazil.[4]

The first step of this new strategy was to slow down the Decision-Making Process (DMP) in the discussion of services. Thus, Brazil and India adopted a policy of muddling through. Indeed, this new policy could already be felt at the end of June 1986 when Brazil and India proposed an alternative draft declaration to the Punta del Este negotiations.[5] Formally, Brazil's intention was to replace the draft produced by Australia, Canada, New Zealand and the European Free Trade Area (EFTA) countries, which had the explicit support of the US and EC. In fact, the G-10 Declaration was inspired by Batista[6] and was illustrative of Brazil's strategy of muddling through.[7]

The main difference between the two draft-declarations was that the Brazilian (G-10) draft, instead of including services in the new Round, suggested a working group to prepare the work in the new issues - such as Intellectual Property Rights (IPRs), Foreign Direct Investment (FDI), etc. Only after the conclusion of this preparatory work would the new Round be launched.[8] Moreover, in the G-10 draft it was implicit that DCs would have to make concessions to the Less Developed Countries (LDCs) as a necessary condition of the launching of the new Round. These concessions would include the end of the MFA and the elimination of other protectionist measures, such as Voluntary Export Restraints (VERs). Brazil also wanted a promise that DCs would not adopt new protectionist measures - a standstill.[9]

Brazil's position can be interpreted at different levels. At the rhetorical and ideological level, Brazil continued to maintain that it was opposed to a deal on services being included in the new Round. However, after realizing that its position was losing support, even among LDCs, Brazilian officials were urged to give interviews declaring that Brazil "did not want to block things".[10] This, in diplomatic language, meant that Brazil wanted a compromise solution, where the interests of all parties would be protected. This position was part of a propaganda effort, whereby the actor tries to keep his image and credibility intact for a later phase of negotiations. This also meant that Brazil wanted to avoid being forced into an isolationist position which would accompany any open obstruction to discuss services. Thus, one can see the importance of understanding the propaganda level.

However, on a practical level, Brazil had formed a pressure group of countries with common interests in order to block any progress in the discussions on services. This G-10 was well-known in the GATT negotiations and had been active informally since the 1982 Ministerial Meeting. It is within this perspective of blocking the negotiations that the Brazilian draft should be considered.[11] Indeed, Brazil believed that its goals could be met if it adopted a very radical attitude to try to negotiate concessions. For this reason, Brazil prepared a draft proposal which was not constructive. Indeed, Brazil's draft declaration was considered, even by LDCs, to be unrealistic and too negative.[12] Brazil did not want to make and never had any intention of making any contribution to the discussions on services. Brazil wanted to paralyse the process of decision-making or - if that was not possible - Brazil wanted to try to persuade the DCs and as many supporters as possible to agree to an acceptable compromise on trade in services from Brazil's perspective.

The compromise Brazil had in mind was to discuss services within another forum (viz., UNCTAD), or to create a separate group to discuss services outside the new Round, in order to prevent trade-offs during negotiations on goods and services.[13] As the deadline approached without any compromise in sight, Brazil even hardened its position, using the legalist argument that: "The negotiations can only cover matters within the jurisdiction of the GATT", declared Batista.[14]

The most likely explanation for the G-10 draft declaration is that it was an attempt to make the Preparatory Committee (of the new Round) miss the deadline. It may thus be considered part of the obstructionist policy. In fact, it was only the personal intervention of Dunkel that lent impetus to the discussions, which were deadlocked. He announced that the Preparatory Committee would enter into permanent session after 18 July. With this announcement he gave a sense of urgency to the discussions and contributed to avoiding a new delay in the construction of a declaration.

In Brazil's view, a delay in the elaboration of a final declaration would postpone the beginning of the multilateral trade negotiations. This was one of the main objectives of Itamaraty at that time. As expected, the Brazilian initial proposal was considered unacceptable by the US and the EC. The G-10 then tried to demonstrate flexibility and presented a modified version of its original draft declaration.[15] However, the second draft did not differ substantially from the first one. In both versions the service sector and new issues were not included in the new Round. The second version was presented on 16 July 1986, a few days before the deadline set by the Preparatory Committee for a declaration to be made. The most substantial difference between the declarations proposed by Brazil and India and that supported by the nine industrialized countries was again related to new issues in the GATT, such as services, IPRs and FDI. None of the declarations of the G-10 - inspired by Batista - made reference to the new issues.[16]

Brazil also wanted the negotiations to be controlled by the Contracting Parties to GATT, in order to take the discussions on services to a broader forum, where the likelihood of an eventual defeat could be reduced by the presence of other members. In fact, Brazil was using a tactic which had already been used in the United Nations: a coalition of LDCs against a coalition of DCs.[17] However, the Brazilian strategy did not work because support for the G-10 was in decline, even among the LDCs. Indeed, LDCs from

Asia, such as South Korea, formed the "moderate" group of 20 LDCs. They worked on a kind of compromise between the draft proposal of hard-line LDCs (the G-10) and the DCs (G-9). The mediation of the G-20 was welcomed by European countries, and it was received coolly by Brazil and India. The moderate LDCs and the EC believed that an agreement was better than confrontation - an opinion not shared by Brazil, India or by the G-10. Among LDCs, Southeast Asian countries were in favour of introducing services in the GATT.[18]

This new alliance of DCs in the group of nine and the moderate 20 LDCs gave new impetus to the launching of new Multilateral Trade Negotiations (MTNs). The draft of this alliance had the support not only of the EC and the ASEAN countries, but also of Switzerland and Colombia which submitted it to the Preparatory Committee (PrepCom). This wide support for the compromise draft - it was estimated that at least 49 of the 91 countries which belonged to the GATT took part in its elaboration - contributed to the isolation of the hard-liners, whose views no longer represented the views of the majority of the LDCs. However, it seems that the negotiators representing the moderate LDCs had their negotiating hands weaker than they would have been had Brazil and India been present.[19]

Despite this, the US succeeded in broadening the spectrum of the DCs-LDCs alliance. In order to co-opt LDCs, many concessions were made. An important concession to the LDCs, for instance, which was agreed in the Swiss-Colombian proposal, was that preferential treatment for LDCs under the GATT framework would be reinforced and that LDCs would not be pressured to make any kind of trade concessions that could harm their development and financial needs. This meant that they would not need to decrease tariff levels in exchange for increased access to the DC markets.[20]

In the polemical discussion of the new issues it was agreed, in the Swiss-Colombian draft, that the introduction of services in the GATT framework would be left open, with its form and significance depending on the prospective new Round. However, services would be discussed in the Round. The compromise draft also proposed the creation of a Trade Negotiating Committee (TNC) which would coordinate the discussions of the groups established by PrepCom. Batista was not impressed by the compromise draft crafted by the alliance of the 9 DCs and the 20 LDCs. He declared that the situation was contradictory and that the paper represented nothing.[21]

Surprisingly, the hard-liners received the support of Dunkel. He opposed a movement in the GATT led by the US to isolate Brazil, India and the G-10. He also tried to work as a mediator between the US, on one hand, and Brazil and India on the other, but he was not very successful. A group that sympathized with Brazil and India was the EC, which were trying to find solutions acceptable to the US and to G-10. The EC suggested dividing the negotiations into two parts. The negotiations on goods already covered within the GATT framework would remain under the aegis of the GATT. Services would be dealt with separately, but using GATT procedures.

While Batista maintained Brazil's tough position against the inclusion of services, he sought to obtain the support of other countries to put agriculture at the centre of the new Round. In order to achieve this, Batista was instrumental in arranging a meeting of twelve countries in Thailand in July 1986.[22] Following this meeting they issued a warning stating that unless agriculture was at the centre of the new Round, they would boycott it. All twelve countries were important agricultural exporters and wanted an end to US and EC subsidies, through the Common Agricultural Policy (CAP). They wanted to see reform in the farm regimes of the US and the EC. It was ironic that the movement in favour of free-trade was supported by Brazil, one of the most protectionist countries in the world.

With this policy of support for a coalition of agricultural exporting countries, Batista achieved three objectives at once. First, he ensured that one of the main issues of concern to Brazil - that of opening up the markets of DCs to its exports of agricultural products - would be treated as a central point. Second, Batista - whilst pressing for a complete phasing out of export subsidies by the US and EC - knew that this would cause a delay in launching the new Round, which had been the Brazilian goal from the beginning. Third, Batista managed to remove the new issues from the focus of attention. Now, all countries would wait to see the EC's reaction of the issue of export subsidies.[23] However, the US, which also wanted reform in the agricultural regime of the EC, threatened to withdraw from the new Round if two topics were not included. One was the reform of the CAP, and the second was the new issues. The US considered Brazil's opposition to the inclusion of services within the GATT as irrational.[24]

In the end, Brazil refused to accept the compromise draft suggested by Colombia and Switzerland. Therefore, the Preparatory Committee did not reach agreement on a final text. Three texts were proposed as a basis for discussion. First, the Colombian-Swiss compromise, mentioned above. Second, the modified version of the Indo-Brazilian draft, which made no reference to services. Third, there was a text proposed by Argentina which aimed at being a compromise between the Swiss-Colombian proposal and the revised Indo-Brazilian draft. The Argentinean proposal suggested that trade in services should be discussed in a separate forum. The EC was the most enthusiastic supporter of a fusion of all proposals. They suggested, as Argentina had done, that services should be discussed in a separate forum. This forum would respect national legislation. The US position was that this procedure was too restrictive.[25]

An acceptable solution: the twin-track proposal

The twin-track proposal was not entirely dead in 1985. When the Meeting at Punta del Este began, Colombian officials suggested the creation of what came to be known as the "twin-track" approach. According to this suggestion services would be discussed "separately and distinctly" from trade in goods, but both issues would be discussed using GATT procedures. Brazil and India insisted on discussing services outside the GATT, and suggested UNCTAD, which the US considered unacceptable. In an attempt at compromise, the US delegation proposed that each country could decide about joining an eventual GATT agreement on services.[26]

In a similar concession, Brazil and India agreed to withdraw their draft proposal and to work with the Swiss-Colombian draft compromise. However, they wanted amendments to the text to exclude services from negotiations in the GATT. The G-10 also wanted to include a phasing out of barriers in DCs which infringed the principles of the GATT. They insisted that the MFA be ended as a pre-condition to the negotiations. The amendments proposed by the G-10 were seen as an obstructionist tactic by the US and the EC.

Nevertheless, Brazil and India did not want to be responsible for the collapse of the negotiations, already nearing the deadline. At the last moment, both countries accepted that services could be negotiated at the same time as goods. It was also agreed that services would be treated under the same political undertaking, the Uruguay Round. Clayton Yeutter, the new US Trade Representative, accepted that services could technically be excluded from the GATT negotiations on goods. However, services would be tackled using GATT procedures. Therefore, it was necessary to reach an agreement on the forum within which services could be discussed, whilst maintaining GATT procedures. The US delegation then suggested that services could be tackled by a "neutral" committee outside the framework of the GATT.[27] The compromise reached determined that goods would be tackled in the new Round, launched by GATT members. However, a Ministerial Meeting would call a separate negotiation to discuss trade in services, under a trade negotiation committee. This solution, sought and suggested initially by Brazil in 1985, became known as the dual-track approach.[28] The sole difference was that the negotiations on goods were to be carried out by the Contracting Parties to the GATT under the GATT aegis. The negotiations on trade in services would be carried out by the governments of countries which could be Contracting Parties to the GATT. As a result, a ministerial meeting - open to all countries, even non-Contracting Parties to the GATT, began to discuss services. The two main players in this game, the US and the G-10, claimed victory. The US delegation argued that it managed to include services in a multilateral negotiation. More important, these negotiations would be compatible with the practices and procedures of the GATT.[29]

Batista maintained that the G-10 had prevented services being included in the GATT. Both countries believed that they had separated the negotiations on goods from the negotiations on services. Therefore, it meant that any concession they received in market access from DCs, for instance, would not require a concession in the area of services. Batista claimed another victory by the fact that the negotiations on services would respect national policies and law. The negotiations on services would also use the relevant studies of other organizations, such as UNCTAD.

It is worth noting that the launching of the Uruguay Round was seen in a different light by the two groups of countries. In the view of DCs and moderate LDCs a new Round was launched which included services and other new issues. For Brazil and India two different negotiating processes were being launched at Punta del Este: one on trade in goods, and another on services.[30] The Declaration which launched the Uruguay Round was divided into two parts (13): trade in goods (Part I), and trade in services (Part II). The most controversial aspect of the first part (Trade in Goods) was the commitment by GATT Contracting Parties not to adopt any new trade restrictions or measures inconsistent with the provisions of the GATT (viz., VERs). This was the standstill commitment. The second controversial commitment - the roll-back - stated that all measures inconsistent with the GATT should be eliminated at the end of the Uruguay Round.[31] Furthermore, subjects for negotiation in the new Round would be broadened to include not only tariffs, but also Non-Tariff Barriers (NTBs), tropical products, natural resource-based products, textiles and clothing, and agriculture. Other discussions would include GATT articles, Intellectual Property Rights-IPRs (TRIPs) and Trade-Related Investment Measures (TRIMs).

The role of the US in the compromise accepted by Brazil at Punta del Este

It is difficult to prove that Brazil accepted the inclusion of services in the Uruguay Round solely due to US pressure. The US had threatened Brazil with sanctions in Information Technology (IT) in 1985, and the threat did not work as imagined. If the US wanted to step up pressure on Brazil to make a deal (or threaten retaliatory measures at the issue of services) the last opportunity to do so was during the visit of Brazilian President Sarney to the US at the beginning of September 1986. However, during the negotiations preceding the launching of the Round, at the end of September, there was no agreement in sight.[32]

It is true that Brazil made several gestures of goodwill towards the US in the IT sector. The most famous of these was the authorization of two IBM projects, at a time when the autonomy of Transnational Corporations (TNCs) was extremely restricted in Brazil in the IT field. However, this gesture was made to coincide with the visit of President Sarney. These concessions cannot be considered to be a result of the visit, rather they were a result of previous US pressure. Their acceptance was made to create a good atmosphere for the visit. Nevertheless the visit of President Sarney did not produce expected results.

Indeed, the five-day visit of Sarney was considered a failure. There was no reasonable agreement in the IT field. The aim of the US was no longer to change the Brazilian Law on IT (1985), but rather to guarantee its transparent application, an appeal process, and a guarantee that it would not be extended to other sectors. The US wanted better copyright protection for software, and the expansion of investment possibilities for TNCs.[33] Therefore, the Brazil-US dispute in IT was not confined to the discussions of services in the GATT. This dispute would continue for several years. On the other hand, Brazil did accept changes in its copyright law and tried to accommodate US critics. However, the conflict between the two countries exploded in October and November of 1986 when the GATT preliminary discussions had already been concluded. This corroborates the point of this chapter that the threat of using Section 301 and Super 301 against Brazil by the US was the Brazilian Law of 1985 on IT - and the lack of IPRs - and not the Brazilian stance in the discussions on services.[34] The Brazilian attitude in the GATT was in complete accord with the Law on IT (1985). And this law became the central point of the Brazil-US dispute because it had an impact on trade policies (import of computers and components), on production (the TNCs were forbidden from producing micro and minicomputers), and on IPRs (whose legal protection was considered to be insufficient).

Indeed, in the middle of October (two weeks after the launch of the Uruguay Round) the United States imposed provisional anti-dumping duties of up to 8.541% on Brazilian exports of orange juice. Meanwhile, within the GATT the US began a complaints procedure against Brazil's protectionism in the IT sector. This shows that the link between retaliation and negotiation on whether to include services in the Uruguay Round is fluid.[35]

Brazil's opposition to the inclusion started in the 1982 Ministerial Meeting and went on up to 1987, while Batista was the main Brazilian negotiator. The threats of US sanctions started in 1984 and the US sanctions started *de facto* in 1985. If US sanctions were the sole explanation for the Brazilian position, Brazil would have changed its position during the Ministerial Meeting in Punta del Este in 1986. As it is known, this did not occur. In fact, Brazil's position became more radical in 1986/1987 against an inclusion of services in the Uruguay Round. Brazil's position changed only in 1988, when Brazil's main negotiator in Geneva was replaced. Therefore, the role and the position of the main negotiator are vital to explain Brazil's position related to the GATT.

Batista summarized the advantages of the compromise reached at Punta del Este for Brazil.[36] In his opinion, the main benefit to Brazil was that the decisions taken within the Group Negotiating on Services (GNS) would not be binding on all countries. This would have been unacceptable under GATT rules. The LDCs would be the main beneficiaries. Furthermore, according to him, the fact that the negotiations would adopt GATT procedures, outside GATT's framework, also had some advantages. First, decisions must be taken by consensus. This would guarantee that LDCs would not be ignored in the negotiations. Second, following GATT procedures, any bilateral agreement on liberalizing trade in services between countries would be multilateralized to all countries due to the Most Favoured Nation (MFN) principle.

Odell also supports the view that the US-Brazil dispute on IT did not affect Brazil's position in the GATT. He said that: "All sides were very careful to isolate both these disputes (in IT) from other issue areas. In neither conflict did either official link his demands or proposals to developments in the Uruguay Round of trade negotiations or to security arrangements. Neither did the Brazilian government explicitly link its position on informatics with current debt negotiations".[37]

An overview of the Uruguay Round

To Dunkel, the Uruguay Round is "the chosen means of government to extend and reinforce the multilateral trading system; to make it the vehicle for growth, sustainable development and successful economic reforms in decades to come".[38]

The Uruguay Round was launched in order to continue the work begun by the GATT, especially in the field of reducing tariffs and assuring market access to products from all countries. Although it was created initially to exchange tariff concessions among its members, it became a *de facto* internal organization, since the International Trade Organization was never ratified.[39] The GATT managed to reduce the level of world tariffs from about 40% to around 5% in industrialized goods in DCs.

However, the Uruguay Round went far beyond the work begun by the GATT. The Punta del Este Declaration specified that the new Round aimed, *inter alia*: to bring about further liberalization and expansion of world trade and to strengthen the role of the GATT and improve the multilateral trading system.[40] The Uruguay Round was divided into two parts. The first part should discuss not only tariff-related subjects (such as tariffs and Non Tariff-Measures), but also the Functioning of the GATT System (FOGS), specific rules which were part of the GATT, Textiles, Agriculture, TRIPS and TRIMs. The second part of the Round discussed services.[41] To enumerate the issues gives an idea of the comprehensiveness and importance of the Uruguay Round. In fact, the Uruguay Round went beyond the GATT in many fields. The Uruguay Round managed to include in the world trade system many fields that had not been covered by the GATT, such as Agriculture, due to the opposition of the EC and the US, on Textiles, due to the existence of the MFA. In agriculture, Dunkel estimated that DCs spent an average of US$320 billion per year, creating an extremely subsidized market.[42] The MFA also created a derogation from the GATT.[43]

The Uruguay Round exceeded its own mandate in at least three other fields: the FOGs, TRIMS, TRIPS and Services. The FOGS Group suggested nothing more than the creation of an organization more powerful than GATT itself, the Multilateral Trade Organization. The TRIPS Group, due to US pressure, managed to include not only trade related aspects of IPRs, but a new code of IPRs which has made the World Intellectual Property Organization (WIPO) almost useless. The same thing can be said about the TRIMs. As most of FDI nowadays is in the field of services, the acceptance by Brazil of the right of establishment, which assures the right of any firms to invest in another country in a specific area, made the TRIMs discussions lose part of their original importance.

Finally, the Uruguay Round managed to establish a set of multilateral rules for services, which the International Trade Organization (ITO) had partially completed, but which had never been ratified. As already mentioned, during the negotiations of the ITO the US feared that a multilateral agreement on services, as LDCs wanted, to limit Restrictive Business Practices (BRP), could limit the work of the service firms of DCs. This explains the US opposition to a multilateral agreement on services at that time.[44] In the case of the Uruguay Round, however, due to the insistence of the US, and in spite of opposition from LDCs such as Brazil and India, a multilateral agreement in services based on GATT principles of free-trade and trade liberalization was established. Even in services the final agreement exceeded the initial Declaration. Indeed, the initial Declaration did not foresee the presentation of offers in specific services. In the end, the services agreement covered most fields, with the important exceptions of transport and financial services.

Brazil's position on specific fields: "old issues" and tariffs

Old issues: agriculture and the Multi Fibre Arrangement (MFA)

Although these two issues are not of equal importance to Brazil, they were considered together because Itamaraty supports the application of the same principle of free-trade to all three areas. In fact, these three sectors were the only ones where Brazil supported free-trade. This can be explained by the fact that Brazil had more to gain than to lose through trade liberalization in these three sectors. Zietz & Valdis (1986) estimated that if there were no barriers in agricultural trade, Brazil's exchange gains would be $617 million for sugar exports, and $1,370 million for beef exports.[45] Brazil was in favour of trade liberalization by DCs but this did not mean that Brazil would liberalize its markets in these above mentioned sectors to imports. It only signifies that Brazil wanted DCs to open their markets to its exports. Overall, some authors estimate that Brazil would have increased its exports by $1.5 billion per year in the early 1980s with the end of agricultural protectionism.[46] One should not forget that in 1987 agriculture represented 40% of Brazil's exports.[47]

As a result, the Brazilian position in agriculture, as articulated within the Cairns Group, was the same as that of the US. Both were in favour of the elimination of all subsidies in the export of agricultural products by the EC.[48] Brazil also wanted to see the end of State support programmes. One of the targets of the US, Brazil and the Cairns Group was the ending of the EC's CAP. The Cairns Group, which comprised grain exporters, is an example of a coalition formed by middle powers, including DCs and LDCs.[49] Tropical products were the major concern of some countries, such as Brazil and Indonesia.[50] This sector includes not only commodities, but also some industrial goods. Thus, the concept of tropical products varies, depending on the definition used. DCs exclude those items that they consider politically sensitive from the definition. Brazil claimed that the Ministerial Declaration which launched the Round had already conceded the complete liberalization of trade in those products and the ending of all restrictions - whether tariffs or NTBs.[51]

DCs wanted to negotiate any concessions to LDCs against concessions from these countries, based on the principle of graduation. The US did not want to make concessions without a clear commitment from the EC to remove their subsidies. This was only partially obtained. Analysts have estimated that Brazil would have a gain in net economic welfare of about US$4.7 billion from global liberalization in agricultural products. Brazil would benefit, in those commodities areas in which it has a comparative advantage, for example sugar.[52]

With regard to textiles, the situation is the same. According to UNC-TAD (1986), the costs to LDCs of protectionist measures in textiles and clothing are very high. UNCTAD estimates that if there was a complete removal of tariffs and NTBs, textiles exports would rise by 49.1% and clothing exports by 128.9%.[53] Brazil was in a peculiar situation because it did not know if it would gain from the liberalization of textile exports because the MFA guaranteed a market for Brazilian exporters without requiring LDCs to open their markets. Aggarwal (1985) considered Brazil just a partially competitive country, with some competitive products due to comparative advantage.[54] Brazil's share of world trade in textile exports fell from 11.3% in 1955 to only 4.9% in 1982, and as such, Brazil became a secondary exporter of such products. A study conducted by the International Textile Manufacturers confirmed the lack of competitiveness of Brazil's textile industry compared to the industry of other LDCs.[55]

As a result, it was believed that Brazilian firms were not competitive enough to face a sudden liberalization of imports in this sector, except in some specific sectors. It was mentioned, as proof of this, that Brazil had not completely filled its quota allocation under the MFA. Indeed, in 1978 Brazil used only 72.4% of its quota, and in 1983 it used around 94.3%, while some countries, such as Peru and Pakistan over-fulfilled their quota allocations by 2.9%.[56] Brazilian firms regard their quotas under the MFA as a guarantee of their export market-share. In principle, they oppose the ending of the MFA and should the MFA be ended, they expect Brazil to use provisions in the GATT - such as Special and Differential (S&D) treatment for LDCs or Balance of Payments (BOP) Restrictions - to stop imports. In fact, the importance of textiles and clothing for the Brazilian economy is in decline. Indeed, textiles and clothing output represented only around 11.5% of industrial production in Brazil in 1975 and has fallen since then.[57] Employment in the clothing and textile sector accounts for less than 20.5% of industrial employment in Brazil, below the average for LDCs.[58] This fact also explains why Finlayson & Weston (1990) do not mention Brazil among the countries which had a keen interest in an early end to the MFA. They mention Pakistan, Hong Kong, Turkey, South Korea, Indonesia and India.[59] Furthermore, Brazilian exports of textile and clothing were falling steadily. In 1973 they represented 18.9% and 7.4% of Brazilian exports of manufactured goods; in 1982 they accounted for only 6.8% and 1.3% of Brazilian exports respectively.[60] As Abreu & Fritsch (1988) noted, this average was well below the average of textile exports of other LDCs.[61]

However, while Brazil strongly supported the ending of the MFA in the Uruguay Round, in an internal seminar Itamaraty declared that it was necessary for the Brazilian textile sector to decide whether it was ready to pay the price to obtain concessions outside the framework of the MFA, or if it would adapt to the existing structure (the MFA) leaving a definition about the future regime for textiles after 1992. This illustrates the contradictions of the Itamaraty's attitude in the Uruguay Round.[62]

How can it be explained that Brazil was supporting the ending of the MFA so eagerly if Itamaraty was not convinced about possible gain from complete liberalization, whilst the Brazilian textile sector remained undecided about supporting the ending of MFA? The first explanation is consistency. From this perspective, Itamaraty supported the ending of the MFA in order to be consistent with its position in other areas, viz., agricultural commodities and tropical products. As a result of this position, even if Brazil had to open up its market to textile imports the increase in its exports of agricultural and tropical products would compensate for higher textile imports.

An alternative explanation is not to be found in Brazil, but in the coalitions formed in the Uruguay Round. In this context, the alliance Brazil-India starts to make sense. If for Brazil textiles were a secondary sector, they constituted India's main source of manufactured exports. On the other hand, for Brazil, the export of tropical products is clearly very important, while it is irrelevant for India. Therefore, both countries united to support each other's interests. Brazil strongly supported the end of MFA while India put pressure to end restrictions on exports of tropical products. This is one of the main features of the Brazil-India alliance and was exploited by the G-10 coalition.[63]

Tariffs and Non-Tariff Barriers (NTBs)

The Brazilian position was that DCs should reduce or eliminate all tariffs on products originating from LDCs. However, DCs claimed that they had already reduced most of their tariffs in previous Rounds and, therefore, their contribution in this field would be minimal. However, Brazil argued that there were still two problems to be solved: tariff escalation and tariff peaks. Tariff escalation refers to the fact that the real rate of tariff protection increases with the rate of value added in the product. As a result, manufactured exports from LDCs were suffering discrimination since it was cheaper to import raw materials and process them than to import the final product. Brazil also pointed out that although tariffs in DCs were on average low, there were tariff peaks affecting products exported by LDCs to DCs.[64]

Brazil proposed to DCs a general schedule of reductions of their tariffs on products from LDCs to zero, without exception. According to this proposal, all DCs would consolidate their tariffs on products from LDCs over a ten year period. After this period, the same tariff would be applied for products originating from other DCs. In return, LDCs would consolidate some of their tariffs over products originating from DCs after a period of ten years.

The position of the US and of other DCs was that as they had already consolidated their tariffs in most product areas, further reductions should be followed by a consolidation of the tariffs of LDCs, in particular the most developed among them. The US also proposed that countries with a low level of consolidation of tariffs, such as Brazil, should apply a general formula to reduce their tariffs. On the other hand, DCs wanted to reduce their remaining tariffs on a request and offer basis.[65]

It can clearly be seen that the US and Brazilian proposals were not compatible. While the Brazilian proposal was based on the principle of S&D treatment, the US proposal was based on the principle of graduation. Moreover, DCs maintained that tariffs should be discussed along with NTBs. To the US, better market access for products of LDCs should be part of a global process of liberalization. The US would reduce its NTBs if the access of its products on the markets of LDCs was improved. In fact, the US wished to gain access to other countries' markets on the same terms that it offered to imports coming into the US, based on the principle of fair trade.

On the one hand, the US had in mind the markets of Brazil, India and South Korea. On the other hand, Brazil maintained that when the Uruguay Round was launched, DCs promised to remove all their NTBs which were GATT inconsistent. Therefore, Brazil would refuse to exchange concessions in return for the removal of such NTBs. Furthermore, Itamaraty argued that tariff barriers and NTBs were distinct and negotiations should be dealt with separately. However, Itamaraty was ready to negotiate reductions in NTBs consistent with the GATT if the principle of S&D treatment for LDCs was accepted in the negotiations. Eventually, the principle of S&D treatment for LDCs was accepted during the Uruguay Round negotiations.[66]

With regard to NTBs, Brazil's position was that it was necessary to differentiate between those measures which were GATT inconsistent, which should be withdrawn unilaterally as part of previous commitments, and those measures which were GATT consistent. Only the measures which were consistent with the GATT should be discussed in the Group of NTBs. The position of the US is that it is very difficult to make such differentiation, and they claim that the lack of data on this jeopardized the negotiations. The US presented a detailed list - per tariff line - to the negotiating group on NTBs of the measures adopted by each country that it would like to negotiate, product by product, on a request and offer basis, in an attempt to bilateralize the discussion. This was not accepted by Brazil.[67]

Brazil's initial position in the Group Negotiating in Services (GNS) in the Uruguay Round[68]

The initial Brazilian position on services: Main features[69]

The main arguments advanced by Batista can be split according to their nature into technical, political, legal, and economic ones. They have been divided here only to allow their analysis from different perspectives. This book has as one of its assumptions that Itamaraty initially opposed the inclusion of services in the Round, and, therefore, Brazilian arguments were part of an obstructionist tactic seeking to delay the negotiations on services. Certainly, the Brazilian opposition to the inclusion of services derived from the Brazil-India alliance.[70]

Technical aspects of the Brazilian position

Brazil's technical arguments can be summarized as follows:

> 1) There were several conceptual obstacles to be overcome, such as the definition of services, and consequently, what is meant by international trade in services. It is also necessary to differentiate between trade and investments. Poor or unreliable information remained a potential problem as well.[71]

2) Less powerful countries, such as Brazil, had a structural weakness in terms of negotiating strength. In the case of services, this weakness was increased by the lack of knowledge of what was being discussed and by the lack of expertise in this 'new field'. LDCs may need more time for their preparation of the meetings[72].

3) LDCs had few data about their respective service sectors, while DCs had accumulated data in OECD and other fora.

The technical arguments raised by Batista clearly show the lack of enthusiasm on Brazil's part for the negotiations on services. Although there was no commonly accepted definition of services this was not a reason for preventing an agreement.[73] Thus, Brazil turned the search for a definition that could be accepted, at least tentatively until a better one could be developed, into an impossible task. Indeed, it became a weapon in Brazilian hands to delay the negotiations. A policy which can be characterized as stalling. The same can be said about the definition of trade in services and the differentiation of investment and trade.[74]

Although difficult, such ideas can be agreed if there is political will to negotiate them. This was not the case. Moreover, it should also be noted that other international organizations, such as OECD and even UNCTAD, had already developed some possible frameworks, but Brazil refused to rely on either of them. Naturally, Brazil maintained that the negotiations should not go ahead without an agreed definition. This led to a circular argument: negotiations could not continue without a definition, and Brazil used all its influence to prevent the agreement on a definition. However, as will be seen later on, this kind of tactic could not last for ever, and eventually a definition would have to be agreed. Brazil opted for a very narrow definition of services, which excluded the right of establishment, because it knew that this definition was unacceptable to the US which supported a broad concept, including the right of establishment.[75]

Batista also argued that because data was poor and unreliable LDCs had little information. This put Brazil and other LDCs in a weak position during the negotiating process. Batista maintained that as a result of these facts, it would need more time to prepare for the meetings than DCs. This argument was also a smoke screen to hide Brazil's lack of interest in the negotiations on services and to string DCs along. After the 1982 Ministerial Meeting, the possibility was discussed of services being eventually included in the GATT framework. At that Meeting it was suggested that GATT members carry out national studies of their service sectors.[76]

At UNCTAD the discussion on services had started long before, between the end of the 1960s and the beginning of the 1970s, when some service sectors such as tourism were studied in that organization. As a result, by the 1980s UNCTAD had acquired expertise in many areas of the service sector, such as transport, technology, and financial transactions. By the mid 1980s UNCTAD had started to collaborate with national studies of countries, not including Brazil, which were interested in services. Moreover, UNCTAD had lent its support to UN Conventions,[77] with Brazil's participation. This invalidated the argument that there was no expertise to negotiate in services.[78]

Therefore, Brazil had the opportunity to develop its expertise in the field of services at least since the 1970s through UNCTAD, or since the beginning of the 1980s through the GATT. Even if these two organizations had not dealt with services Brazil could have sent experts to the OECD to train them on how to carry out studies in services. The same can be said about the lack of negotiating skills in the field of services of Brazilian diplomats.

Brazil is part of the ICAO[79] and through UNCTAD and other organizations had negotiated several international conventions which had a direct effect in the area of services such as shipping, IT, IPRs, business restrictive practice, FDI, etc. Thus, to argue that Brazilian diplomats had no experience in negotiating in the service sector is either disingenuous or shows bad faith. Certainly, Brazilian diplomats could negotiate on services in international fora if they had enough data to do so. If there was no data the responsibility lay with the Brazilian government which did nothing to overcome this problem, which they had been aware of since the 1970s through UNCTAD, and after 1982 through GATT.[80]

Finally, Brazil always claims that it is a powerless country. However, market access can in some instances be a viable bargaining tool for LDCs. Some LDCs, such as Brazil and India, have domestic markets which are large by any standards.[81]

The political aspects of the Brazilian position

Brazil used all kinds of political arguments to block the service negotiations. The most important can be summarized as follows:

1) Negotiations on services had political implications that could affect the constitutional principles and the internal organization of some countries as sovereign States. The solutions reached should respect the sovereignty of all countries[82].

2) Trade liberalization on services is not an end in itself. Thus, negotiations should not be concerned with the best allocation of resources, but with growth and development. The development of LDCs should not constitute a derogation from GATT, as in the case of goods, but a central part of any eventually agreed rules.

3) Brazil had aspired to becoming a producer and supplier of high technology goods and services (infant-industry argument), especially in IT.[83]

4) Since TNCs were the most dynamic sector of world trade, Brazil wondered if the absence of legislation to regulate trade between branches of the same TNC could affect the national interest in either host or home country.

5) Although Brazil supported the adoption of the GATT principle of unconditional MFN treatment, Brazil was convinced that the application of other GATT principles to services may have unforseen consequences. The principle of national treatment to goods, for instance, implies the acceptance of products while the adoption of national treatment and right of establishment to trade in services implies the acceptance of investments or production itself in home territory. As a result, to give automatic right of establishment to TNCs would violate the right of each country to regulate FDI. Moreover, it was argued, one cannot accept free movement of capital and deny free movement of labour.[84]

On the other hand, it could be argued that the concept of sovereignty is vague and can be developed in international fora to express the position of a government in any sector, from the cinema to nuclear-power stations. In the case of services, sovereignty is used in three situations: a) liberalization of services opens the door to more FDI of TNCs in traditional domestic sectors; b) the removal of control on FDI, and c) state-owned firms would be subject to greater international competition.[85]

The principal effects, which Brazil probably had in mind, are in the field of FDI affecting constitutional principles. Indeed, in Brazil, the property of the sub-soil belongs to the State, and therefore foreigners cannot be owners of certain natural resources, such as uranium, oil and waterfalls. Batista feared that if FDI was included in the negotiations on services by way of the principles of right of establishment and national treatment, Brazil would have to allow FDI in fields which are a State monopoly. This issue is the subject of fierce debate in Brazil between ultra-nationalist groups - who support the monopoly - and liberal groups - who support the entry of FDI. This explains Batista's insistence in the GNS that a paragraph be included in any eventual agreement guaranteeing that national legislation should be respected. However, defence of the State monopolies was justified on political and security grounds, which are not economic concepts.[86]

However, instead of basing its position on dated slogans and poor economics, Brazil would have been better off if it had used the discussions in progress, within the Uruguay Round, to re-examine the validity of such principles. Furthermore, Brazil had agreed to take part in several international agreements and institutions that in one way or another limited its room for manoeuvre, such as the Law of the Sea and the IMF. To appeal to constitutional principles to prevent a fruitful negotiation was certainly a Brazilian tactic to obtain the support of other LDCs where nationalism played an important role, such as in Latin America.

The second argument has two important aspects. First of all, when it is argued that trade liberalization is not an end in itself, and therefore by implication that negotiators should not seek the best allocation of resources, it shows not only a deep lack of respect on the part of the Brazilian authorities for the most basic economic principles, but also demonstrates that the ideological heritage of UNCTAD, which believed that political decisions could abolish economic principles, was still alive. Indeed, this belief was confirmed by Brazil's first negotiator, Batista, who stated that development should be at the centre of GATT and not supplementary. As a result, Brazil wanted to put an ideological principle - support for development - as the main pillar of international trade, rather than economic efficiency.[87]

Although the third argument advanced by Batista seems to emphasize the economic aspect, it is based on the principle of economic nationalism and the infant industry argument. These principles were the pillars of the Import Substitution Industrialization (ISI) model which contributed to Brazilian industrialization, and are basically political and not economic concepts.[88] Although it is possible for most countries to build an industry of high-technology products, such an industry would have high economic, social and political costs. These costs would be increased in a country which does not have comparative advantage in the field of high technology, or abundance of resources to develop it. Even if such an industry is built, there is no guarantee that it can be maintained without State support.[89] This latter possibility emphasizes the political aspect of the possible development of a new industry by the State. One should not forget that the 1980 Brazilian government was very much involved in the growth of an indigenous IT industry using national technology, an arms industry, and a nuclear industry. Brazil also had important projects in the fields of bio-technology, missiles, satellites and telecom. The high technology service sector would be no exception to this effort.[90]

National interest was the fourth main political argument used by Batista to try to stop negotiations on services. The notion of "national interest" is imprecise to include any objective of any government and could, thus, obtain the maximum amount of support of LDCs. In the specific case of Brazil, there was a fear that intra-company trade from TNCs could affect the growth of trade in services in Brazil. However, Batista did not produce any evidence to testify that TNCs' intra-company trade was already affecting the growth of Brazilian trade in services, since Brazil had not conducted a comprehensive study on this. Thus, Brazil was using a hypothetical argument to conjure up fears in LDCs about would-be threats to national interest, without giving any evidence to substantiate these fears.[91]

The fifth main political argument raised by Brazil during the negotiation on services had two aspects. First of all it pandered to the prejudices some LDCs still had concerning concerning TNCs and the lack of power of the State before them if an agreement on services were concluded. From Brazil's point of view, the State would become a powerless entity, in charge of internal administration but unable to control or even to orientate FDI toward certain activities considered to be priorities. TNCs would choose the sectors they considered to be most important to invest in. As most LDCs already had some degree of bias against TNCs, the only thing Brazil had to do was to increase the apparent threat which TNCs represented for them. One should also not forget that UNCTAD had carried out a comprehensive study on restrictive business practices of TNCs and the United Nations had created an agency - the United Nations Centre for Transnational Corporations (UNCTC) - both with support from Brazil, in order to monitor the activities of TNCs.[92]

The second part of the argument was directly linked to the controversial issue of migration, which Brazil knew was unacceptable to DCs. Therefore, when Batista proposed the link between free movement of capital and free movement of people (labour) he wanted to politicize the issue of services and at the same time generate a negative response among DCs. This is why this issue should not be seen in its economic aspect, but in its political one. Moreover, by bringing this political debate to the negotiations on services, Brazil wanted to show that the DCs, and in particular the US, just wanted to negotiate on the matters that they considered to be in their interests, for example, free movement of capital, while they left issues of interest to LDCs, such as free movement of labour untouched.[93]

The legal aspects of the Brazilian position

Brazil's main legal arguments in the negotiation on services were:

. 1) Services were not formally part of the GATT framework, which encompassed only trade in goods. Furthermore, service negotiations were not being carried out under the aegis of GATT, but within a separate, *ad hoc*, legal frame of references. As a result, there should be no trade-offs between services and goods. It was argued that such trade-offs were economically unjustifiable and technically unfeasible. Moreover, negotiations also depended on other commitments assumed by DCs, such as standstill and reversal of protectionist measures.[94]

2) Brazil supported the view that a multilateral approach was better than bilateral or limited plurilateral solutions, since these two imply discrimination, which would be at odds with the aim of the negotiations (trade liberalization) and GATT principles.

3) Negotiations should consider existing agreements and the work carried out in other organizations, such as UNCTAD and the International Maritime Organization (IMO).[95]

4) There are intrinsic problems of a technical as well as a legal nature in the negotiations on services that cannot be put aside. Therefore, these negotiations should not proceed faster than the negotiations on goods. On the contrary, the negotiations on goods should go quicker than the negotiation

on services. Both negotiations should provide a balanced distribution of advantages among participants. [96]

The first argument is the most typically legal in the sense that it aimed at determining where the negotiations were to be carried out and what should be expected from them. This position has several aspects that can also be specified. First, Brazil never lost an opportunity to call attention to the fact that the negotiations on services were not formally part of the GATT. It meant that legally there was no question of just incorporating the negotiations on services automatically within the GATT. This stance placed a sword of Damocles above the heads of the negotiators in the sense of not being certain of an inclusion of services in the GATT framework. From Batista's point of view, there was not even certainty to make a deal. This uncertainty can be discerned in the Batista's Declaration. Indeed, one can read that: "Brazil agreed to explore the possibility of arriving at a set of multilateral rules...".[97] This is confirmed when it says that: "... the very nature of any possible agreement that may hopefully emerge at the end of our deliberations...".[98] At a certain point, Batista is more explicit and states: "we have committed ourselves to negotiate, but we are not bound to come to a final agreement at any price".[99]

Secondly, it slowed the negotiations down and each aspect had to be carefully negotiated and ascertained. As the negotiations maintained the GATT principle of reaching decisions by consensus, Brazil remained assured that no agreement would be achieved without its support.

Thirdly, a practical consequence of the formal separation of services from the GATT framework was that Brazil wanted to prevent trade-offs between the negotiations on services and those in goods. This was important to Brazil because it felt that it had a fragile industry in the service sector. Thus, Brazil did not want to make concessions in services to obtain advantages in goods in such areas of interest to Brazil as market access, agricultural liberalization, and the ending of protectionism in DCs, as practised in the textile sector.[100]

Fourthly, Brazil also argued that trade-offs were economically unjustifiable and technically unfeasible, but did not say why. These are not legal arguments and therefore they cannot be analyzed as such. However, from a legal perspective, when a very comprehensive agreement such as the Uruguay Round is being negotiated, it is much more difficult to prevent compromises than to reach them, because although Brazil maintained the negotiations on services were parallel but separate, they were part of the same political undertaking, as Brazil itself recognized.[101]

Batista's attitude proved to be naive and trade-offs between services and goods did occur, with Brazil's blessing. US pressed Brazil to present an offer in financial services. Brazil agreed, but its offer was a delaying tactic, as were most of its offers in services. Eventually, Brazil offered concessions in financial services in exchange for market access, without success.[102] In the case of a policy of no trade-offs between services and goods, Brazil would be the main loser, because it would lose the opportunity to receive advantages from its concessions. Moreover, from a practical point of view, such compartmentalized negotiations (no trade-offs) are unworkable, and trade policy does not operate in an arena of such legal abstractions.[103]

The second legal argument had an important implication, in the sense that the shape of any agreement (bilateral, plurilateral or multilateral) would determine not only discrimination, as Brazil suggested, but the exclusion of any country from a future world trade system in services. This is an important aspect because the rules of GATT allowed countries which were not so important in international trade to participate actively due, amongst other reasons, to the principle of consensus building.[104]

This principle differs strongly from majority rule because it requires that all countries (or almost all) agree on a basic agenda. This legitimizes GATT decisions and policy-making because these cannot then be considered the result of the will of DCs, as Brazil used to argue, but the product of a collective decision. Only once did GATT use the mechanism of majority vote: in 1985 when the US asked for a postal ballot to call a Special Session of the GATT in order to decide the inclusion of services in the Uruguay Round. However, this only occurred because Brazil and India were using the principle of consensus building to slow down the DMP in order to paralyse the system.[105]

Therefore, the position of Batista concerning Brazil's participation in a multilateral mechanism to regulate international trade in services was very delicate indeed. Batista did not want the inclusion of the subject in the Uruguay Round, and at Punta del Este this inclusion was approved only after tortuous negotiations. On the other hand, Brazil could not radicalize the process too much because it did not want to be excluded from it. This risk was quite real and the US declared several times that if LDCs (viz., Brazil and India) did not wish to adopt a constructive role in the process, the US would withdraw from GATT and negotiate a parallel agreement with like-minded countries.[106] However, the position of the US in private meetings, according to GATT officials, was that Brazil and India were not obliged to take part in the process and if they did not want to negotiate services they should leave and not try to block it.[107] Certainly, choosing between having some influence (a lot for an LDC) in a multilateral agreement or being excluded from an eventual limited plurilateral agreement, Brazil opted for the former. These are some aspects of the discussion and arguments which were behind the choice between a bi-, multi- or pluri- lateral option. The option of a multilateral solution was legally superior for Brazil because it allowed some principles to be included which would assure a fair representation of all countries. Besides the MFN principle, Brazil wanted the inclusion of mechanisms that would guarantee S&D treatment for LDCs. This principle would allow Brazil to proceed slowly with the process of liberalization in services, should it decide to take part in it at all. Thus, Brazil insisted on S&D, though this treatment had worked against the interests of LDCs.[108]

Moreover, a would-be organization with a wide representation such as the negotiated Multilateral Trade Organization (MTO) would have to contain general principles which reflected not only the concerns of DCs, but also those of LDCs. And last but not least, Brazil wanted this multilateral trade organization to be rules-oriented, so that "The Law of the Jungle" did not prevail. However, the limited plurilateral agreement of like-minded countries, as the one suggested by the US, would probably reflect a composition of economic power of DCs against the interests of LDCs, whilst a multilateral rules oriented agreement might be more in the interests of LDCs.[109]

The third legal argument used by Brazil maintained that the work of other international organizations should be taken into consideration. Brazil wanted to try to limit the room for manoeuvre of any future organization in services, calling attention to the fact that there were already other organizations working in this field and, as a result, any future agreement would have to be limited by work already carried out by these other organizations. Brazil's final goal would be the establishment of the clear legal competence of any organization which would deal with any aspects of services. Brazil expected that international law and existing agreements, such as those on aviation, copyrights, shipping would be respected and thus would be excluded from the service negotiations. Although some of these were being discussed in other negotiating groups, such as TRIMS, they had a clear link with services, since most FDI was in the field of services. Besides, the fact that Batista mentioned other organizations strengthened Brazil's position that the GATT was not the only forum which was able to deal with services technically and legally, as Batista emphasized in his statement.[110]

Brazil wanted a multilateral agreement sponsored by, or with the participation of, UNCTAD because Brazil considered it reliable and it was rule-oriented and not power-oriented as the GATT. This also reflects a contradiction in Brazil's position. Brazil was in favour of the principle of consensus building in the GATT because it knew that DCs could count on the support of the majority of its members. If the principle of consensus did not apply, radical views such as Brazil's position on services would have no chance of succeeding. However, in other organizations which were controlled by the LDCs such as UNCTAD, due to the criterion of representation by geographical areas, Brazil did not support the principle of consensus, but the rule of the majority since the LDCs could easily obtain a majority of votes in the main decisions. Therefore, this argument concerning the participation of other organizations should be examined in its several implications which go beyond the legal field, encompassing economic and technical arguments.[111]

The fourth legal argument reflects a principle of law: reciprocity and a balance of rights and obligations of all members in an international agreement and as a result, of burdens and benefits. Naturally, Brazil wanted to prevent a situation where the DCs would take advantage of liberalization in services and the LDCs would receive nothing in exchange. It is in this field that Brazil expected the principle of reciprocity to work. Although not declaring it in public, Brazil wanted the effort it was making in taking part in multilateral negotiations recognized in a field where it believed it had no competitive industries. The concessions it was making in services would have to be reflected in a global agreement, which should balance benefits and burdens amongst all parties. Nevertheless, whilst Brazil was obstructing the negotiations on services, by means of philosophical and technical discussions as to what services and trade in services constituted, it recognized that eventually an agreement on services would be reached with or without its support.[112]

In this context, Itamaraty wanted a guarantee that the text agreed would include the sectors of importance to Brazil (viz., market access in agricultural products and textiles) alongside the new issues (viz., services). As a result, by linking the speed of the negotiations on services to the old GATT discussions, Brazil ensured that there would be a global agreement (in services and goods) or there would be no agreement at all. However, this position of 'all-or-nothing' is a clear contradiction of other Brazilian arguments of no trade-off between goods and services. Indeed, one cannot at the same time declare that there is no link between the negotiations in services and the negotiations in goods (no trade-offs) and simultaneously make an agreement in each section of the negotiations conditional on the speed and results of a favourable agreement in other parts.[113]

Moreover, if the negotiations on services were concluded before the negotiations on goods, this would create a problem: which legal framework should regulate services? Legally, the GATT could not absorb an eventual agreement on services since they were not formally covered by the GATT. Although it was possible to overcome this legal limitation of the GATT, negotiations would have to be carried out and Brazil knew that. The easiest solution would be a general understanding that when GATT texts refer to goods, the meaning is extended to goods and services.[114]

Nevertheless, this possibility assumes a high degree of consensus that did not exist in GATT on the issue of services. Another possibility would be to add the word services to the GATT text when the word goods is mentioned. However, this would be equivalent to reforming the text of GATT. This would again require consensus, or the support of at least two thirds of GATT members. If the changes already had support from most LDCs, it would be necessary only to pass a resolution by majority vote to determine that the GATT would also be in charge of supervising the agreement on services. Naturally, Batista was aware of all these legal constraints on GATT and would not allow any legal reform of the GATT to include an agreement on services without a similar agreement on goods.[115]

Economic aspects of the Brazilian position

Brazil used four main economic arguments to slow down the speed of the negotiations on services:

> 1) Brazil refused to endorse statements that services had become the dynamic axis of international trade. For Brazil, goods were still the centre of international trade. The main reason for this was that services were not tradeable.[116]

2) DCs had a more competitive service industry than LDCs. Besides, DCs had more comprehensive regulations than LDCs. In this respect, there was an asymmetry between DCs and LDCs. Negotiations should overcome this asymmetry and not institutionalize it.[117]

3) Brazil rejected as naive the assumptions of the free-trade school that unilateral liberalization is intrinsically beneficial. Brazil believed that imperfect competition prevailed in international trade and free-trade theory was very debatable and perhaps totally irrelevant when applied to trade in services.

4) Brazil maintained that it would be a contradiction to apply the Theory of Comparative Advantage (TCA) to services, since the TCA had assumed the immobility of factors of production (capital, labour and land), while trade in services assumes the existence of movement of capital, persons or money.[118]

Before analyzing each one of these arguments, it should be recalled that even if one assumes that Brazil had no comparative advantage in any service sector, which is hard to imagine, the gains from the liberalization of trade in services would then manifest themselves in a greater participation of LDCs in the trade in goods.[119] However, studies suggest that Brazil has comparative advantages at least in some service sectors.[120]

The first argument raised by Batista was based on the fact that trade in commercial services was very unstable. Indeed, while in 1970 commercial services corresponded to 19% of all world trade, they fell to 17% in 1980, and increased again to 19% in 1989.[121] Therefore, Batista argued that there was no clear trend suggesting that trade in services would overtake trade in goods as the engine of world trade. Moreover, Batista maintained that growth of trade in services during the 1980s occurred at a similar rate to growth of trade in goods. There was no basis, Batista believed, to maintain that trade in services was more dynamic than trade in goods. The average annual change in exports of commercial services between 1980 and 1989 was about 6.5%, the same rate as that in exports of goods.

Thus, if one considers the data mentioned, Batista's argument holds until the end of the 1980s. However, if one notes that the quality and nature of world trade was changing, one will perceive how far from reality Batista was. Not only had the nature of services being exported changed, but also the nature of goods exported was changing. The quality of goods was increasing because they used more higher technology and services within it than before. Moreover, the importance of raw materials in world trade declined by half between 1973 and 1985 from 6% to 3.5%.[122] In some sectors, raw materials have been replaced by man-made products, such as synthetic fibres for cotton and synthetic rubber for rubber. There was also some substitution between products of different origin: steel was replacing wood in the construction industry, plastic was replacing steel in cars and wood in the furniture industry. Since the 1960s, the growth of trade in manufactured goods has been more than twice as large as trade in agriculture or mining. In the 1960s, manufactured goods grew by more than 10%, against a growth of 6% for mining and 4% for agriculture. In the 1970s trade in manufactured goods grew by more than 7% - a substantially higher rate than 2.5% for agricultural products and 3% recorded for mining.[123]

The result is that the role of agriculture in world trade declined. Indeed, while agricultural products represented more than 20% of merchandise trade in 1970, this share had fallen to around 10% in 1985.[124] On the other hand, minerals increased their share from around 15% to around 20% and manufactured goods grew from 55% in 1980 to 66.6% in 1986 and almost 70% in 1987.[125]

However, some changes were also happening within trade in manufactured goods. The trade of some products based on high technology, such as cars, was growing at a faster rate than products based on low technology.[126] Moreover, while in the 1960s only 18% of passenger cars were exported, in the 1980s the total reached almost 40%.[127] In the export of cars, not only price but also technology became important, since automobiles made greater use of electronic products. This helps to explain, at least partially, the dynamism of electronic products, which increased their share of world trade from about 4.3% in 1979 to 7.1 % in 1985 in spite of the fall in their final prices.[128]

Even in agricultural trade, high technology was playing a more important role through the use of bio-technology (manipulation of DNA). Certainly this new trend in international trade, based on high technology placed the service sector at centre stage because the service sector is the main supplier of high technology, as in the case of IT. Besides these factors, important changes were occurring within the trade in services category. Shipping declined steadily between 1970 and 1987, with its share in the exports of commercial services falling from 22% to 13% during that period.[129]

As a result, the same effect was felt in port services, with a decrease from 12% to 11%. However, passenger services and travel increased their share from 5% to 6% and from 29% to 30% respectively, in the same period.[130] This data illustrates that Batista was wrong when he argued that services were not important, as had been thought. In fact, it was Batista who noticed the transformation taking place in world trade during the 1970s and the 1980s or the role played by IT and services in those changes. Moreover, FDI in the service sector, which is complementary to trade in services, not only had grown at a faster pace than trade in services, but also an increasing share of FDI from DCs is accounted for by services.[131]

The second main argument used by Brazil was that DCs had too regulated a service sector. This argument could hardly be invoked by Brazil which, since the end of the 1970s, had been carrying out programmes with strong State support in order to develop its own service industry. Although there were restrictions to entry in some service sectors in certain DCs (for example, telecom in the EC), few countries were as protectionist as Brazil was, to the point of approving national legislation to forbid firms which were already in the market from producing similar kinds of goods, as Brazil did with IT.[132] Thus, Brazil was not the best placed country to raise questions about protectionism in DCs.

Another aspect of the issue is that regulations do not mean the existence of a closed market. The US, for instance, has one of the most open markets in telecommunications and financial services, and cannot be accused of protectionism in either field, although it is very regulated in the former. Moreover, if Brazil's argument was true, that there were too many regulations affecting the service sector in DCs, it was not Brazil's answer of greater protectionist legislation that would solve the problem of how to develop a service industry in LDCs or stimulate service trade.[133]

Today it is clear that the Brazilian IT industry is not competitive and that it has not developed indigenous technology. But it has decreased the competitiveness of other sectors of the economy which need electronic components inputs. This is not all. Brazilian consumers cannot import computers and, thus, are obliged to pay at least double the price of an imported computer for one which is less efficient, sometimes even out of date, and probably a clone.[134]

The third argument questions the foundations of the free-trade theory (and the TCA). It is worth noting that Brazil was supporting free-trade and liberalization in other fields, such as agriculture, tropical products and textiles, but not in services.[135] This implies that Batista was not opposed to free-trade (and the TCA) theory in principle, but only its application to sectors where he perceived free-trade was not to be beneficial to Brazil or where Batista felt Brazil had no comparative advantage.

Having said that, Batista argued that free-trade (and the TCA) could not be applied to services.[136] Batista supported this view with three main arguments. First, he noted that the TCA was based on free-trade and free competition. However, as imperfect competition prevailed in trade in services, the TCA could not be applied to services. One could argue that this applies just as well to goods' markets, since a few huge TNCs control the international markets of several products, such as oil and grains. Nevertheless, the TCA is employed as a policy rationale to those sectors and Brazil maintained that the TCA should be applied to grains (viz., agriculture). On the issue of services, Feketekuty (1988) concluded that although restrictions to competition exist in some sectors, they should not constitute a rationale for restricting trade. Free-trade in services forces governments to re-evaluate the regulations in the service sector which restrict competition. Thus, trade is an instrument for improving competition.[137] A second argument used by Brazil to reject free trade was that the TCA is based on the principle that there is no movement of factors of production.[138] As trade in services assumes that there must be movement of either capital, or consumers, (or both), the TCA could not be applied to trade in services. This view has been challenged by many authors besides Feketekuty. Melvin (1989) considers that there is no complete movement of factors of production in any sector, neither of capital nor labour. This occurs because all governments establish regulations to control them. Indeed, almost all countries have immigration laws, which make full movement of labour virtually impossible. The same can be said about capital. Taxation and national legislation have a direct effect on capital flows. Capital flows, thus, are not only dependent on the market, but also on the attitude of central banks, which may adopt rules that restrict trade. It follows that trade and factor flows are not contradictory, but complementary and they affect not only trade in services, but also trade in goods.[139]

Therefore, if one wants to reject free-trade (and the TCA) on the grounds that there is no mobility of factors of production, one should reject the theory as much for trade in goods as for trade in services. As there is still no definitive proof that the TCA cannot be applied to trade in goods or services, one should apply the theorem equally to both sectors. Hindley has a similar opinion. He believes that the movement of people or capital does not invalidate the assumptions of the TCA. He suggests the main feature explaining the existence of trade and the TCA is not the movement of labour or capital but the difference in the distribution of resources between different countries and regions. As long as different factor endowments remain there will be a logic to international trade.[140]

Secondly, it is also possible to argue that even if there was complete movement of capital around the world, which is not yet a reality, this would follow the parameters of the TCA, since capital would flow to the regions where there is a high demand for it (and the returns are higher) and labour would flow to countries where the salaries are higher. This reinforces rather than denies the principles of the TCA. Feketekuty used an alternative approach to tackle the issue of movement of factors of production, suggested by Hindley, to arrive at the same conclusions. He proposed that since it is possible to differentiate between permanent transfers of resources, which can be described as FDI, and temporary movement of capital, which could be considered as a service export, there is no reason to deny a trade status to export in services. As a result, Feketekuty strongly believes that the requirement of movement of capital, or people, to realize export of services does not mean that the logic of the TCA does not apply to services.[141]

A final argument used by Batista to support his view that the TCA cannot be applied to trade in services is that one of the main characteristics of this trade is its invisibility. Since trade in services is invisible, one cannot determine what is being traded. This is more a fallacy than an argument. The fact that something cannot be seen does not mean that it does not exist. And if it does exist, it can be measured, as in the case of financial transactions. If it can be measured, it should be possible to determine what, who, and when a service is being used. Thus, the invisibility of trade in services does not mean that the principles of the TCA do not apply. For this reason, most authors support the view that the TCA can be applied to services.[142]

The point that this section has highlighted is that although the theory of international trade in services is still being developed, there is no valid argument, as Batista claimed, that the TCA should be rejected *in toto* when applied to services. It has already shown how Batista was a strong supporter of the TCA in agriculture and industrial products.

Ideological aspects of Brazilian position

Naturally, the Brazilian position reflected the values and ideologies of Brazil's main negotiator, Batista. For this reason, the Brazilian position emphasized the links with the G-10.[143] Indeed, the G-10 and its core group of Argentina, Brazil, Egypt, India and Nigeria reflected the traditional values of LDCs, expressed in UNCTAD and the G-77.[144] These values could be summarized as self-reliance, econonomic nationalism and the option for the ISI model. On the other hand, the Group of Cairns, which was a coalition of DCs and LDCs had no automatic links with LDCs. Batista sought a compromise between Brazil's participation in the G-10 and the Cairns Group.

It is worth noting that in both Groups (the G-10 and the Cairns Group) Brazil supported agricultural liberalization. The likely difference is that probably Brazil's support for free-trade in the G-10 was more a condition for entering into a negotiation services than support for trade liberalization in agriculture. This helps to explain why Brazil's participation in the Cairns Group was so hesitant. As a result, it could be said that support from Brazil for agriculture during Batista's term as Brazil's main negotiator was more to cause delay in the negotiations than in expectation of results. A proof of this fact is that internal documents from Itamaraty illustrate that it was not confident that Brazil would benefit if there was world liberalization in agricultural trade.[145] Loyal to UNCTAD tradition, Batista believed that Brazil had an industrial vocation and thus, should concentrate its efforts on access for its manufactured goods.[146] This fact is added to the lack of confidence that Batista had in DCs. Moreover, Batista had strong anti-US views, which supported the Cairns Group.[147] All these factors explain why the Cairns Group played only a marginal role when Batista was Brazil's main negotiator in the Uruguay Round, but this position would change dramatically with the arrival of Ricupero to replace Batista, as will be seen in the next chapter.

Conclusions

Although Brazil adopted ISI measures in services domestically, it was a supporter of free-trade for DCs in goods and agricultural products. The logic of the Brazilian position was that if all DCs were protectionist, Brazil could not export its products. However, it is necessary to give some acceptable explanation for the contradiction in Brazil's position between what it proposed other countries should do, and what it was doing itself. It is at this point that the concept of S&D treatment appears. LDCs would be exempt from implementing Brazil's proposals, because they had not achieved the minimum level of development that would allow them to open their markets.

This rhetoric could be clearly seen in the case of agricultural products, where Brazil defended free access to the EC and the US markets, but kept its market closed to most agricultural products. However, it should be clear that it is not being argued that Brazil did not negotiate trade concessions as a result of S&D. As Desai notes, S&D treatment never prevented LDCs from participation in MTN Rounds: countries which wanted to negotiate could always do so as Chile, Peru, Jamaica, South Korea did in the Kennedy Round and Indonesia, Morocco, Colombia, Thailand and the Ivory Coast did in the Tokyo Round.[148] This chapter emphasized that LDCs, and, in particular, Brazil, used the concept of S&D treatment to justify their position of free-riders. LDCs believed that free-trade was good for DCs but the LDCs should be exempted from it, because they needed to protect their infant industries. This is reflected in Brazil's position in the tariff negotiations, where Brazil asked for a reduction in the tariffs of DCs but offered almost nothing in return.

Even in this respect interest in the discussions on services is justified, since at the beginning of the Round and for the first time Brazil was not proposing to DCs the application of free-trade in services, but the complete exclusion of the issue from negotiations. It is Brazil's subsequent conversion to trade liberalization even in services that will be described in the next chapter. This chapter wanted only to emphasize the contradictions of the Brazilian stance in the Uruguay Round when it was launched. Two sectors in particular illustrated the contradiction: in old issues (viz., textiles), Brazil supported free-trade, and in tariffs Brazil supported protectionism. As a result, tariff concessions were avoided in a period of more than a decade, using the principle of S&D treatment. Thus, the Brazilian position in tariffs cannot be taken seriously in tariff negotiations because it did not guarantee real tariff reductions, but only the consolidation of existing tariffs.[149]

In services most of the arguments used by Batista were a smoke screen for his personal opposition to an agreement. He used all kinds of arguments to emphasize the same thing: a service agreement was impossible. This reinforces the point which has been stressed that in the trade negotiations the personality and personal beliefs of the Brazilian negotiator were as important in determining Brazil's position in the trade negotiations as the instructions from Itamaraty.

End Notes

1. Kennedy & Fonseca, 1989, *op.cit.*, pp.42-43.
2. *Financial Times.* 19/06/86.
3. In short, Brazil's requirements were: 1) services would be discussed in any forum but GATT; 2) liberalization in agriculture and textiles; 3) end of protectionist measures - viz. Voluntary Export Restraints (VERs); and 4) commitment by DCs to not adopting new protectionist measures.
4. Martone & Braga, 1988, *op.cit.*, p.94.
5. GATT Document. Prep. Com(86) W 41.
6. *Financial Times.* 27/06/86.
7. Martone, 1988, *op.cit.*, p.84.
8. See: GATT Document. Prep. Com.(86) W 41.
9. See Barros Netto, 1987, *op.cit.*, pp.9-10.
10. *Financial Times.* 19/06/86.
11. Confidential interview with an Ambassador from a developing country.
12. *Financial Times.* 23/06/86.
13. See: Abreu, 1992, *op.cit.*, p.26.
14. *Financial Times.* 11/07/94.
15. Compare GATT. Document: Prep.Com(86) W41/Rev.1 and GATT Document.: Prep.Com(86) W41 Add.1. 22/07/86.
16. Sciama, 1988, *op.cit.*, p.150.
17. *Le Monde.* 21/07/86: 'une negotiation bloc a bloc'.
18. Sciamma, 1988, *op.cit.*, p.151.
19. Oxley, 1990, *op.cit.*, p.138.
20. Martone, C. & Braga, C., 1988, *Brazil and the Uruguay Round*, p.20. São Paulo, USP (mimeo).
21. *Le Monde.* 24/07/86.
22. Argentina, Brazil, Australia, Canada, Chile, Hungary, Indonesia, Malaysia, New Zealand, Philippines, Holland and Uruguay.
23. For a discussion of EC's position, see Wiener, J., 1994, *Making the Rules for Agriculture in the Uruguay Round: A Study in International Leadership.* Canterbury, Kent University (PhD Thesis).
24. Confidential interview with a GATT official.
25. Confidential interview with a GATT official.
26. *Jornal da Tarde.* 15/10/86.
27. *Folha de São Paulo.* 12/10/86.

28. Bhagwati, 1987c, *op.cit.*, p.207.
29. *O Estado de São Paulo*. 17/10/86.
30. *Gazeta Mercantil*. 20/10/86.
31. The Ministerial Declaration on the Uruguay Round. GATT, 1987, *BISD 1986-1987. 35 Sup.* Geneva, GATT. pp.19-28.
32. The visit of Brazilian President Sarney to the US can be found in Itamaraty, 1987, *Relatório 1986*. Brasilia, MRE.
33. *Financial Times*. 08/10/86.
34. See Odell, J. 1992, "International Threats and Internal Politics: Brazil, the US and the European Community". In Evans, P. Putnam, H. & Jacobson,R. *International Politics and Domestic Bargaining: an Interactive Approach*. Berkeley, University of California Press.
35. See Chapter 6.
36. Interview in *Le Monde*. 23/09/86.
37. Odell, 1991, *op.cit.*, p.31.
38. Dunkel in GATT, 1992, *The Uruguay Round. A Giant Step for Trade and Development, and a Response to the Challenges of the Modern World*. Geneva, GATT. p.1.
39. GATT, 1992, *op.cit.*, p.24.
40. GATT, 1987, *GATT Activities 1986*. Geneva, GATT. p.16.
41. GATT, 1987, *op.cit.* pp.15-29.
42. GATT, 1992, *op.cit.*, p.4.
43. The Multi-Fibre Arrangement in practice controlled most of the world trade in textiles and clothing.
44. Abreu, 1990, *op.cit.* p.12.
45. Zietz, J. & Valdis, A. 1986. The Cost of Protectionism to Developing Countries. An Analysis for Selected Agricultural Products. (World Bank Staff Papers n. 769) p.17. Quoted in Abreu & Fristch, 1989, *op.cit.*, p.47.
46. Abreu & Fritsch, 1989, *op.cit.*, p.19.
47. Finlayson & Weston, 1990, *op.cit.*, p.41.
48. Itamaraty, 1988a, *op.cit.*, p.15.
49. Finlayson & Weston, 1990, *op.cit.*, p.40.
50. Finlayson & Weston, 1990, *op.cit.*, p.41.
51. Itamaraty, 1988a, *op.cit.*, p.13.
52. Gunasekera, B Parsons, D. & Kirby, M. 1989. "Liberalising Trade in Agriculture: Some Perspectives for Developing Countries". in Whalley, J. 1989. *op.cit.*, pp.247-248.
53. UNCTAD, 1986, *op.cit.*, p.25, Part I.
54. In Abreu & Fritsch, 1988, *op.cit.*, pp.22-23.
55. In Abreu & Fritsch, 1988, *op.cit.*, p.22.
56. Koekoek, 1989, *op.cit.*, p.77.
57. Abreu & Fritsch, 1988, *op.cit.*, p.20.

58. GATT data, quoted in: Abreu & Fritsch, 1988, *op.cit.*, p.20.
59. Finlayson & Weston, 1990, *op.cit.*, p.49. .
60. Abreu & Fritsch, 1988, *op.cit.*, p.20.
61. Abreu & Fritsch, 1988, *op.cit.*, p.20.
62. Itamaraty, 1988a, *op.cit.*, p.24.
63. Confidential interview with a Brazilian diplomat.
64. Itamaraty, 1988a, *op.cit.*, pp.5-6.
65. Finlayson & Weston, 1990, *op.cit.*, p.26.
66. Balasubramanyam, 1991, *op.cit.*, p.139.
67. Itamaraty, 1988a, *op.cit.*, p.13.
68. This section will not analyze the changes in Brazil's position in the GNS or the reasons for this change, which are the subject of chapters 5 and 6.
69. The main source for the discussion of Brazil's position is the well-known statement made by Batista during the Uruguay Round in the GNS. This Declaration was made public by way of an article, from now on, referred to Batista, 1987, "Brazil's Perspective on service negotiations" in *SELA Capítulos* 16. This chapter also uses other sources, such as various Brazilian Communiqués in the GNS, documents from Itamaraty and GATT, confidential interviews with Brazilian and foreign diplomats and with Itamaraty and GATT officials.
70. Abreu, 1992, *op.cit.*, p.33.
71. Batista, 1987, *op.cit.*, p.63.
72. Batista, 1987, *op.cit.*, pp.61-62.
73. During the founding of the UN, there was no consensus on the use of the word war, which was then replaced by the expression "armed aggression against a State".
74. See Abreu, 1990, *op.cit.*, p.148.
75. Oxley (1990) noted that the EU and the US supported the view that an agreement in services should cover every single service transaction, while LDCs were concerned about the umbrella approach and wanted to exclude some sectors and even the right to waive the obligation to liberalize (See: Oxley, 1990, *op.cit.*, pp.186-187). A more limited definition would have the sympathy of LDCs since it would obviously limit the final scope of an agreement on services.
76. For the complete text of the 1982 Ministerial Declaration see GATT, 1983, *BISD 1981-1982 and 38th Session*. Geneva, GATT. pp.9-23, esp. pp.21-22.
77. Examples of Conventions discussed at UNCTAD are: The Code of Conduct for Linear Conferences, The International Multi-modal Transport of Goods and Restrictive Business Practices Code.
78. For UNCTAD activities in the field of services, see Taylor, 1987, *UNCTAD and Trade in Services*. Geneva, GATT.
79. The International Civil Aviation Organization (ICAO) was established in the 1940s to regulate air transport. For a review of ICAO Activities, see, ICAO, 1981, *Memorandum in ICAO. The story of International Civil Aviation*. Geneva, United Nations.

80. Abreu (1990) also supports this view that Brazil used the argument of lack of information to obstruct the negotiations. See: Abreu, 1990, *op.cit.* p.325.

81. McMillan, 1989, "A Game Theoretical View of International Trade Negotiations: Implications for LDCs". in Whalley, *op.cit.* p.38.

82. Batista, 1987, *op.cit.*, pp.61-62.

83. Batista, 1987, *op.cit.*, p.62 and p.66.

84. Batista, 1987, *op.cit.*, pp.64-65.

85. Schott and Mazza, 1986, *op.cit.*, p.262.

86. In 1987, Brazil had state monopolies in oil, waterfalls, power stations, telecom and uranium. The monopoly in oil was set up in the 1950s after a nationalist campaign.

87. The idea of putting development as the centre of world trade was the 'leitmotiv' of the creation of UNCTAD in the 1960s. In the 1970s, Brazil brought this issue to GATT with the nomination of Maciel as its Representative in the GATT. For a summary of Brazil's positions then, see: Maciel, 1978, *op.cit.*

88. Except infant-industry, but this is not widely accepted.

89. Deardoff, 1984, *Comparative Advantage and International Trade and Investment in Services.* Michigan, University of Michigan.

90. For an analysis of Brazilian efforts to increase the competitiveness of its computer industry, see Tigre, P., 1991, "Política ou Não Política: Os Descaminhos da Informática no Brasil". In Velloso, R., 1991. *op.cit.*, p.15.

91. For an analysis of the importance of political arguments, see Hillman, A.(ed.), 1991, *Markets and Politicians. Politicized Economic Choice.* Boston, Kluwer Academic Publishers.

92. See: UNCTAD, 1981, *The Set of Multilaterally Agreed Equitable Principles and Rules for the Control of Restrictive Business Practice.* Geneva, GATT.

93. However, Brazil did not mention that many LDCs do not have laws to protect labour rights, which keep wages down.

94. Batista, 1987, *op.cit.*, p.61.

95. Batista, 1987, *op.cit.*, pp.62-63.

96. Batista, 1987, *op.cit.*, p.65.

97. Batista, 1987, *op.cit.*, p.61.

98. Batista, 1987, *op.cit.*, p.65.

99. Batista, 1987, *op.cit.*, p.65.

100. Batista, 1987, *op.cit.*, p.61.

101. Batista, 1987, *op.cit.*, p.65.

102. Confidential interview with a Brazilian Ambassador.

103. Schott & Mazza, 1986, *op.cit.*, p.270.

104. See: GATT, 1986, *The Text of the General Agreement on Tariffs and Trade.* Geneva, GATT. (Art.XXV and XXX).

105. Martone & Braga, 1988, *op.cit.*, p.37.

106. For the US position, see: GATT Document. L.5838 9/7/85.

107. Confidential interviews with GATT officials.

108. Balasubramanyam, 1991, *op.cit.*, pp.139-141.
109. OECD, 1989. *Trade in Services and Developing Countries.* Paris, OECD.
110. Batista, 1987, *op.cit.*, pp.62-63.
111. For an analysis of the shortcomings of the group negotiations techniques employed at UNCTAD, see: Weiss, T., 1986, *Multilateral Development Diplomacy in UNCTAD. The Lessons of Group Negotiations: 1964-1984.* Basingstoke, Macmillan.
112. Brazil could not block the negotiations for ever, as a Brazilian Ambassador remarked privately.
113. Interview with Dr. Jarrod Wiener.
114. See: Jackson, J., 1988, *International Competition in Services. A Constitutional Framework.* Washington, American Enterprise Institute for Public Policy Research.
115. On GATT rules, see: Hudec, R. 1990, *The GATT Legal System and World Trade Diplomacy.* New York, Butterworth.
116. Batista, 1987, *op.cit.*, p.64.
117. Batista, 1987, *op.cit.*, pp.61-62.
118. Batista, 1987, *op.cit.*, p.62.
119. In any goods sector, due to gains in productivity allowed by a more efficient service industry. See: Jones, R., & Kierskowsky, H., 1990, "The Role of Services in Production and International Trade". In Jones, R. & Krueger, A. *The Political Economy of International Trade.* Cambridge (MA), Basil Blackwell. p.45.
120. See chapter 2.
121. GATT, 1990, *International Trade. 1988-1989.* Geneva, GATT. Vol.II p.1.
122. GATT, 1986, *International Trade 1984-1985.* Geneva, GATT. p.40.
123. GATT, 1986, *op.cit.*, p.13.
124. Ibid. p.139 (Appendix).
125. GATT, 1988, *International Trade 1986-1987.* Geneva, GATT. Vol.II p.87. Table AA1.
126. GATT, 1986, *op.cit.*, p.63.
127. Idem. p.35.
128. Idem p.65.
129. GATT, 1989, *op.cit.*, vol.I p.30.
130. GATT, 1989, *International Trade 1987-1988.* Geneva, GATT. Vol.I, p.30.
131. Balasubramanyam, 1991, *op.cit.*, p.121.
132. Brazil. Congresso Nacional. Lei de Informatica. 1984. In *Anais do Congresso Nacional.* Decembro 1984. Brasilia, Camara dos Deputados.
133. See a discussion of protectionism in LDCs in Mckee, D., 1988, *Growth, Development and the Service Economy in the Third World.* New York, Praeger.
134. See Tigre, 1991, *op.cit.*, p.17.
135. See Gatt document L.5818 07/06/85.

136.   Batista, 1987, *op.cit.*, p.64.
137.   Feketekuty, 1988, *op.cit.*, pp.110-111.
138.   Batista, 1987, *op.cit.*, p.64.
139.   Melvin, 1987, *Trade in Services: A Theoretical Analysis*. Halifax, Institute for Research on Public Policy. p.13.
140.   See Hindley, 1984, "Comparative Advantage and Trade in Services". In *The World Economy* v.7 (4):pp. 369-390.
141.   Feketekuty, 1988, *op.cit.*, p.104.
142.   For a general review, see Bhagwati, 1987c, *op.cit* and Melvin, 1989, *op.cit.*
143.   For a detailed discussion of the G-10, see Chapter 3.
144.   On G-77, see: Williams, M., 1991, *Third World Cooperation. The Group of 77 in UNCTAD*. New York, St. Martin's Press.
145.   Itamaraty, 1988, *O Contexto de Acesso a Mercados na Rodada Uruguay*. Brasilia, Itamaraty (MRE).
146.   Tachinardi, 1993, *A Guerra das Patentes. O Conflito Brasil-EUA sobre Propriedade Intellectual*. São Paulo, Paz e Terra.
147.   Confidential interview with a Brazilian Ambassador.
148.   See A. Desai, 1987, *op.cit.*, p.53.
149.   Brazil. Itamaraty. 1988a, *op.cit.*, p.36.

4. The Development of Brazil's Stance

Introduction

The objective of this chapter is to analyze the development and final position of Brazil in the Uruguay Round. It is divided into five parts. The first section focuses on the evolution of Brazil's position in services in the Uruguay Round, concentrating on Itamaraty's view of the process. The most important individual development in this sector was the replacement of Brazil's first negotiator, Batista, by Rubens Ricupero, who had a completely different style, personality and perspective on the service discussions.

The second section focuses on the evolution of the US position during the negotiations. When the technical discussions started, the US realized that its ambition of a complete and immediate liberalization of services was not possible. This is described in the second part, which explains why the US position evolved during the discussions. The third part describes how the US and Brazilian positions began to converge after the arrival of Ricupero. This was through a process of mutual bargaining between Brazil and the US.

The fourth part of this chapter refers to Brazil's final position, in particular with respect to the proposal submitted by the Director-General of the GATT, Arthur Dunkel, the Draft Final Act (DFA). It compares Brazil's initial and final position. It also demonstrates how Brazil influenced the outcome of the process. Finally, the fifth section of this chapter makes a comparison between Brazil's final position on tariffs and agriculture, with its initial position on the same issues. This illustrates the extent of change in Brazil's position during the Uruguay Round. This is followed by a concluding view of the position adopted by Itamaraty in the Uruguay Round in the above mentioned sectors.

The evolution of Brazil's and Indian position in the Group Negotiating on Services (GNS)

The Brazilian position

After a surveillance body was set up to supervise the application of the standstill and roll-back of protectionist measures, the discussions on services started, in January 1987. The GNS met on 28 January. Five elements were chosen as the most significant to be discussed by the Group: 1) definitional and statistical issues; 2) broad concepts on which rules for trade in services might be based; 3) coverage of the framework for trade in services; 4) existing international arrangements; 5) measures or barriers limiting the expansion of trade in services.[1]

The first official meeting of the GNS was in February 1987. At this meeting (23-25 February), Batista maintained a high profile position and blocked any significant discussion. Batista used all the obstructionist tactics available. Initially, he discussed the legal basis for the negotiations and the general objectives in seeking a framework of rules and disciplines for services.[2]

At the second Meeting of the GNS (8-10 April) Batista insisted on discussing the role of statistics in the service sector. Batista constantly reminded other participants of the work of other institutions - read UNCTAD - in collecting and analyzing statistics on services. He suggested that it could take years before any relevant statistics could be structured in a credible way.[3] Batista accepted that the concepts used in the GATT framework for goods could be used in the discussions concerning services, such as mutual advantage, transparency, national treatment, increasing international competition and trade liberalization. However, in a rather negative attitude, he proposed that these concepts should be redefined to be applied to services. In his first attack on the GNS, Batista noted that the goals of the negotiations were economic growth and development promotion, and not trade liberalization. The latter should be seen as a way of achieving those two goals and not an end in itself.[4]

The third Meeting (29 June to 2 July) concentrated on the statistical issue; its main conclusion was that they needed to be improved. Some suggestions were made on how to improve them. The discussion also considered whether the concept of unconditional Most Favoured Nation (MFN) should be applied to services. The general perception was that it would not be practical to do so.[5]

As a result of Batista's (and the G-10) hard-line position, the negotiations after the first six months were blocked. The Chairman of the GNS, Colombian Ambassador, Felipe Jaramillo, declared in the bulletin of GATT that differences prevailed on the importance of arriving at an agreed definition of trade in services.[6] This meant that after almost six months of negotiations, the GNS could not achieve a consensus on the role of a definition in trade in services, let alone the definition of services itself. The blocking strategy continued. In September 1987, the GNS had no definition of services and did not know which concepts of GATT should be applied to an agreement on services - if there was to be an agreement at all.[7]

In November, the US tried to push for the adoption of a framework to achieve trade liberalization in services as soon as possible, which would include as many countries as possible.[8] The US proposed the application of the concepts of transparency, non-discrimination and national treatment to a prospective code on services. In other words, foreign firms should receive exactly the same treatment or privileges that Brazilian firms received. This also implied that the Brazilian government could not discriminate against US firms. If this kind of requirement had already been in place, Brazil could never have launched an industrial policy to create national firms of Information Technology (IT), because it discriminates against Trans-National Corporations (TNCs).

This caused alarm in Brazil, which believed that there was an imbalance in the negotiations, with discussions on services going faster than on goods. As a result, India and Brazil decided to maintain their policy of obstruction.[9] However, some progress was made in December. At the 14-15 December meeting the GNS agreed a provisional definition of services and concepts that could be applied to that sector. The discussions progressed offering the prospect of agreeing concepts to apply to specific sectors. The EC proposed a standstill on the introduction of national regulations to control trade in services, the main barrier to international transactions in services in their opinion. Switzerland proposed that MFN should not be applied to a prospective agreement in services. On the other hand, Brazil and India (and the G-10) continued to obstruct the discussions when they had a chance to do so. They argued that the GNS gave little attention to development issues. The impact of an agreement on the development process remained unclear to them. Moreover, Brazil insisted that international agreements should be examined more carefully. In order to delay the proceedings, India and Brazil also proposed that the polemical issue of labour mobility be included in further discussions.[10] In spite of this, Jaramillo managed to approve an agreement on how to continue the negotiating process in a second phase, to be started in January 1988. In its report to the TNC, he noted that the GNS would have to continue to work on the basis of the five elements suggested early in 1987.[11]

In 1988, the first Meeting (27-29 January) concentrated on the discussion of the proposals presented by the EC and Switzerland. It was suggested that instead of a multilateral agreement there would be bilateral agreements which could be extended, or not, to third parties through an optional MFN clause.[12] Brazil considered the EC proposal more balanced because it conciliated a liberalization of market access with national regulations. Since in Brazil several sectors were excluded from international competition due to barriers to imports or market access, the EC draft fitted Brazil's autarkic policies. Moreover, if the Swiss proposal was accepted the result would be the exclusion of Brazil from international service markets. Indeed, Brazil would have to negotiate the liberalization of its market in each sector discussed in the Uruguay Round and would probably prefer to keep its market closed than to open it to other countries, as the case of goods illustrates. However, Brazil considered that the weak point of the EC proposal was that the situation of Less Developed Countries (LDCs) was being ignored.

In order to overcome this gap, a document was presented by Argentina to the Meeting of 22-25 March 1988, where the development concerns of LDCs were expressed. Basically, the paper proposed that a future framework in services should include a principle ensuring that national legislation and policies would not be questioned. It also sought Special and Differential (S&D) treatment for LDCs. This proposal had the strong support of Brazil since Argentina was also a member of the G-10. At the same Meeting, Nordic countries presented their proposal for an agreement on services. The Nordic paper included a MFN clause and a requirement that rules should not restrict trade in services beyond the level required to fulfil national goals.[13]

At the Meeting of 16-19 May the proposals from Canada, the US and Japan were discussed. The proposals suggested liberalization measures as the first step to a multilateral service framework. The Japanese proposal had some provisions which considered the needs of LDCs. However, the LDCs believed that the provisions were not sufficient and Mexico presented a comprehensive document at the Meeting of 18-22 July. The Mexican proposal included the idea that development should be an integral part of the framework of any sectoral agreement. It also suggested that the polemical issue of the right of establishment should not be covered by a prospective agreement and measures should be taken to speed up transfers of technology from Developed Countries (DCs) to LDCs. Besides, the Mexican proposal also included the concept of relative reciprocity, which is very important to LDCs.

Australia also made its contribution to the discussions. The Australian proposal was an example of how a framework would look. It was divided into three parts: a) concepts and scope; b) obligations and benefits; c) institutional provisions. It was based on strong rules of general application incorporating a balance of rights and obligations.[14] However, this was exactly the kind of approach Brazil was against since it would mean that all countries would necessarily have to present lists of regulations that would be excluded from the general agreement. Later on, these lists would have to be shortened until all regulations were harmonized within the framework through multilateral negotiations. Simultaneously, the GNS was discussing a glossary of words to be applied to the negotiations on services. The glossary also included the national positions concerning each of the terms.[15]

This was the means found to narrow the divergences between DCs and LDCs, such as Brazil and India, who had been obstructing the negotiations with their insistence on discussing concepts and definitions. These discussions continued at the Meeting of 19-23 September. Basically, Brazil wanted the GNS to adopt a narrow definition of trade in services. This meant that only services which crossed borders should be considered international transactions in services. DCs, however, wanted a broader definition of services to include transactions realized inside a country when the agent had to move to effect it.[16] This discussion was vital since the preparations for the Montreal Meeting in December 1988 were going on and the GNS was probably the only group not to have agreed even on a definition. However, in November 1988, when Ricupero was already leading the Brazilian team, the negotiations reached a crux and it was possible to formulate an agreement on a definition and on a framework to govern trade in services.

This broad definition was finally accepted by Brazil. Brazil also accepted the concepts of national treatment for foreign suppliers, MFN, as well as progressive liberalization. On the other hand, the framework agreement included provisions to guarantee the growing participation of LDCs in trade in services.[17] The Montreal agreement on principles in the GNS was quite a significant achievement. Not all the Groups in the Uruguay Round reached an agreement. From fifteen areas being negotiated in goods, four of them remained open to discussions: agriculture, textiles, Intellectual Property Rights (IPRs), and reform of the safeguards system. Thus, the agreement on principles was quite unexpected since the service issue was considered to be by far the most problematic. However, the lack of results in those four above mentioned fields caused all results to be put on hold pending a global agreement in April 1989 in Geneva.[18]

The Montreal agreement was a set of principles to be applied to negotiations on a prospective framework for services. These included transparency, progressive liberalization, national treatment, market access, increasing participation of LDCs, safeguards and exceptions, and the regulatory situation.[19] In April the GNS discussed the application of the concepts agreed in Montreal,[20] and in June, they were applied to two sectors: telecom and construction.[21] Discussions in these two sectors were particularly important due to the fact that construction involved the movement of labour. In July, the areas of transport and tourism were examined,[22] and in September it was debated whether the principles could be applied to professional and financial services. At this Meeting, New Zealand and Switzerland presented a detailed proposal for a General Agreement on Trade in Services, GATS.[23]

Thus, what seemed to be unthinkable two years before began to be realized: the negotiation of a legal framework for services. This was a clear step forward when compared to the text agreed in December at the Montreal Mid-term Review. At the October Meeting it was the turn of the US to present a detailed and near complete proposal of a legal text for an agreement on services. However, Brazil, India and other LDCs believed that although the US proposal could be considered comprehensive, it did not include provisions for the development of LDCs.[24]

For this reason, Brazil decided to present its own proposal for an agreement on trade in services at the Meeting of 20-24 November.[25] It is worthwhile noting that Ricupero, being presented with either the prospect of an agreement on services which Brazil considered against its fundamental interests, or with participation in the negotiations to try to influence the outcome, opted for the latter alternative. As a result, Brazil's draft proposal included questions that it considered to be the most relevant to its development and excluded controversial issues. The Brazilian proposal for a framework to regulate services was based on a strict definition of trade in services. Indeed, trade in service was defined as the cross-border movement of services, consumers and factors of production. Cross-border movement of factors of production were accepted only where it was essential for suppliers and was subject to certain criteria. The main aspects of the Brazilian draft rested on four principles: respect for national policies; consistency with development objectives; balance of benefits among participants; and exceptions. The Brazilian proposal excluded the polemical question of Foreign Direct Investment (FDI) and labour immigration. In principle, there would be no service sector that would be excluded from the draft framework, and measures would be adopted in order to increase the participation of LDCs in world trade in services. Those would include the strengthening of domestic service industries, transfer of technology, and preferential financial mechanisms. The proposals presented by Brazil and other countries were summarized in a paper prepared by the GATT secretariat in order to narrow the differences between the various positions.

At the Meeting of 18 December the GNS adopted a draft version of a framework on services. This fell into four parts. The first part outlined the scope of the agreement, and gave a definition of trade in services. The second one described the principles and rules, for example, market access, transparency, progressive liberalization, MFN, increasing participation of LDCs, and other provisions. The third part included alternative approaches to progressive liberalization, and comments about the framework.[26] The last part described institutional features of a prospective framework. However, Brazil and other LDCs felt that development interests were not sufficiently reflected in the framework and they would try to expand them at the next Meeting of the GNS in January 1990. Indeed, at the January Meeting, India proposed some changes to the framework to emphasize its development aspects. To some it incorporated some features of the Brazilian draft proposal, but it went even further. For instance, India considered that trade liberalization in services should be based on the following principles: respect for national policies; development and technological objectives; expansion of service exports from LDCs; and the possibility for LDCs to adopt a slower pace of trade liberalization. National treatment would be a goal and not a commitment; DCs could give preferences to LDCs without extending them to other DCs and freedom would exist for LDCs to impose rules on foreign service providers. The increasing participation of LDCs would be achieved, in the Indian proposal, by way of an end to restrictions on labour migration; the requirement to transfer technology by foreign service providers; and special access to DCs markets for the exports of LDCs.[27]

The Indian position and its techniques of muddling through

The Indian proposal apparently had the goal of strengthening the position of LDCs in the discussions, and of obliging the DCs to make more concessions in the framework negotiations. It had been agreed that these negotiations would be concluded by July 1990. It was not a coincidence that the ending of immigration restrictions, which was not mentioned in the Brazilian proposal, was included in the Indian draft. In the service negotiations, there was a kind of 'division of labour' between Brazil and India. Brazil and India would alternatively play the role of the hard-liner among the hard-liners, as this example showed. Brazil presented a draft which was considered by DCs to be radical. Afterwards, India presented another proposal which was even more radical than the draft submitted by Brazil. As a result, the Brazilian proposal began to be considered moderate and no longer radical. Brazil and India were at the same time initiators and mediators between themselves in the G-10, and on behalf of LDCs in general. This was a complex negotiating technique that could be used only by countries with a fine diplomatic service, such as Brazil and India. The technique was noted by GATT officials and was used at a time when the subject being discussed was considered to be vital by one of the two players.[28]

The GNS Meeting in February discussed a possible structure for a framework in services. The discussions considered what initial commitment should be made, and how trade liberalization should be adopted. Brazil presented a proposal elaborated by the Latin American Economic System (SELA), on behalf of 11 LDCs. The text incorporated GATT principles (progressive liberalization, MFN, transparency), but its strongest feature was the stress on the development needs of LDCs. Basically it proposed relative reciprocity, flexibility for LDCs in the opening of their markets, technical assistance for LDCs industries, and the right of LDCs to provide support for their domestic service providers.[29]

The SELA proposal showed that Latin American countries were coordinating their positions again, and Brazil could use this to increase its bargaining power in the negotiations. Moreover, the discussions also considered how to reconcile the work carried out by other organizations (such as UNCTAD) and existing arrangements (such as International Civil Aviation Organization (ICAO) with trade liberalization. This aspect was a point of honour for Brazil, and it was clear that it would use UNCTAD's work to obtain concessions from DCs. Indeed, Brazil and other LDCs insisted that all development provisions should be included in the framework, while industrialized countries suggested that those provisions could be included in an annex or in the preamble. At the March Meeting DCs complained that the proposals from LDCs, and in particular those emanating from SELA, incorporated too many exclusions and exemptions and few commitments. DCs believed that this was not the best way to build a strong and competitive industry in services. On the other hand, LDCs denied that they were trying to be free-riders. Brazil and LDCs argued that they did not have proper data and this would jeopardize their ability to negotiate.[30] Naturally, DCs interpreted this as a play by LDCs to obtain concessions. In spite of this, in May 1990 the GNS set up Working Groups to consult on service sectors already covered by the principles approved at the Montreal Meeting in 1988: telecommunications, construction, transportation, tourism, financial services, and professional services.[31]

In another delaying tactic, India and other LDCs[32] presented a new proposal for a legal framework for services. However, this proposal did not include permanent establishment, FDI, or international immigration. The draft suggested the creation of an International Trade in Services Organization to ease the implementation of the agreed framework.[33] It had few possibilities of being accepted, entirely or in parts, and it should be seen as a last effort by LDCs to obtain concessions in the final negotiations of the agreement. Until November 1990, there was no agreement on the definition, viz., application of MFN and sector coverage in services.[34]

In December 1990, the Uruguay Round broke down at the Brussels Meeting due to lack of agreement on agriculture. However, a provisional agreement on services was already realized. It would be clarified, modified and completed by an intensive series of consultations by Jaramillo and the Australian Ambassador, David Hawes. In 1991, due to the lack of an agreement between the US and the EC on reductions in subsidies for agricultural products, an impasse followed. To overcome the impasse, Dunkel was instructed to elaborate a compromise draft, the DFA. The DFA covered all sectors discussed in the Uruguay Round, including services, which were not covered by GATT and was the only sector to be discussed outside the aegis of the GATT.[35]

The negotiations on services from the US perspective

The US had never entirely accepted the idea of keeping the GNS outside the scope of GATT. The US wanted to include services in the Uruguay Round and to withdraw its "special status" in that Round. As a result, the US proposed that a framework should be discussed in order to settle general principles that would regulate trade in services. In the US view, these principles could then be extended to specific sectors, so that by the middle of 1988 liberalization of trade in services would be a reality. The US also demanded the dismantling of regulatory barriers.[36] Brazil rejected the proposal presented by the US to the GNS in November 1987, which aimed to increase transparency and non-discrimination in services.[37]

The US proposal also intended to obtain national treatment for TNCs, that is, the same rights as for national firms. By the end of 1987 the US was aware that its target of opening all service markets by July of 1988 would not be fulfilled. They were now resigned to accepting the completion of the Round as scheduled at the end of 1990. The US proposal was strongly criticized by experts, who considered it dangerous and selective.[38]

The US used the US-Canadian Agreement of 1987 to illustrate the viability of a detailed agreement for trade in services being achieved in a short period of time. National obstacles had been overcome. As a result, the US delegation believed that an overall agreement on trade in services was possible.[39]

The EC proposal for regulating trade in services incorporated some important differences from those presented by the US. While the US proposal started from general principles to arrive at specific sectors, the EC proposals concentrated on procedures as the first step to reduce barriers in services. The EC considered the US proposal too ambitious. They pointed out that few governments would accept the two main features of the US proposal: the right of establishment and national treatment alongside their respective implications, freedom for foreign investment and non-discrimination against foreign suppliers.[40]

The main advantage of the EC proposal was its simplicity. Its main aim was the expansion of trade in services and the prevention of carrying out reforms in the world trading system. Each country would announce to a "regulatory committee", the barriers faced by its service suppliers abroad. Moreover, each country would describe the barriers adopted domestically against foreign suppliers. The regulation committee would then judge the compatibility of the domestic restrictions with market liberalization of trade in services. If a restriction was considered inappropriate, the country which had adopted it should modify or eliminate it. However, the EC proposal was criticized on the grounds that national treatment and non-discrimination should only be goals and not starting points for negotiations. Otherwise, national governments would have too much opportunity to keep access to their markets closed. National governments could also adopt discriminatory measures in opposition to the principles of GATT.[41]

Besides that, the lack of a non-discrimination clause would prevent the agreements established from benefiting all countries. The threat of bilateral agreements, such as those practised during the 1930s, would reappear. This is a paradox, since the EC wanted to prevent the US from adopting bilateral treaties but its proposals allowed it do so. Thus if the US proposal had principles but no procedures, the EC one had procedures but no principle.[42]

Indeed, the EC proposal received little support from other countries. They feared that national legislation would be controlled by the Supra-National Committee proposed by the EC. Moreover, LDCs pointed out that they could not discuss principles without analyzing the impact on specific sectors. Thus, they wanted to discuss principles and the impact on specific sectors at the same time. LDCs also wanted guarantees that the sectors in which they had a greater comparative advantage and expertise, such as civil construction and engineering, would not be ignored.[43]

Argentina showed interest in provisions for transfer of technology. Another concern mentioned in the Argentina proposal was that IPRs should not become a monopoly right of its owners, and, thus, prevent exports of services. Basically, Argentina suggested that each LDC could regulate each sub-sector of services according to its level of development. LDCs should also be allowed to adopt Import Substitution Industrialization (ISI) measures.[44] The Argentinean proposal required that DCs should keep their markets open to service exports from LDCs. The latter would not be prevented from adopting measures to stimulate their exports. Moreover, LDCs would have control of the financial flows linked to projects in the field of trade in services.[45]

The US tried to answer Argentina's proposals and reply to its former critics by presenting, in May 1988, a new paper with several practical measures, in order to adopt a multilateral framework as soon as possible. The new US proposal could be divided into three stages. In the first one, general guidelines would be adopted. In the second stage, studies would be conducted on how to apply those to specific sectors. In this phase, countries would decide which sectors would be liberalized and which would not. The sectors which would be liberalized would be named during the second phase. Those sectors that national governments considered politically or economically "sensitive" would be left to a third phase. In this third phase, countries would have to negotiate an opening of the sensitive service sectors, such as communications in the US.

The advantage of the new US proposal was that it included the three existing proposals in one: the first US proposal, the EC proposal and the Argentinean one. In this way, the new US paper was the most balanced and acceptable compromise for all countries concerned - DCs and LDCs alike. However, the new US proposal did not include the idea of development and the definition of services. LDCs argued that without a definition of services and without a proper framework, no liberalization could take place. LDCs also wanted the negotiations on services to include the mobility of labour. Three areas had already been discussed in the negotiating group: telecom, aviation, and shipping.[46]

Nevertheless, the complexity of air transport demonstrated by the work done by ICAO confirmed that there was no easy answer to liberalizing services in this sector, and the negotiations had to continue. Australia made an important contribution to the discussions on services with the submission of a paper suggesting a compromise. The Australian paper followed the free trade lines of the US, and the EC proposals, and was based on Australia's free-trade agreement with New Zealand. The basic idea of the Australian draft was an international agreement with clear principles that all countries would commit themselves to adopt gradually. However, the degree of gradualism involved would be decided by each country.[47]

The main difference between the Australian paper and that of the US is that the former included a period of time for each country to negotiate market access with other countries. The Australian proposal allowed countries to ask for exceptions on the grounds of national security. However, there would be a requirement under which changes in domestic law would be open to comment from other countries. This aimed to ensure that the principle of national treatment and MFN would be respected.[48]

A controversial point of the Australian document was the lack of any reference to the development of LDCs. It triggered complaints from LDCs about the direction of the Uruguay Round. In the first half of 1988, Brazil's new Ambassador to GATT, Ricupero, formally accused the multilateral talks of having serious imbalances. The sectors where Brazil and LDCs had comparative advantage were obstructed.[49] However, in the service sector, where DCs had a greater comparative advantage, the talks were going too fast. India even accused the EC, US, and Japan of going beyond the agreed mandate in services.[50]

McPherson, US Acting Treasury Secretary, declared that from now on LDCs would have to reciprocate. If LDCs wanted better access for their exports, they would have to withdraw their non-trade barriers to services, and reduce trade barriers.[51] However, less than two months after Brazil and India's criticism of the lack of progress in the talks, the US and the EC made concrete proposals to ease the access of tropical products for LDCs.[52] At the end of 1988 the differences between the US and the EC started to appear. In particular, there was a disagreement between the US and the EC on the principles of trade in services. The US believed that they should be considered obligations, while the EC thought that they should only be guidelines.

Ms Anita Gradin, Trade Minister for Sweden, was in charge of heading a reform group on services. Her main task was to present a new draft summary of the paper on services produced by previous negotiators, which had been considered to be too comprehensive with its more than 130 "points of disagreement".[53]

The basis of the new document discussed at Montreal stated that liberalization in services should be larger than the greater the level of development of each country. Another concession which the US should make in the final document would include general principles, as the EC and LDCs wanted, and not obligations as the US required. On the other hand, the final document included the principles of national treatment, transparency nondiscrimination, safeguards, and exceptions. The document also contained a formula specifying the right of LDCs to adapt an eventual agreement on services to their own legislation, and to maintain their national legislation in some sectors, such as IT in Brazil. However, the lack of agreement between US and the EC over farm subsidies in Montreal led to a rebellion from LDCs, led by Argentina and indirectly, Brazil.[54] Brazil and Argentina refused to accept the 'early harvest' of the Uruguay Round proposed by the US and defended the all-or-nothing negotiating principle. This meant that progress in services was dependent on progress in other fields, that is, agreement on farm subsidies.

The result of the disagreement on agriculture was the postponement of the mid-term review of the Uruguay Round from December 1988 to April 1989. The prospective agreements on services were frozen as were all other agreements. However, the fact that Dunkel decided to work as mediator in the US-EC conflict over farm subsidies was seen as a sign that a compromise could be reached. Dunkel proposed a compromise not only on farm subsidies, but in all other areas which were frozen by the disagreement between the US and the EC. Just after the new mediating role of Dunkel was announced, the EC Commission said it would re-examine its position on the Round as a whole.

The results of Dunkels's mediation became known as the Dunkel Plan. This plan incorporated a freeze on expenditure on farm support policies in the US and the EC. The final goal of the Dunkel Plan would be to eliminate misrepresentations of agricultural exports resulting from various subsidy regimes and protection to farmers.[55] In April 1989, the US and EC accepted the Dunkel plan, ending the deadlock in the trade negotiations. The Dunkel Plan was also accepted by the Cairns Group.[56]

The agreement reached by the US and the EC in agriculture had a direct impact on the service negotiations. It was agreed that a service agreement would be based on the same rules that govern trade in goods. This meant that GATT rules would be used as a parameter; and accelerated the service negotiations. Negotiations would move now to individual sectors since the principles had been agreed. It can be said that the meeting at Geneva (April 1989) was a success in the sense that it marked important progress in the trade negotiations.

Brazil began to accept GATT rules more readily. Brazil started to accept the idea of GATT more easily and its perception of GATT had considerably changed at this point. This was a significant U-turn from the beginning of the negotiations, when Batista was leading the Brazilian negotiating team. At that stage, Brazil had declared the negotiations in services a mere 'exercise' and held the view that they may not be successful. As a matter of fact, one of the arguments used by the US to persuade Brazil to take part in the negotiations on services was that there would be an informal 'walk-out' clause. According to this informal deal, any country which did not feel entirely satisfied with a would-be agreement could either refrain from signing it or ask for exemption. Batista's statement clearly gives the impression that Brazil was only taking part in an 'exercise' and no more than that.[57]

The first test of the rules agreed in Geneva (1989) would be their application in two sectors: telecommunications and construction. These two sectors were chosen because they represented a compromise. The US was very keen on rules in telecom services, while LDCs always considered civil construction as their most competitive sector. Eventually, the negotiations would include transport, tourism, financial services, and professional services.

The LDCs wanted to take advantage of lower labour costs and salaries existent in LDCs to export labour intensive services, such as construction. In the discussion with DCs they managed to include the issue of mobility of labour. LDCs wanted to obtain an agreement that stipulated under which conditions contractors could transfer workers among countries.[58] On the other hand, the US was concerned with a strict anti-subsidy code. Basically, the US position aimed at eliminating support from governments to private national contractors making bids abroad. This was achieved. In telecommunications, the US pressed for and obtained agreement that discussions would include value added products in services, such as electronic mail.[59]

The naming of Brazil by the USTR Office as an unfair trading nation, in May 1989, did not affect its position in the GNS of the Uruguay Round. Brazil insisted that the use of the new 1988 US Omnibus Trade Bill (Super 301) by the US was illegal under GATT. Brazil refused to join "consultations" with the US about its trade policies, in particular its import restrictions. Brazil claimed that it could not discuss its trade policies bilaterally using the domestic law of another country as a basis. Brazil and other countries felt that the US was using its national legislation to achieve its national interests in the Uruguay Round.[60]

The service negotiations continued to make significant progress. The principles which had been used to conduct studies on telecom and civil construction were accepted by both DCs and LDCs. Thus, studies of other sectors such as tourism and aviation started. Moreover, in July 1989 the EC presented a proposal which represented another step towards the complete liberalization of trade in services. The EC proposal no longer aimed at determining principles, since it was considered that these had been essentially agreed, but rather implementation itself.

The EC proposal was divided into three phases. In the first phase, countries would commit themselves not to adopt any norm or law which would contradict the principles agreed. Second, countries which wanted to liberalize trade in services would present concrete proposals on how to abandon existing legislation which prevented liberalization of trade in services. Finally, countries would ensure that their finance sectors did not present any restrictions in terms of market access for TNCs.[61]

The EC proposal recognized that there could be some difference in the speed at which each trade sector was subject to the process of liberalization. This would depend on the kind of market, the level of development, and the degree of liberalization already in existence. After the presentation of the EC proposal it was the turn of the US to present its own. The new US proposal conceived of liberalization based on the agreed rules. There was no provision in the US proposal for S&D treatment for LDCs. Besides the principles defended by the US it included the possibility of derogations, which should be temporary. Finally, the US proposed the creation of a GATS, based on the GATT. In the US proposal, the GATS would have 30 articles, covering all aspects of trade in services.[62]

New Zealand made a contribution to the GNS. Basically, the New Zealand paper accepted that liberalization of trade in services could not be achieved in the short term. Thus, the New Zealand draft accepted the need to create an institution such as GATS, suggested by the US but it went even further. It proposed that each country when joining the GATS could adopt some reservations affecting those areas they considered not ready for liberalization. On the other hand, GATS members would have to specify how they planned to liberalize trade in services in those sectors where they asked for reservations. This could be done in multilateral meetings where concessions could be exchanged. These concessions would be seen as a commitment by the mentioned country. Thus, all countries would be committed to liberalize trade in services, to a schedule of reservations, and to a schedule of concessions.[63]

The main difference between the US and New Zealand's proposals is that the draft from New Zealand included more mechanisms to cover the development needs of LDCs than the US one. The US proposal's lack of flexibility in that area led Brazil and other LDCs to reject it, in favour of New Zealand's draft. Brazil's position was that it would not support any agreement that did not have provisions to protect infant-service industries. Another important difference between both drafts was the inclusion, in the US proposal, of a provision for sectorial arrangements. This provision was not accepted by EC, on the grounds that these sectorial agreements would only take place between interested countries. Thus, its results would not be extended to other parties. As a result, this provision violated the principle of non-discrimination of the GATT, enshrined in the MFN article. However, the US wanted to exclude those sectors they considered to present a threat to their security.[64]

However, most differences in points of view between the two trading partners were overcome and Jaramillo could present a draft text which embraced the different views. Although it contained 160 brackets it was considered to signify progress in the negotiations. All the principles were defined and agreed. The proposed agreement (GATS) would cover all services, though some arrangements should be made to include financial services, transport, and telecom.[65]

Nevertheless, LDCs continued to complain about the lack of concern with their development needs. After some negotiations, the US agreed to include "appropriate provisions" that would guarantee that no TNC would create a monopoly in LDCs. These countries considered that the US proposal was not sufficient.

In January 1990 it was agreed that an international agreement on services would be ready by July of that year. In order to achieve this goal, each government committed itself to suggest by March the sectors that would be covered by an agreement. In May each country would then present its own proposals for opening their respective markets, announcing which sectors would not be included in the agreement. Brazil and India supported the timetable and its content, but they insisted on S&D treatment for LDCs.[66]

In April 1990, the US and EC presented a compromise draft on services. Their main differences of approach were narrowed in order to produce a united front on the part of DCs. The US, for instance, wanted to exclude telecom and transport from the agreement, an ambition which was not shared by the EC. Moreover, the US was against concessions to LDCs, while the

EC admitted concessions in some sectors, according to the level of performance of the LDCs in the sector concerned. The EC did not support the US
suggestion of excluding the telecom sector from an agreement in services and
was determined that it should be included. The EC noted that it had managed
to convince their members not to exclude any sectors from liberalization.
The US should follow the EC example and adopt the GATS agreement in
full. It was argued that if the DCs began their membership of the prospective
GATS with exemptions, they could not prevent the LDCs from doing the
same. In the EC proposal, the LDCs would have three years to comply with
the GATS.[67]

In response to EC criticism, in June the US drew up a list for the EC
of barriers the US considered discriminated against its exports in services.
The barriers covered 17 sectors, including the financial sector, and indicated
a willingness of the US to discuss an eventual inclusion of financial services
in a final agreement. On the other hand, the US wanted to exclude aviation
and shipping from a service agreement due to pressure from domestic lobbies. The US negotiators pointed out that they wanted an agreement on
services as soon as possible, and they regretted the fact that the deadline of
July for an agreement set at the beginning of the year would be missed.[68]

However, some members of the EC started to exert pressure to exclude the audio-visual sector from an overall agreement. It was argued that
the exception had the objective of protecting the "cultural values" of
Europe.[69] Simultaneously, LDCs stepped up their pressure to ensure that the
issue of labour movement would not constitute a barrier to trade in services.
They wanted an annex to the proposed GATS agreement, to include a commitment to allow short-term labour movement. As a result of these divergent
interests and perspectives, the agreement on services announced for July did
not materialize. The US refused to join a GATS if it included all service
sectors. Shipping and oil distribution should be excluded. However, it was
agreed that the liberalization of trade in services would occur in two phases.

In the first phase, countries would select the sectors that would initially be liberalized. In the second, countries would widen the process of liberalization to services not yet covered. In this way, liberalization in all sectors would result. Jaramillo left the question whether or not the GATS
should include all sectors open in his draft.[70]

In order to find a compromise on services, the US proposed that some
movement of labour could be accepted. This would include: managers, ex-

ecutives and experts, for a temporary period of no more than five years. The families of these employees would also be allowed entry. On the other hand, the US blocked liberalization in telecom. The US delegation declared that the US wanted an exemption for its telecom industry from the future GATS. As a result of the US refusal to commit itself to full liberalization, Brazil also decided to protect some of its service sectors. Therefore, it announced that it would not open its financial service markets to foreign competition. This meant that Brazil would seek a derogation - the right of exemption for its banking and insurance companies. The EC Ambassador to GATT declared that the US proposal to exclude some sectors from an overall agreement was a recipe for anarchy.[71]

The US also refused to apply the MFN principle to services. The US argued that it had the most open market in the world. Thus, if a system of MFN was adopted its market would be open to other countries, but these countries would not need to open theirs. As a result, the US would lose the opportunity of using its market to obtain concessions in bi- or multilateral negotiations. The EC considered that the withdrawal of the MFN clause from the negotiations would remove the substance of the agreement. This opposition of the US to the MFN clause halted the service negotiations, and jeopardized the trade talks. It could be said that after the farm impasse, the deadlock in services was the most serious one in the Uruguay Round. This elicited strong criticism from Dunkel. In his report to the heads of the delegations, dated 7 November 1990, Dunkel declared that the key to the negotiations on services was the application of a diluted MFN, without which the framework agreement was an empty shell.[72] A possible explanation for this US position was that the American negotiators had not been successful in excluding shipping and telecom from trade liberalization. Furthermore, the additions to the GATS text would include an exception for a limited period of years. After this period, liberalization would have to occur. The US delegation wanted an assurance that liberalization of its market would be linked to negotiations in individual sectors and increase market access in other countries where State monopolies remained, such as in France and Germany. A second explanation was that the US was unhappy with the lack of progress in farm talks and decided to withdraw prior commitments in other sectors. A third explanation was that the US government was only answering to the pressures of its powerful lobbies in the sectors of air and sea transport. Moreover, the US wanted an immediate liberalization in financial services, which LDCs did not accept.[73]

The EC modified its original position and committed itself to a complete liberalization in financial services and a partial, but progressive, liberalization in telecommunications. As a result, the US reviewed its position and agreed that the MFN principle should be included in a service agreement. The US change of attitude removed the deadlock in the service negotiations. Nevertheless, the US position depended on derogations from MFN in some sectors, such as telecom. After several months of deadlock in the trade talks due to lack of agreement on agricultural issues, the US and the EC delegations renewed negotiations on services in January 1991. However, shipping and telecom were not included in the discussions. The US offered no further concessions in these fields. A proposal from Nordic countries to liberalize shipping, but which required the US to accept the MFN clause, was refused by the US. In order to keep the negotiations moving, countries started to present their preliminary suggestions on services. Brazil presented its suggestions in June 1991.[74]

In December 1991, the US changed its position and declared that the MFN clause could be extended to telecommunications. However, it was conditional on the commitment of other countries in the organization to be created (GATS) to liberalize their markets. These commitments should include liberalization of foreign investment and domestic treatment for foreign enterprises. However, the lack of agreement on farm subsidies jeopardized the conclusion of the Uruguay Round. Following several missed deadlines, Dunkel decided to publish a compromise agreement - the DFA.

The next section will outline the common points between the Brazilian and US positions on services.

The common denominator between Brazil's and US position

In spite of Brazil's radical position within the G-10 opposing the inclusion of services in the GATT, it should be noted that Brazil and some DCs, including the US, shared certain common positions. What had happened was that, during the period that Batista was heading the Brazilian Mission in Geneva, points of disagreement were always emphasized, often with a great fanfare. Thereby, Brazil's individual stance was noticed by DCs. Despite this and several speeches by Batista threatening to sink the negotiations, one should not forget that Brazil had an interest in some kind of multilateral agreement.

A lack of agreement would mean that the "Law of the Jungle" would prevail, which was not in the interests of any country.[75]

The departure of Minister Setúbal from Itamaraty coincided with the decrease in influence of the group linked to Batista. General Secretary Tarso strengthened his position and became the 'de facto' Minister. Brazil's policy relative to the GATT was then altered to emphasize the features which it shared with other DCs, in particular with the US. The removal of Batista from GATT - due to his radical views - was essential to this process. Ricupero, his successor, put into practice this new policy of conciliation. His attitude in the Uruguay Round may be defined as neighbourly, and emphasized common denominators. There is a clear difference between Brazil's position during the period that Ricupero was Brazil's representative and before.[76]

The first common position between Brazil and the US was the respect for national legislation. Initially the US was against it because the US thought that it would be used as a tool for protectionism. But when analyzing its national legislation, the US noted that its own domestic law had many incompatibilities with free international trade in services, as its financial and shipping sectors illustrate very well. Furthermore, general pressure in favour of maintenance of this principle, including that from the EC, made its exclusion politically impractical.[77]

The second common denominator between the position of the US and Brazil concerned the principles to be followed. Brazil, during the period that Ricupero was its main negotiator, realized that the principles of the GATT, if adapted to services, could be an advantage for Brazil. This was because, for example, the MFN principle would mean that any opening of markets in the service sector between two DCs would be extended to Brazil. In practice, this would allow a higher penetration of Brazilian firms in some DCs.[78]

In the same way, the GATT concept of transparency would permit any country, such as Brazil, to verify whether there were any kind of barriers to its service sector exports. Brazil, however, feared the GATT principle of national treatment by which foreign firms must receive the same treatment and advantage given to Brazilian firms. Initially, Brazil was convinced that this principle, combined with the principle of right of establishment, was going to be used by the US to force the entry of TNCs in fields not foreseen by Brazilian law. However, since the principles would allow respect for national legislation, Brazil realized that it did not have to change its national law, and thus, its fears were unjustified.[79] Another common denominator was the matter of the guidelines which would regulate any prospective agreement in services. The US insisted that free trade and liberalization should be the motto for trade in services, while Brazil insisted that liberalization was only a means to achieve economic development, which was the main goal. Later on, both parties agreed that the growth of production and expansion of world trade in services should be the general goal, based on free trade and liberalization as a means of achieving development.[80]

A fourth common denominator concerned S&D treatment. Brazil knew that the appearance of the expression S&D treatment would not be sufficient to guarantee any advantage for it. Thus, Brazil tried to include in the agreement some mechanisms acceptable to the US that could be transformed into concrete economic advantage. Among them, might be mentioned one of the articles which specified that an agreement in services would try to increase the share of LDC trade in international markets. This would be achieved with the help of DCs by means of exchanges of information about niche markets and other data that could be of interest to LDCs. This was acceptable to the US because it did not imply a paternalist attitude, but quite the opposite, a stimulus for LDCs to develop markets in services and eventually compete. This was a very innovative approach and a complete departure from the old S&D treatment rhetoric. In this context, the change in attitude of Itamaraty should be noted.[81]

An interesting common point between the US and Brazil concerned the sectors to be opened up and the speed of such a process. Brazil wanted a slow opening in several sectors. This explains why most Brazilian offers in the service sector were standstill commitments and not really true concessions. On the other hand, the US did not want to make a formal offer in some sectors because it feared that other countries would not match it, as in the case of the financial and securities market. Furthermore, the US government was under pressure from some companies, in particular in telecommunications and in the maritime transport sector, not to make an offer while other countries did not present their own suggestions. Therefore, both Brazil and the US wanted the right to exclude some sectors from the final agreement. In the end, the EC also wanted to exclude the audiovisual sector from the agreement in services for cultural reasons. This was what happened.[82]

Eventually, as Brazil's apprehensions about the negotiations on trade in services were dispelled, the issue of which definition to use for services lost its controversial aspect and Brazil accepted a broad definition of services. This included the right of establishment. This was agreed during the period when Ricupero was the main negotiator for Brazil and it would certainly have been considered anathema when Batista was the head of Brazil's negotiating team. Perhaps one of the main conclusions that could be drawn from the evolution of the Brazilian and US position is that the difficulties concerning reaching an international agreement should not be overestimated and it is possible to find common ground when there is political will and flexibility of both parties. A proof of this is that the final text on services excepting Financial Services and the Audiovisual sector was one of the areas in which agreement was achieved in 1990.

Brazil's final position on service and the Draft Final Act (DFA)

Brazil's final position in Dunkel's Draft Final Act (DFA)

Basically, Brazil's final position in the Uruguay Round was to accept all the proposals of the DFA as it was proposed by Dunkel. Brazil considered that it was a balanced agreement, as it meant that prospective losses in a sector would be compensated by gains in other sectors. Furthermore, Brazil did not ask for an alteration of any part of the DFA because it would mean reopening the discussions in all sectors, which Brazil did not want. This also reflects Itamaraty's new pragmatic approach and its new position towards a multilateral framework in services.

Significantly, the DFA called this framework GATS. Similarity with the GATT was no coincidence. All the provisions of GATS were based on the GATT, from which Dunkel drew its concepts, principles, and structure. Indeed, GATS, as is GATT, is based on MFN rules of transparency, market access, national treatment, and progressive liberalization. If someone had proposed such a draft to Brazil when the negotiations started it would be have been rejected.[83] Now, some brief comments will be made about the GATS in the DFA before examining the differences between the initial and final Brazilian positions in other sectors of the Uruguay Round.

The GATS in the Draft Final Act (DFA) of Dunkel

The GATS proposed by Dunkel and accepted by Brazil contains a Preamble and is divided into six parts: I) Scope and Definitions; II) General Obligations and Discipline; III) Specific Commitments; IV) Progressive Liberalisation; V) Institutional Provisions; and, VI) Final Provisions. In the first part, the point that draws most attention is that the definition supported by Brazil - a restrictive concept of services - was rejected and a broad definition was adopted (Art. I). As a result, the scope of the agreement was enlarged. The fact that Brazil supported this enlargement points to the change in Brazil's position.[84]

In the second part, three important features can be noted. First, it starts with a commitment of the Parties to the GATS to apply MFN treatment (Art. II) - one of the basic principles of the GATT. Moreover, and in second place, for the first time the issue of development was treated without paternalism. The rhetoric in favour of S&D treatment was replaced by specific commitments. Indeed, Art. IV describes ways to increase the participation of LDCs in world trade. The commitments include: a) access of LDCs to technology in services on a commercial basis; b) improved access for LDCs to information networks; and c) liberalization of market access in sectors and modes of supply of information about service exports of interest to LDC.[85] The DCs also committed themselves to recognize professional qualifications of employees from LDCs. Finally, the GATS provisions on the use of Balance of Payments (BOP) restrictions are more stringent than their equivalent in the GATT. Parties to the GATS need an authorization from the IMF (or an equivalent committee) to resort to those provisions.[86] In the third part, two other well-known GATT principles are present: market access and national treatment. Art. XVI determines that Parties of the GATS will allow services and service providers a treatment no less favourable in terms of market access than specified in its schedule. To reinforce this feature Parties extend national treatment for services and service providers to other parties similar to those offered to their own services or service providers.[87] This is important because national treatment is not enough to ensure market access. On the other hand, market access without national treatment implies discrimination towards national providers of services. Thus, the importance of realizing both simultaneously. In the Brazilian case, the main complaint from other countries was market access, and not national treatment.[88]

It is the first part, however, which constitutes one of the most difficult areas of Dunkel's DFA for Brazil. It deals with progressive liberalization, which implies, obviously, free-trade. As has already been seen, Brazil refused to accept the application of free-trade, or the theory of comparative advantages (TCA) to services. However, in the GATS Brazil seems to have finally capitulated in favour of free-trade and trade liberalization. Although Part IV of the DFA has some concessions to LDCs, for example that progressive liberalization should respect national policies and objectives as well as the level of development of the Parties, the fact is that all Parties agreed to open their markets and extend effective market access to foreign service providers (Art.XIX and XX). As a first measure, each Party would make initial commitments in favour of market access. Brazil proposed opening service sectors to foreign service providers, among them the construction sector, engineering, consultancy, and franchising.[89]

The institutional provisions are included in the fifth part. Basically, it maintains the GATT mechanisms, such as consultation, dispute settlement, enforcement, and joint action. However, the GATS tries to strengthen these procedures, with the view of easing their operation (Art. XXIV). One step in that direction was the adoption of the principle of one vote per Party, and decisions taken by majority vote. This mechanism replaces the traditional system of consensus adopted in the GATT system which allowed Parties to block the procedures if the findings of a Panel, for instance, were not favourable to its interests. As a result, many panels were not implemented. One of the most famous cases was in soya beans, where the EC managed not to take any action in this field in spite of the results of the Panel condemning its regime. The sixth part mentions final provisions, for example, entry into force, acceptance, accession, non-application, and withdrawals. It contains definitions, regulations concerning movement of workers, and annexes. These latter include the controversial sectors, for example, financial services and telecom, and sectors where the GATS could not be applied immediately due to the existence of international conventions, for example, air transport. In the financial sector, Parties were authorized to make commitments in an alternative approach.[90]

In this alternative approach to Part III all GATS principles would be respected. However, Parties could also commit themselves not to adopt new domestic legislation (a standstill) and to abolish monopoly rights affecting market access. The understanding meant that in the purchase of financial services by public entities the principles of MFN and national treatment should be respected. This was not required in other sectors of the GATS. Moreover, the understanding had strong provisions concerning the abolishing of all discriminatory measures. The understanding was a compromise between the US, which wanted strong commitments in the financial sector, and other Parties, which preferred a slower liberalization. Brazil was one of the countries which lobbied to transform the commitments in the financial sector into an understanding in the DFA. Itamaraty welcomed the lack of agreement in financial services because it meant that Brazil would not have to open its market in that sector. Thus, there is no formal obligation for Brazil to open its market in financial services to all countries. In the end Brazil presented an offer in services, based on a standstill in order to respond to pressure from the US.[91]

The same happened on air transport. The GATS specifies that the Chicago Convention should be respected.[92] This was a relief for Brazil, it meant that it would not have to open air transport to foreign firms. However, the Annex on Air Transport stipulates that fields not covered by the Chicago Convention, for example, aircraft repair, the sale or marketing of air transport services, and computer reservation services should be liberalized.[93]

As regards the telecom sector, the GATS Annex accepts that there are some characteristics in this sector which prevent it from being fully liberalized. Moreover, the Annex on Telecommunications does require parties to authorize foreign service suppliers to establish telecom networks on their territory. However, it does not require parties to allow the flow of information about market access to their respective national territories (transparency principle). Furthermore, if foreign suppliers are allowed each party should guarantee that there is access in a non-discriminatory way (MFN). The service offered by public networks should also be offered in a non-discriminatory way. Parties should also recognize the role played by the International Telecommunication Union (ITU).

Brazil was also opposed to the opening of its telecom market. However, in this case the situation differed a little due to the existence of a State monopoly, which is mandated by Brazil's new Constitution (1988). However, if Brazil had wanted to decrease the deficit in the number of telephone lines without committing scarce financial resources which could be invested in other sectors (such as education), the opening of the telecom market should have been considered. In this area Brazil lobbied for and, with the support of EC, obtained that, as a strategic sector, telecom should be excluded from immediate liberalization. In short, Itamaraty's position in this sector also conforms to the GATS agreement.[94]

Brazil's ultimate position in some sectors of the Uruguay Round

Agriculture, tropical products, and the MFA

These are the sectors where there was no change in the Brazilian position. Brazil supported free-trade on these issues when the Round was launched and continued to support this when the negotiations collapsed in 1990 due to a lack of agreement on agriculture between the US and the EC.[95] Brazil supported the DFA in those sectors although the DFA does not propose free-trade in agriculture but only a reduction in the level of subsidies and in State supported agricultural programmes;[96] with the refusal of the EC to accept the DFA the section was replaced by the "Blair House Agreement". Brazil accepted this agreement and its 'clarification' as well.[97]

In agriculture, Itamaraty's attitude was very pragmatic. Brazil coordinated its policy on agriculture within the Cairns Group, which has the support of the US, and Itamaraty knew that this is a very complex subject. Itamaraty was also aware that some EC members, for example Germany and France, did not want to make any concession in this field. Therefore, Brazil saw any reduction in the current levels of subsidies (and any reform of the Common Agricultural Policy (CAP) as a step forward. It should also be noted that the Brazilian government - as was the case in the service discussions - had not prepared any study of the impact on Brazilian exports of a liberalization in agricultural trade. As a result, one cannot say if Brazil would be a net exporter of agricultural products or not.[98]

Some authors have suggested that Brazil may benefit from a liberalization in agriculture, but these plans are dependent on several favourable factors. Itamaraty supported the DFA although it was not the ideal outcome. Brazil sought better market access for its export products such as soya. However, in order to remain competitive in this field Brazil required a reduction in the level of subsidies practised internationally today. It is likely that imports of some products in which Brazil is not competitive, such as wheat, would increase. But for this to happen, it would be necessary for

Brazil to stop subsidizing its domestic production of wheat and terminate the system of granting concessions to internal processors and distributors (the wheat mills).

In tropical products the situation is quite different. Since Brazil is a net exporter in this field it has everything to win and nothing to lose from the liberalization of such trade. Brazil could increase its exports without having to increase its imports. Thus, Brazil's position in this area is complete support for liberalization and free-trade. However, Brazil does face competition from other producers. In the case of coffee, for instance, Brazil faces tough competition from both Latin American and African countries, which offer a better quality product for what is sometimes a better price. A contradiction in Brazil's position is that although it favours liberalization of the coffee market, this does not mean that Brazil is in favour of ending agreements in this field. Thus, Brazil supports the work of the International Coffee Organization to regulate the market.

The same can be said about the MFA. Although Brazil does not know precisely whether it is going to win or lose from a complete liberalization of textiles and clothing, it expects to increase at least some of its exports in this sector. However, it is quite likely that some imports of textiles and clothing could grow, which would result in a neutral effect from liberalization. However, Brazil always made the ending of MFA one of the pre-conditions for its participation in the Round. This was one of the pillars of the Brazil-India alliance. As a result, Brazil could not change its mind on this subject without the risk of losing all its credibility in the G-10. Thus, Brazil considers that the DFA in this area also reflects its interests, as perceived by Itamaraty. The DFA proposed that over a ten year period all countries should remove their restrictions on clothing and textile imports.[99]

It is worth noting that according to a study by Erzan, Goto & Holmes (1990), the distribution of gains among countries alters according to the sector, specific products, countries, and trade areas involved. In the case of Brazil, for instance, the study noted that Brazil in the 1980s made greater use of its US market quota with Brazil's rate increasing, on average, from less than 50% to just under 80%. However, in the EC market, Brazil's share decreased from less than 90% to less than 80%.[100]

The best explanation for this seems to be that Brazilian producers altered the pattern of their exports from the EC to the US. This hypothesis is confirmed by the fact that although binding restrictions existed on textile product suppliers from Hong Kong, the Republic of Korea, and Taiwan, Brazil's share in the EC market for those products also fell from 81% in 1981 to 55% in 1987. At the same time its exports of those products to the US increased from 37% to 86%.[101] It is important to note that Brazil is probably not fully competitive otherwise it would have used all its quota. A low utilization of quota shows an anti-export bias or political disruption. The most efficient suppliers always make the best use of the prevailing conditions.[102]

Two hypotheses can explain Brazil's preference for the US market. US importers offer either higher profit margins or better conditions for Brazilian firms than those offered by EC importers. Alternatively, Brazil's exporters use the quota as a last resort to substitute for domestic sales, which is the best explanation. Brazilian exporters see foreign markets as complements to the domestic market. They only export if the domestic market is in recession and if it cannot absorb national production. It works as a guarantee in case of a sudden fall in sales in the domestic market. Moreover, Brazil does not withdraw export quota shares allocated domestically amongst its exporters due to political pressure or corruption. Thus, Brazilian firms can maintain their quota shares even if they do not make full use of them.[103]

Raffaelli's (1990) study seems to confirm this hypothesis. He notes that Brazil is a major exporter of semi-manufactured products (for example, cotton yarns and cotton fabrics), but only a minor exporter of clothing and made-up items.[104] Moreover, he notes that Brazil is a good example of the primacy of the domestic market. When the domestic market improved in 1986, Brazilian exports to DCs members of the MFA fell to $460 million of textiles and $151 millions of clothing. As a result, aggregate Brazilian exports of clothing and textiles in 1986 were less than $610 million, well below the country's export potential. Raffaelli suggests that Brazilian textiles producers consider exports as a safety valve.[105] This is the case despite the fact that among the 250 biggest textile companies in the world, fourteen are Brazilian.[106] Raffaelli explains this contradiction by arguing that Brazilian entrepreneurs lack initiative and incentives to export. Meanwhile, when they are successful the MFA imposes a barrier on further increasing their exports.[107] In any case, the result is that although Brazil has companies which are potentially competitive in the international textile sector, the consequence of an opening of the Brazilian market is probably a high increase in imports, especially from highly competitive countries where entrepreneurs are at the forefront of international competition, for example, South Korea, Taiwan, Singapore. That is why the result of ending MFA for Brazil would tend to be neutral, at least in the short term, although it could be advantageous in the medium and long term.[108]

The main advantage of a decrease in tariffs is that it allows businessmen to renew their machines. Moreover, if Brazil's maximum tariff remains at 35%, this means that the real cost of a product when it arrives in Brazil is at least 50% higher, due to other costs such as transport and insurance.[109]

Tariffs and Non-Tariff Barriers (NTBs)

After 1988, Brazil began to adopt a process of tariff reform. This was followed by a process of unilateral trade liberalization, after 1990, when Collor took power. This indicated a dramatic change in Brazil's traditional protectionist trade policies. The sudden changes in the ISI model during Collor's term had a direct effect on Brazil's position in the tariff negotiation group on at least two points.

First, Brazil agreed not only to restrict, but also to reduce the level of its tariffs on imports. Indeed, Brazil presented to the GATT a proposal for restricting all its tariffs to a maximum of 35%; a low level by Brazilian standards. Moreover, most raw materials have a tariff schedule of 0%, consolidating a trend begun in the 1980s. Recently, Brazil brought forward the implementation of its tariff schedules. Before the Round had finished (1993), Brazil had already reduced its tariffs to no more than 35%, for the first time in Brazil's history.[110]

In the area of Non-Tariff Barriers (NTBs) Brazil agreed to the removal of all its practices which could be considered an obstacle to imports. Brazil ended, for example, the lists of forbidden products and simplified its import procedures. The complex import licences (*guias de importação*) were replaced by simpler forms. Furthermore, it is no longer necessary to obtain an authorization to import any product. Imports are free from such measures. Brazil agreed, which is perhaps the most important and significant point, not to use BOP arguments to prevent imports.[111]

The most significant point is that Brazil used to perceive imports as bad for the economy, but this perception now changed. Brazil also abandoned its previous pretence of being self-sufficient in most products. However, Itamaraty would like to see its process of unilateral trade liberalization considered as a concession in the Uruguay Round and Itamaraty expected to obtain greater market access for Brazilian exports.

Itamaraty is probably going to be disappointed in this because: 1) tariff reductions and market access are completely distinct concepts and one does not ensure the other; 2) if a country has adopted a process of unilateral trade liberalization, other countries feel that they do not need to make concessions on market access since they take unilateral tariff reductions for granted as part of the process.

Conclusions

The Brazilian position in the GATT had undergone dramatic changes between 1986, when the Uruguay Round was launched, and 1991, when Dunkel proposed the DFA. Brazil evolved from a position of free-rider - supporting free-trade by DCs while it adopted ISI - to a position of pro-free-trade, although it still has a long way to go. In the issues studied here - tariffs and NTBs, and services - Brazil's position changed from a protectionist, and sometimes even autarkic, attitude to being a supporter of trade liberalization. The exception to this change was in the sectors where Brazil had supported free-trade since the beginning of the Round, for example, agriculture, tropical products, and clothing and textiles. However, it should be noted that there is a significant difference between these sectors and those sectors mentioned above. In services, and in manufactured goods in general, Brazil came to the conclusion that it would be better off with an international agreement than with no agreement at all.

In the case of agriculture, tropical products, and clothing and textiles, Brazil initially wanted an opening of the DCs markets without opening its own market. From 1947 to 1987 Brazil used several GATT provisions (for example, BOP arguments, infant-industry, quota restrictions, etc.) to prevent the entry of foreign products on its market. Thus, when Brazil claimed that it wanted free-trade in agriculture, tropical products and clothing and textiles, it knew that GATT provisions allowed LDCs to adopt protectionist measures against imports. However, in 1991 Brazil agreed to stop using such measures to prevent imports and adopted a process of liberalization.[112]

Due to its opposition to services, Brazil used its influence in the GATT first to postpone the launching of the new Round, and later on, to try to keep services out of it. When it was no longer possible to do this, Brazil tried to block any progress in discussing the subject from 1986 to 1988. Initially Brazil argued that the theory of comparative advantage did not apply to services due to the special characteristics of the service sector. Therefore, Brazil argued that first the service sector should be studied in greater depth and a theoretical frame of analysis should be found. However, in 1991 Brazil not only accepted a multilateral agreement negotiated within the GATT, but also made offers to open certain service sectors, for example, construction.[113]

The same may be said about Trade Related Investment Measures (TRIMs). Initially Brazil refused to discuss TRIMs because it feared that the GATT might formulate rules which would oblige its members to liberalize investments. However, Brazil's position also changed on this issue, and it agreed to eliminate all measures affecting FDI which were inconsistent with the agreement on TRIMs. This was not an easy task if one notes that Brazil suffers from internal constraints which hamper the executive from concluding agreements in certain areas, for example, oil.

However, no other issue demonstrates the changes in Brazil's position in the GATT more than its final stance on tariffs and NTBs. Brazil abandoned its protectionist policies and high tariffs which had made Brazil one of the most protectionist countries in the world, and adopted a process of unilateral liberalization. As part of this process all tariffs were gradually reduced and today the highest tariff is no higher than 35%. This means that Brazil has decided to reduce its tariffs without negotiating with other countries bilaterally. Therefore Brazil has broken with the GATT negotiating principle that reductions in tariffs should be based on mutual action arrived at on an offer and request basis.[114]

The adoption of unilateral trade liberalization also implies that Brazil has started to believe that free-trade and unilateral trade liberalization are essentially good and imports should not be prevented. Indeed, Brazil also stated that it would no longer limit imports based on such weak arguments as BOP restrictions - when it is known that Brazil has a surplus of more than US$10 billion per year and foreign reserves of almost US$40 billion. Another direct effect of Brazil's ideological shift is apparent in its position on NTBs. While at the beginning of the 1980s Brazil wanted to prevent imports, at the beginning of the 1990s Brazil simplified its procedures to allow imports to enter the country more easily.

It seems clear that there were radical changes in Brazil's position in the GATT between the launching of the Round (1986) and the DFA of Dunkel (1991). The change in Brazil's position was not only formal, in the sense that it demonstrated a difference of emphasis, but also qualitative. Indeed, the perception at the GATT was that after 1988 Brazil changed the nature of its influence in GATT negotiations. Until 1987 Brazil's influence in the GATT could be described as essentially negative, in the sense of blocking the negotiation of issues which Brazil did not favour. After 1988, however, Brazil became essentially positive and it offered a real contribution to the service negotiations in the Uruguay Round.

End Notes

1.   See GATT, *Focus Newsletter*, Jan./Feb. 1987, n.43, pp.7-8.
2.   GATT, *Focus*, March 1987, n.44, p.6.
3.   GATT, *NUR*, 16/04/87, n.3, p.5.
4.   GATT, *NUR*, 13/04/87, n.3, p.4.
5.   GATT, *Focus*, July-August 1987, n.48, pp.6-7.
6.   GATT, *Focus*, July-August 1987, n.48, p.5.
7.   GATT, *NUR*, 27/10/87, n.9, p.5.
8.   GATT, *NUR*, 10/12/87, n.12, p.5.
9.   Martone, 1988, *Brazil and the Uruguay Round. São Paulo, USP*. pp.39-45.
10.   GATT, *NUR*, 21/12/87, n.13, pp.7-8.
11.   GATT, *NUR*, 21/12/87, n.13, pp.2-3.
12.   GATT, *NUR*, 26/02/88, n.14, pp.2-4.
13.   GATT, *Focus*, June/July, 1988, n.55, p.10.
14.   GATT, *Focus*, August 1988, n.56, p.11.
15.   GATT, *Focus*, September/October 1988, n.57, p.7.
16.   See the different perspectives of services in Chapter 2.
17.   GATT, *Focus*, January/February 1989, n.59, pp.1-2.
18.   GATT, *Focus*, January/February 1989, n.59, p.1.
19.   See GATT, *Focus*, May/June 1990, n.71, p.6.
20.   GATT, *Focus*, January 1989, n.59, p.3.
21.   GATT, *Focus*, July 1989, n.63, p.12.
22.   GATT, *Focus*, August/September 1989, n.64, p.11.
23.   GATT, *Focus*, November 1989, n.66, p.8.
24.   GATT, *Focus*, December 1989, n.67, p.7.
25.   GATT Document.MTN, GNS/W/86, 21/11/89.
26.   GATT, *Focus*, February 1990, n.68, p.12.
27.   For the Indian perspective see: S. Bhalla, 1990, "India". In Messerlin, P. & Sauvant, K. *The Uruguay Round: Services in the World Economy*. Washing-

ton/New York, IBRD/UNCTC.

28.   Confidential interview with a Brazilian Diplomat.

29.   GATT, *Focus*, April 1990, n.70, p.11.

30.   GATT, *Focus*, April 1990, n.70, p.11-12.

31.   GATT, *Focus*, May/June 1990, n.71, pp.4-8 and n.72 pp.9-12.

32.   Cameroon, China, Egypt, Kenya, Nigeria and Tanzania.

33.   GATT, *Focus*, July 1990, n.72, p.9 and 12.

34.   GATT, *Focus*, November 1990, n.76, p.2.

35.   See GATT, 1991, *Draft Final Act (DFA)*. Geneva, GATT.

36.   For the US position, see GATT Doc.L, MTN.GNS/W/7.

37.   See Communication from Brazil, MTN.GNS/W/27.

38.   In particular by Prof. Jackson. See Jackson, J., 1988, *International Competition on Services: A Constitutional Framework*. Washington, American Enterprise Institute for Public Policy Research (AEI studies).

39.   For a discussion of US position, see Lazar, F., 1990, Services and the GATT: US Motives and Blueprint for Negotiations. *In Journal of World Trade Law* 24 (1): pp. 135-145 . February.

40.   For the EC position see: GATT Document. MTN.GNS/W/29.

41.   For a discussion of the competitive advantage of EC see: Oulton, 1984, *International Trade in Services and the Comparative Advantage of E.C. countries*. London, Trade Policy Research Centre.

42.   *Financial Times*, 18/12/87.

43.   For a discussion of the LDCs position, see: Sampson, 1989, "Developing Countries and the Liberalization of Trade in Services" in Whalley, J., 1989, *op.cit.*

44.   Communication from Argentina GATT.Doc. MTN.GNS/W/33 and 35.

45.   *Financial Times*, 25/03/88.

46.   GATT Document. MTN.GNS/W/36-37.

47.   Communication From New Zealand and Australia. GATT Document. MTN.GNS/W/47.

48.   GATT, *Focus*, August 1988, n.56, p.11.

49.   Tropical Products and Textiles, for instance.

50.   *Financial Times*, 27/07/88.

51.   *Financial Times*, 28/07/88.

52.   GATT, *Focus*, September/October 1988, n.57, pp.5-6.

53.   For a review of the developments on the GNS see GATT, *Focus*, September/October 1988, n.57 pp.3-4 and 7.

54.   About the results of Montreal, see: GATT, *Focus*, January 1989, n.59, pp.1-2 and 4.

55.   For more details of the Dunkel Plan, see: GATT, *Focus*, January 1989, n.59, p.2.

56.   See Chapter 4. At this point, Brazil started to link its participation in the Uruguay Round with the results in Agriculture.

57. See Batista, 1987, *op.cit.*, p.21.
58. GATT, *Focus*, June 1989, n. 62, p.3.
59. GATT, *Focus*, July 1989, n.63, p.12.
60. GATT, *Focus*, July 1989, n.63, pp.6-8.
61. See GATT Document. MTN.GNS/W/65.
62. See GATT Document. MTN.GNS/W/64.
63. GATT, *Focus*, August-September 1989, n.64, p.11.
64. GATT, *Focus*, November 1989, n.66, p.8.
65. GATT, *Focus*, February 1990, n.68, p.12.
66. GATT, *Focus*, March 1990, n.69, p.8.
67. GATT, *Focus*, May/June 1990, n.71, pp.4-8.
68. GATT, *Focus*, July 1990, n.72, pp.9-12.
69. *International Herald Tribune*, 21/06/90.
70. GATT, *Focus*, August, n.73, 1990.
71. *Le Monde*, 13/11/90.
72. GATT, *Focus*, November 1990, n.76, p.2.
73. Confidential interview with a Brazilian Diplomat.
74. See GATT Document. MTN.GNS/W/116.
75. See OECD, 1989, *op.cit.*, about the advantages of a multilateral agreement on services for LDCs.
76. Compare GATT Doc. MTN.GNS/W/27 with GATT Doc. MTN.GNS/W/48.
77. For other aspects of the US position see: Low, P., 1993, *Trading Free: The GATT System and the U.S. Trade Policy*. New York, Twenty Century Fund.
78. Sciamma, C., 1988, La Posizione del Brasile nell'Uruguay Round dell GATT con Particular Riferimento al Commercio Internazional di Sirvizos. Milan, Universita Com. Luiggi Bocconi.
79. See Brazilian position in GATT Document MTN.GNS/W/48.
80. See Balasubramanyam, 1991, *op.cit.*, pp.134-139.
81. See Balasubramanyam, 1991, *op.cit.*, pp.139-141.
82. The Text of the Uruguay Round is in GATT (TNC), 1991, *Draft Final Act Embodying the Results of the Uruguay Round of Multilateral Trade Negotiations*. Geneva, GATT. (MTN/TNC/W/FA).
83. See GATT Document MTN.GNS/W/FA.
84. Brazilian diplomats argue that Brazil did not change its position, but that there was an 'evolution'.
85. See GATT.TNC., 1991, *op.cit.*, p.8.
86. Art.XII of the *DFA*, in GATT(TNC), 1991, *op.cit.*
87. See Art XVII of the *DFA* in GATT(TNC), 1991, *op.cit.*
88. Confidential interview with a Brazilian Ambassador.
89. Brazil, MRE. Secretaria Geral de Pol. Exterior. DE-GETEC. *Diplomacia Economica*. Agosto/Novembro 1991, n.9., p.37.
90. See Understanding, in Commitments in Financial Services, in GATT(TNC),

1991, *op.cit.*, p.51.

91. Confidential interview with an Itamaraty Official. The Central Bank was against an offer but Itamaraty was in favour. Itamaraty prevailed.

92. See GATT(TNC), 1991, *op.cit.*, p.45.

93. See GATT(TNC), 1991, *op.cit.*

94. For a discussion on service liberalization in telecom, see Sacerdoti, 1990, *op.cit.*, pp.117-177.

95. Confidential interview with a Brazilian Ambassador. See also: Brazil. MRE, 1993, *Boletim de Diplomacia Economica.*

96. See: GATT(TNC), 1991, *op.cit.*

97. The Blair House agreement was modified due to a request from France. Brazil supported any agreement between the US and EU which implied an opening of European markets to Brazilian imports.

98. Brazil, MRE, 1988a, *op.cit.*, p.26. However, recent studies estimate that Brazil would benefit from farm liberalization.

99. See GATT(TNC), 1991, *op.cit.*

100. See Erzan, Goto & Holmes, 1990," Effects of the Multi Fibre Arrangement on Developing Countries's Trade: An Empirical Investigation". In Hamilton, C., 1990, *op.cit.*, pp.73-74.

101. Erzan, Goto & Holmes, 1990, *op.cit.*, pp.79-80.

102. Erzan, Goto & Holmes, 1990, *op.cit.*, p.75.

103. Confidential interview with a Brazilian Ambassador.

104. Raffaelli, 1990, "Some consideration on the Multi-Fibre Arrangement: Past, Present and Future". In Hamilton, C., 1990, *op.cit.*, p.288.

105. Rafaelli, 1990, *op.cit.*, pp.288-289.

106. Rafaelli, 1990, *op.cit.*, pp.290-291.

107. Rafaelli, 1990, *op.cit.*, p.289.

108. For the complete discussion about ending MFA, see Hamilton, C., *1990, Textiles Trade and Developing Countries. Eliminating Multi Fibre Arrangement in the 1990s.* Washington, IBRD.

109. See Velloso, 1991, *Aquarella do Brasil. Ensaios Politicos Economicos sobre o Governo Collor.* Rio de Janeiro, Rio Fundo.

110. GATT, 1993, *Brazil, Trade Policy Review, 1992.* Geneva, GATT. p.32.

111. GATT, *Focus*, August 1991, n.83, p.1.

112. See GATT, *Focus*, August 1991, n.83. p.1.

113. GATT Documents MTN.GNS./W/116 and MTN.GNS/W/116 Rev.1.

114. GATT, 1993, *Brazil, Trade Policy Review, 1992.* p.15.

5. The Evolution of Brazil's Position

Introduction

The objective of this chapter is to analyze the mains reasons which contributed to the change in Brazil's position in the Uruguay Round, with particular emphasis on the service sector. This evolution occurred, basically, during the Sarney government (1985-1990). For this reason, this chapter will concentrate on this period.

This chapter is divided into two parts. The first part discusses the domestic factors which influenced Itamaraty in its decisions. The second part of this chapter analyzes the external factors which contributed to the change of Brazil's position vis-à-vis the Uruguay Round.

The role of domestic reasons for the change in Brazil's position

Cultural reasons, press and intellectuals

The role of the press and of the intellectuals was not an important factor in the change in Brazil's position in the Uruguay Round. The reason for this is that the press is not a mass phenomena in Brazil.[1] Moreover, GATT Rounds did not occupy a lot of space in the news.

However, the Brazil-US dispute in the field of Information Technology (IT) did. For the first time, public opinion could discuss the role of the IT Law and protectionism in general, in Brazil's strategy of development.[2] Until then, there was a nationalist consensus against imports in Brazil, especially when sovereign interests appeared to be attacked.[3]

On the other hand, the use of Portable Computers (PCs) started to spread in Brazil during the 1980s, specially through smuggling.[4] Moreover, many users of PCs, in particular firms, started to ask why they should pay high costs for local PCs, technologically *passé*, if they could import cheaper and better ones. Later on, an association was created in order to lobby for liberalization in the IT sector. This was also the first time Brazilian consumers organized themselves to press for free-trade. This movement was supported by the press. The press accused the Law of IT of preventing Brazil from modernizing its industries and cutting costs. Since the first discussions in 1984, TV popularized the issue and highlighted its results, including the US sanctions.[5]

The Law of IT raised nationalist feelings. The members of the Brazilian Parliament who were against the law were called pro-US. They concluded that after each declaration by the US, the support for the law increased in Parliament. On the other hand, intellectuals decided to join the debate and they were deeply divided.[6] Some intellectuals challenged the efficiency of protectionism in the long run, and believed that the Import Substitution Industrialization (ISI) model was exhausted or even dead.[7] They argued, for instance, that protectionist measures could decrease the competitiveness of Brazilian firms, since they did not have access to modern technology while their competitors did. Moreover, Brazilian development in IT was not guaranteed, or even best served, by the mere existence of the Law. If Brazil wanted to have high technology, it would have to import it, or to allow Trans-National Corporations (TNCs) to enter into the domestic market through joint-ventures. The Law of IT wanted to recreate the wheel, they argued.[8]

Tarso and his group followed the discussion with interest because he was in charge of the negotiations with the US. They were aware that there was no unanimity around the Law. But during the negotiations with the US the nullification of the Law was considered out of the question for two reasons. First, because the IT Law was based on a principle accepted by the GATT: infant industry. Second, since the Law had already been approved and ratified, the only action that could be taken by the President was to send a new draft-law to Parliament. But there was no guarantee that the draft law would be approved. The US accepted this argument in principle.[9]

The US-Brazil dispute was used by the group led by Tarso to show Sarney that Brazil could reach a compromise with the US. But Parliament did not understand the message and tried to approve a Law of Software.[10] The US said it was ready to use sanctions again and the debate restarted. But now there was a consensus against a 'Law of Software', and it was not approved. Again, Tarso became the main partner of the President in the Brazil-US IT dispute. This fact strengthened his position in Itamaraty against the protectionist trend, led by Batista.[11] Tarso was also very skilful in using the criticism in the press against protectionism in IT to focus his attacks against the nationalist group in Itamaraty. His position in Itamaraty was consolidated in 1987, and in 1988 he went to Canada to take part in the Montreal Meeting[12] and confirmed Brazil's new position.[13]

Economic reasons

Although there was no study in Itamaraty of the costs and benefits of each position that it took in foreign affairs, it seemed clear that its position in favour of protectionism and pro-Less Developed Countries (LDCs) did not make sense any more. Tarso, the main critic of the pro-LDCs policy, realized that the costs of protectionism and close liaisons, especially with Africa, were not paying off.[14] First, Tarso, with his economic approach, noted that African and most socialist countries apart from China, which was adopting free-market policies, were not a significant market for Brazil. As a result, if Brazil wanted to export more, it had to sell its exports in mature markets, that is, markets that could buy Brazilian products now and not some time in the future. These markets were not in Africa, but in North America, Europe, and South East Asia.[15]

Therefore it was necessary to improve the economic and political relations between Brazil and market oriented countries (including China). However, in order to improve relations, Itamaraty had to abandon its rhetoric pro-LDCs and talk the language of Developed Countries (DCs): trade and investment opportunities in Brazil. This business approach was to replace the rhetoric approach in vogue at Itamaraty then. Tarso was in favour of a positive agenda with DCs, in particular the US. He favoured the end of political disputes, such as the refusal of Brazil to discuss services.

Tarso also knew that in the real world no one offers anything for free. Thus, in his perspective of constructive engagement with DCs, one concession should be exchanged for another. If DCs wanted the inclusion of services in the GATT, they should pay for it with another concession. He did not think Brazil had anything to gain in services. As Brazil needed market access for its exports and the US wanted services in the GATT, it had to offer market access in exchange for concessions in services. The world imagined by Tarso was not a world without conflicts, but a world where there would be no unnecessary or artificial conflicts. In his view, all conflicts, in principle, could be negotiated and a compromise reached.[16] Batista supported a complete different view. He followed the 'complain approach'. Following this angle, LDCs would make a list of what they wanted and would offer nothing in return. DCs would feel guilty about the non-development of LDCs and make concessions based on notions of how the world should be.[17]

Another aspect of Tarso's approach is that he challenged the view that Brazil should, following the line of the ISI school, concentrate on the exports of manufactured products only. He argued that traditional commodities, such as soya, orange juice, coffee, cocoa and sugar represented more than 40% of Brazil's exports, and it would be insane to abandon them just because they were not manufactured goods. Tarso's pragmatist group believed that it was in Brazil's best interest to protect the export of these products and try to increase them. Thus, another point made by the pragmatic group was that if the US wanted the introduction of services in the GATT, Brazil wanted the inclusion of agricultural products. His group fought for the inclusion of agricultural goods in the Uruguay Round and against the 'early harvest' theory in Montreal.[18]

However, the strategy of Tarso was to assure not only the formal inclusion of agricultural products in the GATT but also a commitment of market access from DCs, in particular for tropical products. He wanted a *quid pro quo* arrangement. An indirect alliance was then established between Brazil and the US, through the Cairns Group, in the sense that both wanted the inclusion of agricultural products in the Uruguay Round. They fought together for the end or reduction of the subsidies used by the EC.[19] This alliance replaced the previous informal alliance between Brazil and the EC before the launching of the Uruguay Round which was based on the following arrangement: Brazil would not press hard for the end of subsidies in agriculture and the EC would not press for the inclusion of services in the new Round.[20]

Political reasons

There was no interference of political actors as such to press for a change in Brazil's position in the Uruguay Round on services. But on the other hand the consensus in favour of protectionism and against imports vanished after 1985.[21] Itamaraty adapted itself more quickly to the new mood in the country through a series of internal reforms.[22] These reforms had the aim of increasing the power of individuals or sections which did not favour ISI policies.[23] These reforms were launched when Tarso was the General Secretary of Itamaraty and are described in Chapter 1.

An important aspect was the social forces which favoured protectionism. An indirect and positive effect of the threat of sanctions from the US in IT was to help to alter the equilibrium between the social groups which supported protectionism.[24] Although these changes did not affect negotiations on services directly, they showed the costs of protectionism, such as in IT, to sectors threatened by sanctions, such as orange juice and shoes exporters. As a result, the Group of Thirty was created to improve US-Brazil relations.[25] These sectors put pressure on Ministers and Itamaraty's decision-makers to make concessions.[26] They did not directly influence the service discussions due to the decentralized system of Itamaraty, but supported a more internationalist approach in foreign affairs, represented by Tarso and his group, as mentioned in Chapter 1.

Internal reasons (The Role of Itamaraty)

It has been suggested in Chapter 1 that Itamaraty's beliefs are the single most important factor explaining Brazil's position on the issue of services. Between 1983 and 1987 when Batista was Brazil's representative to the GATT, and, therefore, during the Uruguay Round, the Brazilian position did not change. This can be verified in GATT Documents.[27] In all GATT Documents from 1984 to 1987, Batista used the most diverse arguments to block the negotiations in services.[28] However, the arguments advanced by Batista were only a smoke screen used by him to try to prevent the opening of the Brazilian service sector to the world economy.[29] This fear of exposing the Brazilian economy to international competition showed his indifference to the Theory of Comparative Advantage and free-trade.[30] Moreover, Batista was well-known within Itamaraty for his ultranationalist views.[31] He was also considered to have been an obstacle to full negotiations at the GATT and during the Uruguay Round.[32] He also had a very unique perspective of the importance of the GATT and of the Uruguay Round for Brazil. He believed that a failure of the Uruguay Round, or of the GATT, would not affect the world trading system or Brazil's exports.[33] Despite the fact that Batista's perceptions no longer corresponded to Itamaraty's, it was only when

Batista disobeyed the directives he received in 1987 that his situation in the GATT became very difficult. He ignored directives from Itamaraty at the end of 1987 to temper his opposition to the discussion of services in the Uruguay Round.[34] He refused to do so. For this reason, he had to leave the Brazilian Mission in Geneva, against his will.[35]

With Ricupero at the Head of the Brazilian Mission in Geneva, the negotiations on services in the Uruguay Round started to improve very quickly. At the end of December, Brazil started to present more constructive proposals and the Brazilian delegations stopped discussing what were, and what were not, services.[36] At the end of 1988, by the Mid-Term Review of the Uruguay Round, the main concepts and principles to be used in the negotiations on services had already been agreed. This led Brazil's new representative, Ricupero, to complain that there was an imbalance in the Uruguay Round: the negotiations on services were going too quickly, while the negotiations on the 'old issues', for example agriculture and textiles, were going too slowly.[37]

During the period that Ricupero was leading the Brazilian Mission (1987-1989) there was, thus, clear progress in the negotiations on services. It is no exaggeration to say that in this short period, of less than two and half years, the negotiations advanced more than in the previous five years. This was due basically to three main factors. First, the personality of Ricupero. In contrast to Batista, Ricupero was very flexible and did not have any strong ideological bent against other countries. In short, he was the essence of a diplomat. Secondly, the directives issued by Itamaraty had changed. Tarso had become the powerful General Secretary of Itamaraty, and 'de facto' Brazilian Minister of Foreign Affairs, with complete control of all key positions through a process of nominating allies and co-opting former opponents to his group. He wanted to impose his view of international relations. He believed in dialogue and was, therefore, less confrontational than Batista. Moreover, Tarso believed that Brazil should not fear other countries or international competition, and although not a true free-marketeer, he believed there was space for more integration of Brazil in the world economy.

Thirdly, also in contrast to Batista, Ricupero followed international developments and was aware that most countries in the world were adopting pro-market reforms.[38] Ricupero supported the integration of Brazil in the world economy as a signal of the maturing of the Brazilian economy. He also considered that the era of protectionism and ISI was over.[39]

Ricupero's successor in Geneva after 1990, Celso Amorim, was also a liberal, who supported a closer integration of Brazil in the world economy. He, therefore, basically continued the work already begun by Ricupero. There was no significant change in Brazil's position once Ricupero left the Mission in Geneva. Amorim can be considered a proponent of the policy of integrating Brazil in the world economy, which was introduced by Ricupero. This was the first time this policy was pursued by Brazil since its membership of the GATT.[40]

The point being made here is that it was a domestic cause, the replacement of decision-makers at Itamaraty, which was the main single explanation for the change in Brazil's position on services in the GATT and the Uruguay Round.

External factors which helped Brazil to change its position

In order to understand the role of external factors, it will be illustrated first how game theories can be applied in GATT negotiations. These game theories lay behind the rationale of Itamaraty's work during a certain period, when Batista was its representative to the GATT, from 1983 to 1987. Batista behaved as a player and considered the world trade as a zero-sum game. Brazil should not cooperate, especially if this cooperation implied victory for another player and Brazil's defeat. When Itamaraty adopted pro-UNCTAD policies (1947-1987), it also was playing a zero sum game: it is necessary to defeat 'the North'.[41]

However, it is possible to find an equitable solution where both players cooperate and neither of them win (a draw), or both win because they prevented the other player from achieving a total victory. This theory can be used to analyze what happened in the field of services. Between 1983 and 1987 Batista believed Brazil would win more if it adopted a non-cooperative stance. As a result, Brazil blocked service negotiations, first in the GATT, then in the launching of the Round and later in the Group Negotiating on Services (GNS) until 1987.[42]

As a good player Itamaraty could not refuse to cooperate all the time, because this would allow the other player, the US, to win, since a "Super-GATT" would be a total defeat for Brazil.[43] On the other hand, Brazil, as a player, could alternatively negotiate, adopt a radical stance, then negotiate again, to obstruct the negotiations, and then reach an agreement. The important feature of this tactic is to be ready to make concessions if necessary. But, the problem with this strategy is to know when the right moment has arrived and when a country can no longer bluff.

In the Brazilian case it is clear that obstruction and bluff had limits, as the launching of the Uruguay Round showed. For Brazil the non-launching of the Round would have been the worst of all the outcomes of the 'game' and thus it was to be avoided at any cost. The launching of the Round in the GATT framework would be better than the "Super-GATT" alternative, but far from the best outcome: the inclusion of services in the UNCTAD, which would represent an absolute victory for Brazil.[44]

The launching of the Uruguay Round on a separate track from the negotiations on services represented a draw and an acceptable outcome for Brazil, because neither side won. This kind of idea prevailed when Batista was Brazil's representative in the GATT. When Paulo Tarso and his group started to become more influential, the idea that began to prevail was that international trade was not a zero sum game, but a game with a positive outcome, where all players could win. This kind of thinking helped Brazil to accept a position which did not isolate it from other countries.

Batista's strategy worked in the sense that the final outcome of the negotiations was nearer Brazil's interests than could have been expected by the toughest negotiators. On the other hand, it had a high cost. Itamaraty became isolated in the Uruguay Round and in the GATT. At the same time that Brazil won, in terms of concessions in the Round, politically it was isolated. Batista broke with at least two traditions of Itamaraty: Brazil could not represent Latin American countries any more because Batista was considered to be too anti-American, and Brazil stopped speaking on behalf of LDCs. A diplomat accused Batista of being personally responsible for the destruction of Latin American coordination in the GATT, due to its autocratic behaviour.[45]

After 1987 Itamaraty abandoned the zero-sum game approach and adopted a constructive approach where the all players could win. It is considered that game theories may be useful in the analysis of the relations between two actors (or players). However, in reality, most of the situations have more than two players. In the case of Multilateral Trade Negotiations the number of players should be multiplied by dozens. Moreover, the players also vary according to the issue and to the interest involved. For this reason, it has been brought forward the middle powers's perspective for this chapter.

If Batista had considered that Brazil was middle power, he would have realized that Brazil had some bargaining power.[46] However, in his perception, Batista saw Brazil as a poor country, a member of the 'South', which should fight against the countries of the 'North', such as the US.[47] Batista ignored, therefore, the important role that middle powers can and occasionally do play.[48] Although Higgott & Cooper (1990) were referring to the case of Australia, it seems that it also applies to Canada and Brazil. Now the role of external factors were discussed, which helped Brazil to change its position and break this zero-sum game rationale and the middle powers' perspective.

The risk of plurilateral solutions which excluded Brazil

Together with the threat of sanctions, the risk of plurilateral solutions which excluded Brazil was one of the main threats used by the US against Brazil. This was part of a US strategy to either revitalize the GATT or to create a network of free trade arrangements.[49] This network, also known as "Super-GATT", would include only OECD countries and a few others.[50] Itamaraty took this threat very seriously. As a Brazilian diplomat put it: "Brazil is basically a systemic actor on the international scene, and it cannot live without multilateral institutions".[51]

The future of Brazil in the GATT has been sealed since 1986, before the Round was launched, when a spokesman of Itamaraty said that Brazil would stay in the GATT even if it included services, but it would not accept services in the new Round.[52] He justified it on the grounds that Brazil needed open markets.[53] "Super-GATT" would damage Brazil's economic future, not only because the US would be expected to do this in the field of services, but also because it could be extended to goods. It would be a disaster for Brazil since 27.1% of its overall exports go to the US and 25.2% go to the EC.[54] Moreover, Brazil faced more anti-dumping actions than most DCs.[55] This closed many markets to Brazil in a number of sectors, since many importers cancel their orders when an anti-dumping process starts.[56] This threat of a "Super-GATT" put a new card in the game. Its importance was noted at Itamaraty. As the pro-UNCTAD approach was losing its charm, the group led by Tarso saw the advantages that the strengthening of the world trade system could bring and Brazil's position in the GATT became more constructive.[57]

Certainly it could be argued that the threat of a pluralist solution excluding Brazil was used only before the launching of the Uruguay Round in order to 'convince' it to join the discussions on services. However, the threat was quite real and not limited to the launching of the Round.[58] In fact, it could be carried out at any time if the service negotiations failed, or if there was a collapse of the Uruguay Round negotiations.[59] Brazil was aware of it and decided not to call the US bluff on this issue.

William Brock, ex-Head of the United States Trade Representative (USTR), repeatedly threatened Brazil with a "Super-GATT" in 1985, before the launching of the new Round.[60] This kept Brazil participating all the time even when its position was not constructive at all. This was the case when Batista was leading the Brazilian negotiating team, between 1986 and 1987. During this period, Brazil's contribution to the negotiations on services was made of ideological speeches, without any concrete proposal. The speeches were part of the obstructionist policy created by Batista when he was the Brazilian representative to the GATT.[61] Although Batista was personally against any kind of concession in services, before, during and after the launching of the Uruguay Round,[62] the risk of a plurilateral solution excluding Brazil kept it at the negotiating table. The stakes were too high for Brazil to just leave the negotiations and wait and see what might happen. On the other hand, Brazil was not powerful enough to ensure that the negotiations would be carried out under the umbrella of UNCTAD - the organization preferred by Batista. Brazil would nevertheless continue obstructing the negotiations.[63]

It is worth noting that as Brazil spent such a long time negotiating in GATT, its legitimacy increased, even in the eyes of the pro-UNCTAD group. GATT started to be seen as second best, even by the group led by Batista. If for this group the best option was UNCTAD, the worst option was a "Super-GATT". Indeed, there was a growing concern that a "Super-GATT" would lead to a deterioration in the market access for Brazilian products to OECD countries.[64] If Brazil could not choose the negotiating forum preferred outside the GATT formal structures, it could negotiate at GATT and try to reduce concessions to a minimum. But these concessions would have to accommodate both the US and Brazil. This is what happened. Indeed, Brazil wanted to avoid any agreement outside the existing structures of the world trading system, such as a "Super-GATT", promoted by the US within the OECD between like-minded countries. Brazil also wanted to benefit from an agreement in services as it did in the GATT with goods: sharing the benefits and making light commitments in return. Brazil reached its two main goals. The GATS is not directly linked to the GATT, but to the prospective World Trade Organization and allows LDCs to open fewer sectors, according to their level of development.[65]

Changes in the international political environment

Diplomats explain the evolution of Itamaraty's position on the grounds that it was not Brazil who changed, but the world. They exemplify with the fall of the Berlin wall, the end of communism in Eastern Europe, the disintegration of the ex-USSR, and the adoption of pro-market reforms all around the world including Latin American countries and socialist countries such as China. This shows that something had changed in international affairs. But what do these changes have in common and how did they affect Brazil's position?

First of all, it should be noted that Brazil changed its position in the Uruguay Round only after 1988. Some of the above changes, such as the Solidarity movement in Poland, had started to develop from the beginning of the 1980s. Others, such as the fall of the Berlin Wall in Germany, happened after Brazil had already changed its position in the Uruguay Round. But the changes around the world were of such magnitude that they helped the pragmatist group to consolidate their position in Itamaraty and make it difficult for the pro-UNCTAD group to return to power.

China flirts with capitalism Although China had adopted pro-market measures to some degree since the 1970s, it was only in the 1980s that the reformers took control of the state apparatus, and that reforms were firmly entrenched.[66] It is difficult to assert that the pro-market reforms in China are irreversible, but they have been adopted for more than a decade. Although China opted for market reforms without democracy, it appears that central planning is not very high on the Chinese agenda.[67] This explains why China adopted an outward oriented policy to attract Foreign Direct Investment (FDI) and capture markets for its exports, as any capitalist country does. China also let it be known that, in order to provide a stable environment for investors in the region, it did not plan to alter capitalism in Hong Kong. China also applied to join GATT. This shows China's commitment to pro-market reforms and will certainly have a strong impact in Latin America.[68]

For Latin America the effects will be multiple. First, there are many opportunities for Latin American countries to export products and services to a huge market of more than 1 billion people. Second, the low wages in China mean that Chinese exports will have a comparative advantage over Latin American exports. Third, if China is accepted in GATT (or in the World Trade Organization (WTO), Latin American countries will have to apply Most Favoured Nation (MFN) to Chinese exports.[69] Consequently, Brazil may have to face cheap imports from China, as already happened with the US and Mexico. The result is that many firms may have to close, especially in the textile sector. While Chinese products were conquering other markets, the former Brazilian Ambassador to China, from the pro-UNCTAD group, gave an interview to an important Brazilian magazine saying that diplomats were not salesmen ('*mascates*'), and they should not be concerned about commercial and trade issues.[70] How Brazil would justify its open door policy if such an invasion of cheap products happened is something that he did not mention. The pressure from the textile industry to reintroduce tariffs can be politically unbearable, if the end of the Most Favourable Arrangement (MFA) does not compensate it.[71] It is surprising to realize that while the biggest socialist country on the planet was increasing its share in the world economy based on competitiveness and free-trade, Brazilian negotiators in the GATT were combating these same principles, and fighting for Special and Differential (S&D) treatment based on ISI strategy and infant industry arguments.[72]

The assumption of power by Gorbachev: Perestroika, Glasnost and the Pro-Reforms in Eastern Europe.   As a result of, and as part of "Glasnost" and "Perestroika", a movement to democratize the ex-USSR and to broaden the scope of existent freedoms arose. Parts of the Soviet Union, such as Latvia and Lithuania asked for independence. The Soviet empire collapsed, and former parts of ex-USSR became independent States. The result of this movement was the rise to power of Yeltsin and the adoption of pro-market reforms in ex-USSR, including Russia.[73]

The collapse of ex-USSR did have an impact in Eastern Europe-Latin America relations. Initially, this impact was stronger in political aspects, such as the relative decline of socialist movements in Latin America, which are still extensive.[74] In the future, when and if Russia stabilizes its economy, it might import Brazilian products such as grains, and light manufactured goods such as textiles. Brazil could import Russian oil. This fact was ignored by Brazilian policy-makers, which saw events in ex-USSR as isolated from the world economy. They did not see them as part of the changes in the international environment and they did not note the opportunities for Brazil.

Overall, the end of soviet hegemony over the regimes of Eastern Europe had three main effects on the world economy. First it meant that there was no such thing as a centrally planned economy, or an alternative economic system, since socialist regimes in Eastern Europe were adopting pro-market reforms throughout the region.[75] Second, as the countries of this region wanted to rebuild their infrastructure, they would compete for foreign capital, from private and official banks, more aggressively than before. Third, as emerging markets, these countries would offer an alternative for foreign investors, who wanted high returns on their capital, thus competing with Latin American privatization programmes.[76]

Policy-makers in Itamaraty who supported an approximation with LDCs and socialist countries (the pro-UNCTAD group) were slow to assimilate these facts. They had a chance in the 1980s to update their beliefs to the new reality. Indeed, it was necessary to adapt to the new environment quickly or to run the risk of being overcome by events. The pro-UNCTAD group, who ruled Itamaraty until 1985, did not review their position and learnt nothing from international events. They became more and more isolated and were eventually excluded from some key economic positions at Itamaraty.[77]

The emergence of the Pacific Rim and the Four Asian Tigers as the most dynamic area of the world economy   Although the emergence of the Asian Non-Industrialized Countries (NICs) did not happen in the 1980s, it was in this period that the difference between their performance and that of Brazil became more evident. Indeed, since the 1960s Korea and Singapore managed to maintain high rates of growth, of more than 9% per year.[78] In the 1970s the average increased to around 10% per year.[79] In the 1980s their rate of growth was around 8% per year,[80] higher than in most DCs.[81]

While some Brazilian economists kept saying that their model could not be exported to Latin America, they successfully created the most economically dynamic region in the world, together with Japan. These countries had at least one thing in common: the adoption of pro-market reforms.[82] The level of exports of Korea surpassed the Brazilian level,[83] although their GDP was much smaller.[84] In 1980 Korea's GDP was around one fifth of Brazilian GDP. However, by 1990 it was almost half.[85]

Brazilian diplomats agreed that there were tigers in Asia, which were more aggressive than Brazil in world markets. But they argued that national businessmen had a less aggressive temperament. They also claimed that their development was due to the presence of a local superpower, namely Japan.

Pro-Market reforms in Latin America   It was difficult for Brazilian diplomats to believe that countries from Eastern Europe were adopting capitalism. It was not easy for Itamaraty to accept that the model sought by Yeltsin for Russia did not conform to the declarations of UNCTAD, but rather to the prescriptions of the IMF. Even the fact that China was adopting capitalist measures could be easily explained by diplomats arguing that it was due to the existence of a very competitive capitalist market in the region. But when the movement for pro-market reforms reached Latin America, the position of the pro-UNCTAD group at Itamaraty became really difficult.

Chile was the first to launch pro-market reforms successfully in Latin America in the 1970s. The results came fast and it presented a higher growth rate of its GDP than Brazil after 1980.[86] It was argued then that this could happen because of a dictatorial regime. Pinochet adopted reforms because of the small size of the Chilean market.[87] Thus, it could not be applied to Brazil. After Chile, Mexico adopted pro-market reforms and signed a free-trade zone with the US.[88] Diplomats from Itamaraty argued then that this was due to Mexico's strategic importance to the US and such reforms would not be repeated elsewhere in Latin America. But subsequently, pro-market reforms reached Argentina, Colombia, Bolivia, Venezuela and Uruguay.[89]

As a result, all Latin America jumped on the bandwagon of market-reforms except Brazil.[90] Even Nicaragua abandoned pro-UNCTAD policies and opted for pro-market reforms. Some Brazilian diplomats also failed to perceive these changes. Brazil remained apart from market reforms and isolated in negotiations in the GATT. This was the beginning of the collapse of the G-10.

Conclusion: The world changed   As a result of all the above mentioned changes, the pro-UNCTAD lobby, led by Batista, lost ground at Itamaraty, in Brasilia, and at GATT and UNCTAD in Geneva.[91] The world developed in a certain direction, and Brazil did not follow. The world adopted democracy as its main value and had opted for pro-market policies.[92] These policies became considered not an ideology but a reality that had to be accepted.[93] Itamaraty had to accept that market reforms were receiving wide approval. Brazil could either embrace this new world or join the socialist club, formed by Cuba, Vietnam and North Korea. It was difficult to argue that all the countries in the world were wrong except Brazil. Since Itamaraty could not adapt the world it had to change and adapt itself.

There was no sense in Brazil maintaining pro-UNCTAD policies if even socialist countries were embracing free-trade. Itamaraty had to adopt a pro-market approach at GATT if it wanted to keep its influence and not be isolated. Itamaraty came around to this view slowly, with Tarso as one of its main protagonists.[94]

The risk of becoming isolated and the role of pragmatism

One of the most sacred characteristics of Brazilian diplomacy is pragmatism.[95] It tries to be reasonable and to obtain what is possible in a certain situation. Itamaraty put this technique into practice through a constant assessment of the position of other countries, in order to know which position to adopt. In other words, Itamaraty tried to represent a middle-of-the-Round position between many countries. This prevents Itamaraty from being isolated from other countries. As a result, pragmatism and the fear of being isolated can be considered two sides of the same policy.

If Itamaraty realizes that Brazil is becoming isolated, it tries to ac-commodate its position with other countries in order to avoid isolation. Some diplomats go even further and declare that one of the main guidelines of Bra-zilian diplomacy is not to let the country become isolated.[96] Thus, in any in-ternational negotiation, Brazilian diplomats are constantly asked by Itama-raty about the position of other countries and what Brazil could do to help or how to adopt a middle of the road course.[97]

This policy has a positive side in the sense that the country will al-ways follow international trends and will never be left out of any important discussions which take place in international fora. The negative side is that it reflects a deep lack of principles and as a result, a lack of confidence in its own opinions, positions and judgements.[98] Indeed, some Brazilian diplomats argue that Itamaraty suffers from a very strong complex: it has a deep lack of confidence. The result of this is reflected in Itamaraty's positions abroad.[99]

The strategy of blocking the service negotiations can be considered to represent a break with the tradition of pragmatism. Indeed, it implied that Itamaraty was taking a position which was not represented by most coun-tries. The result of this policy was obvious: either Itamaraty would break away from its previous policy of pragmatism or it would have to abandon its tactic of blocking negotiations, which cannot last for ever.[100]

The agreement to negotiate constructively in the GNS after 1988 rep-resented a break away from Brazil's policy of adopting radical positions and confrontation. It was possible, due to two reasons. First, due to ideological change at Itamaraty. This was solved with the replacement of the pro-UNCTAD policy for a more pro free-trade view. Second, due to Itamaraty's wish to re-launch its policy of not allowing Brazil to be isolated from other countries. However, it was necessary to make a clear option. If Itamaraty wanted to keep its policy of not becoming isolated it would have to change its negotiators in Geneva. There, Batista had became famous for being a tough negotiator. Although negotiators recognized that Batista knew how to obtain concessions, he was not seen as a diplomat.[101] Some analysts of the GATT believed that after leading the blocking policy for four years (1983-1987), Batista's position and Brazil's standpoint were becoming unsustain-able.[102] Finally he was removed from Geneva and sent to New York.[103]

It is right to say that Tarso and his group were better exponents of the Itamaraty tradition of pragmatism, moderation and the need to avoid the isolation of the country, than Batista's group. Due to the facts mentioned in the last section, among them the style of the Brazilian negotiator Batista, Itamaraty became very isolated. It was difficult to maintain Brazil's position. Indeed, after Batista's removal from Geneva, Ricupero took a moderate line and Brazil started to participate in a more positive way in the negotiating process.

UNCTAD's lack of effectiveness

The absence of concrete results of UNCTAD had already been noted in Brasilia. In the 1970s Maciel had already seen reports to Itamaraty warning about UNCTAD's lack of a future.[104] He considered the discussions at UNCTAD to be too superficial.[105] These reports were not well received by the pro-UNCTAD lobby in charge of the Economic Department during that period. UNCTAD's lack of concrete results, however, did dislodge the pro-UNCTAD lobby from their key positions at Itamaraty.[106] Although there was another set of principles to replace the ISI approach,[107] it was not accepted by Itamaraty, which emphasized the importance of shared values.[108]

Only in the middle 1980s, with the debt crisis and the collapse of the ISI model, was it possible to think about a change. Itamaraty, as a very conservative institution, is not favourable per se to new thinking. In fact, it does not seek new ideas and they are not welcome. The new ideas must be imposed by a new ruling group, preferably with inside support.[109] In this respect, inertia plays an important role in Itamaraty. If a principle reaches a crisis, as in the case of Brazil's support for UNCTAD, it does not mean that another principle will replace it immediately. Even if there is a group to suggest a new strategy, as the military did in 1964, it is necessary that a new idea develops according to a process which can take years or even decades, because it needs to be 'understood' by all ranks.

Although Itamaraty has a significant degree of autonomy within the State and from other Ministries, it rarely adopts initiatives on its own, that is without political support from powerful individuals outside or within the Ministry. In the case of UNCTAD, the issue was very complex. In the same way that the GATT reflects US trade policies, Itamaraty's support for UNCTAD reflected Brazil's ISI policies. Indeed, there was wide belief among Brazilian economists that the adoption of measures which favoured an ISI process was the best policy for LDCs. As a result, most decision-makers in Brazil followed the ECLA school. Diplomats in Itamaraty were no exception to this general rule.[110]

This explains why when UNCTAD entered a period of crisis at the end of the 1970s and at the beginning of the 1980s, it was difficult to replace the support for the ISI with other ideas. There was no lack of alternatives, but the idea that was current, viz., the adoption of pro-market reforms, was strongly rejected in Brazil by both economists and diplomats. Brazilian economists in general had a deep bias against free-trade. Indeed, free-trade in Brazil had few supporters either among diplomats or economists. An economist who appeared in public to support liberal reforms in Brazil would be considered reactionary or a Friedman disciple.[111]

This background makes the takeover of Itamaraty by the group led by Tarso still more fascinating, because they did not present themselves as the supporters of free-trade against supporters of protectionism (the pro-UNCTAD lobby). If they had done so, they would have isolated themselves from most diplomats. They presented themselves as the 'moderates' and 'pragmatists', who were seeking compromises and acceptable solutions to the conflicts that Brazil was getting involved in.[112] They were against the ultranationalist group who were jeopardizing Brazil's interests.[113]

The theoretical framework used by Tarso's group was a mixture of a policy based on results enhanced by a strong sense of *realpolitik*.[114] They argued that the policy of supporting UNCTAD was taking the country nowhere.[115] In fact, the discussions of interest to Brazil[116] were taking place in the GATT and not in UNCTAD. Itamaraty was wasting time and precious diplomatic effort focusing on an organization which could offer nothing but resolutions which were completely ignored by the US. Instead, the group wanted Brazil to participate more positively in the GATT, making concessions where necessary in order to obtain gains where desired. Instead of making unreal demands Brazil should present practical suggestions, without ideological content. In order to achieve this, Brazil should abandon the pose, adopted by UNCTAD, of LDCs as a 'victim' of the world trade system.[117]

In the eyes of the group of pragmatists led by Tarso, Brazil had to stop thinking that it was a powerless country without any influence on bargaining or incapable of shaping the events in world trade. In this group's opinion, Brazil should behave as a mature country, aware of its international assets: the capacity to engage in an articulate debate with foreign countries, the existence of a racially diverse democracy at home; diplomatic tradition;

excellent representation abroad; good negotiators, good domestic technicians; economic assets, such as the size of its market, high GDP and industrial production, high capacity to export and import, a high level of reserves after 1985, reasonable per capita income, plenty of natural resources and low labour costs, a capitalist system. These factors were tempered, however, by constraints which affected the government's capacity of manoeuvre: high foreign debt, unequal distribution of income, social problems, macroeconomic instability, poverty, high rates of illiteracy, etc. On balance, if Itamaraty entered into an international negotiation conscious of all these aspects, it would not have to fear a negative outcome, since Brazil had more assets than most LDCs.[118]

According to this school of thought, Brazil should stop waiting for a new international division of labour, abandon the defeatist discourse associated with UNCTAD and fight for a better position in the international system. The same can be said about the G-77. There was no point Brazil being part of a group with such different, and sometimes even divergent, interests as the G-77. The divergence of interests had become clear during the negotiations for the International Programme of Commodities (IPC) and the Common Fund (CF), promoted by UNCTAD, where Brazil's position clashed with that of other LDCs. At that time, Itamaraty preferred to ignore this episode and continue to work inside the UNCTAD framework, but it could not do this for ever.[119]

The approach suggested by Tarso was to work on a sectorial basis, according to the balance of interests in each field. An example was the Cairns Group. The pro-UNCTAD lobby was opposed to the Cairns group, because they saw it as a betrayal of UNCTAD ideals because it involved allying with DCs such as the US, Australia, New Zealand and Canada.[120]

In this way, the group of pragmatists adopted a case-by-case approach by which it disrupted and undermined the main principles and positions of the UNCTAD lobby. The strategy of Tarso and his group was to climb to positions of power slowly, as his political origins recommended.[121] Even in a crisis situation Tarso would never interfere, because it was not in his personality. He would only interfere when his service was requested.[122] Certainly, the defeat of the supporters of UNCTAD in Itamaraty was only finalized during the Montreal midterm review, when Tarso, as the General Secretary of Itamaraty, was able to dictate personally the Brazilian position and complete Brazil's U-turn towards the GATT. Of course, this was immediately reflected in the negotiations.[123]

The need of a legal structure of services

Itamaraty did not support the idea of an agreement on services. However, when it became inevitable, it opposed such a negotiation being carried out under the aegis of the GATT. Brazil felt that the GATT did not have sufficient provisions to deal with economic development.[124] However, Brazil had to face reality. What was on offer was not a matter concerning in which organization the negotiations should be carried out. What Brazil was faced with was an agreement following the general lines of GATT procedures and principles or an agreement without Brazil in a "Super-GATT".[125]

Initially, the nationalist group led by Batista supported the view that since an agreement negotiated within UNCTAD was not acceptable to the US, no agreement was better than an agreement under the aegis of the GATT. As this position became indefensible, so the position of the group evolved. Eventually the point was reached that if it was not possible to negotiate within UNCTAD, Brazil would agree to negotiate if this were done outside the GATT, even if it followed GATT principles and procedures. Batista started to support a 'Service compact' outside the GATT. This idea was linked to a dual-track procedure, supported by the EC.[126]

The idea of a "compact", or more specifically an organization to deal with services only, outside the GATT structure and framework, became the second best option to this group.[127] However, this position faced strong resistance from the US, which wanted a service agreement inside the GATT framework. While Batista was leading the Brazilian delegation no progress was made towards any kind of agreement, even on principles. His replacement by Ricupero eased the discussions on the question of the principles which should guide the negotiations for an agreement on services.[128]

The advantages of an agreement on services as it was seen by Ricupero, and eventually Amorim, who replaced him, were very clear. First of all, an agreement offers a stable environment. All sectors need some kind of regulation to avoid the presence of disturbances which can jeopardize development. This is valid for all economic sectors, and international trade in services was no exception.[129]

Second, an international agreement offers stability for investors. Investors want guarantees so that if they decide to reconsider their positions and invest in other sectors or countries they may do so. An international agreement offers this guarantee. A unilateral declaration by a country or a domestic legislation which protects FDI against expropriation does not provide the same guarantee because it can be modified by a new administration.[130]

Third, an agreement creates a set of harmonized rules that all countries have to follow. This fact prevents a country from offering special deals or advantages to foreign investors that other countries cannot offer. It also inhibits any country from trying to pressurize a foreign investor into making FDI or interfering in administrative decisions which are the sole responsibility of foreign investors. A standard set of rules also ensures that foreign investors can think in terms of global markets and do not need to change strategy to adapt a company to a specific market in order to meet rules that were created for that market and which imply a hindrance to FDI.[131]

Fourthly, an international agreement prevents a country from being pressurized by a powerful country into entering into bilateral agreements which better serve the interest of the powerful country. The most powerful country can indeed force the less powerful to open its market, as the US did with South Korea. This is probably the strongest argument in favour of a multilateral agreement. In a multilateral agreement, all countries have to follow the same rules and it makes it much more difficult for a powerful country to use its power to convince another country to adopt policies that are not in its own interests, or to implement measures that it would not have implemented without outside pressure. In short, a multilateral agreement although it restricts all the countries that subscribe to it, does not oblige any country to take measures that it would not normally take if the agreement did not exist. In bilateral negotiations, on the other hand, the country with less bargaining power is at the mercy of the more powerful country.[132]

However, being party to an international agreement has two main disadvantages. The first disadvantage is that a country can no longer adopt national legislation in the field covered. All future legislation will have to be consistent with what was accepted in the agreement. In such a case, if a country were trying to protect its market in order to develop its indigenous industry, and the international agreement it was preparing to endorse deals with market access, it would have to make concessions in its protectionist policy. It would have to establish priorities and goals in order to choose which industries would be covered by the agreement and which would not.

Sometimes countries may not have much choice and the agreement will cover all sectors, though this is uncommon. In general, most agreements accept the inclusion of derogations, exceptions, reserves or safeguards.[133]

The second disadvantage is that once a country is party to an agreement, it is very difficult to renounce it. Although most agreements have clauses specifying under which conditions a country may abandon the contract, this is not very common in international law. Once a country ratifies an international agreement the pressure to remain party to the agreement is very strong and inertia plays a very important role in maintaining the treaty, that is, keeping the country inside the treaty. Furthermore, the industries or sectors which benefit from the agreement will also constitute a powerful lobby for the country to remain party to the treaty even if it jeopardizes other sectors.[134]

All groups at Itamaraty (nationalists and pragmatists) were aware of both the advantages and disadvantages of an international treaty. However, the nationalists were less aware of the benefits of an international treaty since it had not carried out any relevant study about the impact of a service agreement for Brazil.[135]

The group of pragmatists was aware of potential benefits from an agreement in services, and was also more concerned about the consequences of a lack of agreement for Brazil. This group believed that in the case of a collapse in the Uruguay Round and/or a trade war between Brazil and the US, Brazil could not retaliate against the US because Brazil was not the main supplier or the main importer of any US product.[136] Therefore, a US-Brazil conflict would be more prejudicial to Brazil than to the US.

They noted that constant disagreements with the US were creating a bad climate for FDI in Brazil and were jeopardizing Brazilian exports, since the Brazil-US dispute in IPRs was causing the cancellation of orders by US importers. Although the service sector was not directly linked to the dispute in IPRs, the bad political climate between the two countries was having an effect on business confidence in Brazil. The sooner Itamaraty could solve the dispute in services and in IPRs, the sooner Brazil could attract more FDI, which was at a very low level.

Therefore, the position of the pragmatists was that if an agreement in services, though unfavourable from Brazil's point of view, could contribute to improve Brazil-US relations and increase business confidence in Brazil it would be better than no agreement at all. The worse of all possible worlds for this group was the situation in which Brazil was currently living; namely: US-Brazil dispute in IT, low FDI, and the perspective of losing part of the US market due to the cancellation of orders from US importers.[137]

The pro-UNCTAD group, on the other hand, believed that the risk of a trade war, even in the case of a collapse of the Uruguay Round, would be very small.[138] This statement shows the lack of importance given by this group to the Uruguay Round, and also the low commitment to a multilateral trading system. It seems that this group could not evaluate the negative impact that the collapse of the Uruguay Round would have on world trade, since protectionism and bilateral agreements would be able to spread again.

The role of sanctions

Sanctions play an important role in explaining Brazil's change in trade policies.[139] Helleiner also pointed out that bilateral pressures have recently been employed by the US, most vigorously against some of the better-off LDCs, for example, South Korea and Brazil.[140] Before the launch of the Uruguay Round, the US unsuccessfully threatened to withdraw access to the GSP from Brazil.[141] During the Uruguay Round, the Brazil-US disputes in IT and in pharmaceutical products are two examples of the use of sanctions.[142]

Case 1: Sanctions in the US-Brazil Dispute in IT Policies[143] In   March 1985, the US showed disapproval for Brazil's IT policies[144] and threatened sanctions to weaken Brazil's position in the Uruguay Round. The strategy used by the US was to take the conflict to the GATT. Michael Smith, Deputy- Representative of the USTR said that:

> "The US is insisting on discussing the protection of software in the GATT because the trade in software is as important as the trade in shoes and other products. The US has problems with Brazil in the field of high technology due to Brazil's law on IT. We are concerned that the pharmaceutical sector could also be protected. The best way of solving the problem of the Transfer of Technology is to stimulate foreign investments in Brazil. I hope that Brazil will take part in the new Round of negotiations and will adopt a more positive position".[145]

As Bastos noted, it had already been made evident that the Americans had no clear case against IT policy when in June of 1985 they called Brazil for consultation on the issue at GATT.[146] On 7 September 1985, the US started official investigations into Brazil's IT policy. Initially the US wanted the end of this policy. The use of sanctions against Brazil was a possibility. However, less than two weeks after the threat was launched, a spokesman from the Ministry of Commerce Industry (MIC) -gave a declaration saying that Brazilian IT policy was consistent with the GATT.[147] This position was kept throughout the negotiations. Therefore, if the objective of the US's threat to use section 301 was to oblige Brazil to make concessions in the service negotiations, it did not work.

Brazil refused to negotiate bilaterally with the US for five months and kept its tough position in Geneva. The first consultive meeting took place in Caracas in February 1986.[148] Brazil's official position was that the law on IT was not negotiable.[149] Odell notes that 'the tone of the bilateral dispute changed somewhat after May 1986 when the superpower, not the developing country, pulled back'. Officials said that the US did not want to change the law. It rather objected to the arbitrary way that the Secretariat in charge of the IT policy for IT issues in Brazil (SEI) interpreted the Law.[150] After the clarification, the negotiations started and were divided into three parts (a) administrative procedures, (b) market access and (c) IPRs.[151]

Brazil made minimum concessions on the two first issues.[152] In September 1986, at the end of twelve months, superpower coercion had changed very little in Brazil. The only significant concession Brazil would make in all the US-Brazil disputes in IT was related to IPRs.[153] As Bastos noted, it was in IPRs that Brazil made the most significant concessions, among them the adoption of copyright protection for software and the licensing of the later version of MS-DOS by Microsoft.[154]

When the dispute started, there was no link between the US-Brazil dispute in IT and the service negotiations at the Uruguay Round. All sides were careful to isolate both these disputes from other issue areas. In neither conflict did the official negotiator link his demands or proposals to developments of trade negotiations or security arrangements.[155]

In November 1987, the US announced sanctions against Brazil due to the decision of SEI not to accept a request for US firms to license the program MS-DOS due to the existence of a similar one.[156] The main products affected by the sanctions were textiles, shoes, orange juice, paper, electronic products and airplanes. In January 1988, after the sanctions had started, SEI altered its initial position and accepted the licensing of Microsoft's MS-DOS last version. After this concession, the US government announced suspension of sanctions in February, although Brazil had not changed its position in the Uruguay Round.[157]

Case 2: US-Brazil Dispute in Pharmaceutical Concerning Intellectual Property Rights (IPRs)[158] In April 1986 the US sent a document to Itamaraty asking for consultations on the lack of protection for pharmaceutical products. In June 1987 the Pharmaceutical Manufacturers Association (PMA) submitted a petition to the US government, noting that Brazilian practice was unreasonable.[159] The petition was accepted by the USTR which started an investigation based on Section 301 of the US Trade Act. In February 1988, the first consultation started between Brazil and the US. In that month Brazil's new trade negotiator, Ricupero, had already arrived in Geneva, but Brazil's position in the service negotiations was still unclear. In the same month Itamaraty announced that an Inter-Ministerial Meeting had been formed to examine the domestic policy of not giving protection to pharmaceutical products.[160]

Only four months later, the Group would present its report suggesting the creation of protection for process only.[161] This position did not satisfy the US. In July, Brazil was accused of unreasonable trade practice by President Reagan and in September the public audiences started.[162]

It is interesting to note that Brazil had more than three months - between July and September - to negotiate with the US, but it preferred not to change its initial position. It is possible that Brazil expected that the US would, at the last moment, change its initial position and accept minimum concessions, as had happened in IT policies.[163] Another explanation is that there was a strong lobby against concessions in IPRs for pharmaceutical products in Brazil.[164] On 20 October 1988 Reagan ordered the sanctions to enter into force on 30 October. Again, the Brazilian government had ten days to offer some concession, but nothing was proposed. On 30th October, Reagan used Section 301 to justify the application of a 100% tariff ad valorem on chemical products, papers and electronic products.[165] The most interesting aspect is that Brazil had already changed its position in services in the Round, but not in IPRs.[166]

Indeed, as Kumar notes, there was considerable progress in the negotiations on services, as evidenced by the document sent by the president of the group to the Montreal review. But in Trade Related Intellectual Property Rights (TRIPs), however, there was no agreement until Montreal, as India insisted that World Intellectual Property Organization (WIPO) was the proper forum for such negotiations.[167]

In Montreal there was no agreement on TRIPs, since Brazilian and Indian positions had not yet changed. The Itamaraty's answer to the US sanctions was to ask in the GATT for the opening of a panel at the beginning 1989, but the US was slow to answer, and the panel was only created in the early 1990s.[168] The result of the panel was that the US was criticized for failing to use GATT machinery.[169] The conflict would only be solved bilaterally, with retaliatory tariffs withdrawn, when Brazil confirmed that it would change its legislation on IPRs.[170]

Conclusion: Is there a link between sanctions and services? Therefore, it is very difficult, if at all possible, to establish a direct link between the threat of sanctions and Brazil's position in the service negotiations. It is quite clear that the main target of the US was the lack of a law in Brazil to assure IPRs for pharmaceutical products. The US threat in 1985-1986 of withdrawing Brazilian products from its GSP did not work, and Brazil only changed its position on services in 1988.

Between 1985 and 1988 Brazil changed its position in the Uruguay Round partly as a result of US pressure and partly due to its interest in an open trading system to service its debts.[171] The change in the guidelines of international trade policy defended by Itamaraty abroad reflects the loss of interest in the G-10 and in the pro-UNCTAD positions maintained by some of its members. The GATT and the Uruguay Round became the main fora of negotiations in Brazil's diplomatic economic agenda. This position was occupied by UNCTAD until the 1970s. Thus, the sanctions accelerated a process which already existed in the 1980s of an approximation between Brazil and GATT.[172]

On the other hand, it could be said that the use of Section 301 against Brazil had an indirect impact on service negotiations because it helped to change the social forces which supported ISI policies in Brazil. The groups which could be affected by sanctions started to lobby for the opening of Brazilian markets to imports and for the elimination of measures which could cause conflict in the US-Brazil relations. Brazil's largest export products destined for the US could suffer if there were of sanctions due to IT.[173]

This was also the case in the pharmaceutical dispute. It is worth noting that before communicating with the GATT about the US intentions of applying sanctions against Brazilian products in 1986, Clayton Yeutter gave an interview directly from Washington to Brazilian journalists by satellite. In the interview he stated that IT was a maximum priority for the US government.[174] He also mentioned that a gesture from the Brazilian government which would soften US pressure was a law on copyrights on software, and a very tough law against piracy and fake products.[175] This statement of Yeutter confirms our point that the main aspect of the US-Brazil dispute in the IT was centred on IPRs and not on services. He did not make any link between IT and services.

The change of position of other countries

When the negotiations on services began, Batista was adopting Brazil's tough stance against discussing services, and continued to refuse to submit positive suggestions. However, other countries were being flexible. Even taking Brazil's reservations into consideration, Itamaraty noted that it would be difficult to maintain its tough stance forever.[176]

Indeed, Brazil could block the negotiations, but it could not stop them for good. Moreover, if the negotiations were advancing, despite Itamaraty's tactics, it was wiser for Brazil to join the negotiations than to be left out in the cold.[177] Brazilian diplomats liked to argue that Itamaraty did not change its attitude in the negotiations on services. There was only an evolution of its original stance as other countries also changed theirs. Here, Itamaraty has a point. In a negotiation, all parties, by definition, try to be flexible in their stance in order to accommodate their interests and the interests of other parties. For instance, before the launching of the Uruguay Round, Brazil refused to negotiate services in the GATT, but agreed at Punta del Este to negotiate under the aegis of a Trade Negotiating Committee (TNC) that used GATT procedures and principles.[178]

The same thing happened during the actual negotiations. Brazil argued that it was not possible just to adapt GATT definitions and concepts to services because they were created to deal with products or visible goods. As a result, all the GATT principles and procedures were redefined in order to fit the new sector under discussion, viz., services. This happened because the US changed its original stance of just wanting to use GATT principles straight away in services. The US realized that negotiations in a field where there was no ready multilateral framework, that is, services, was much more complex than expected.[179]

Another instance of changes was on the question of trade liberalization. When the US entered the negotiations, it was very eager to obtain immediate liberalization which was opposed by almost all countries and by the EC. In short, the US wanted other countries to commit themselves to all the GATT principles (MFN, non-transparency, reciprocity, etc.). Most countries wanted a set of procedures to be established before starting liberalization, in order to guarantee a kind of standard, slow and controlled path towards liberalization. After arduous discussions, the US accepted that liberalization could be achieved by means of a phased process, as the EC and most countries wanted, and not as a package of measures to be adopted immediately.[180]

Another point of contention was related to liberalization commitments. In the US initial position, all countries had to commit themselves to the GATT principles (MFN, free-trade, etc.) and to adopting liberalization measures. The main opposition to this idea came from the EC. The EC supported the view that the GATT principles should not constitute commitments, but goals to be achieved by all countries according to their capacity. Brazil supported the EC in this matter. When the US realized that it did not have the support for its position from other countries, it had to change its original attitude and accept GATT principles as a goal and not rules. The EC position was due to the fact that many of its markets were covered by regulations, and a liberalization in all sectors would require the unlikely support of all EC members.[181]

The first result of this change of positions during the negotiations was to create a positive atmosphere for discussing a general framework for services. Indeed, in the period following the initial two years, when Brazil had maintained a blocking strategy, the atmosphere in the negotiations improved considerably.[182] The second result is that during negotiations, some proposals, even if they were not accepted, had the effect of creating confidence between negotiators. They are called Confidence Building Measures (CBM). This happened many times before and during the negotiations on services. Examples of CBM are: the agreement by the US not to conduct the negotiations in services under the aegis of the GATT; the choice offered to countries not satisfied with the final outcome of the negotiations of not signing the agreement; and even the acceptance of liberalization and other GATT principles as principles to be followed and hopefully achieved rather than as firm commitment. These measures eased tensions and decreased the degree of apprehension of many LDCs, especially those of Brazil.[183]

A third result is that, due to the GATT procedure of consensus building, all countries feel that they are also obliged to follow general decisions if there is a commitment in that direction. As other countries showed a disposition to listen to suggestions from Brazil and the willingness to meet some of its proposals, it would be very difficult for Itamaraty to remain inflexible. After the rise of Tarso as the main decision-maker at Itamaraty in 1985 and the replacement of Batista in 1987, Tarso allowed Brazilian negotiators in Geneva to be more flexible.[184]

These factors helped Itamaraty to alter its initial stance. Itamaraty can claim, as it does today, that Brazil reviewed its initial positions as other countries did - in particular the US - and showed flexibility in the negotiations, by changing some of its initial positions and even accommodating some Brazilian concerns. However, it seems that the change in the Brazilian negotiating team in Geneva eased the process considerably.

The agreement reflected Brazil's interests and concerns

Many factors during the negotiations contributed to the decrease in Brazil's resistance to an international agreement on services. The most salient are[185]:

a) The fact that the agreement was formally independent of the GATT.

b) The definition of principles to be used in the agreement.

c) The respect of sovereignty and national legislation.

d) The issue of rights of establishment was clarified.

e) The perspective of Brazilian companies was taken into account.

f) The participation of private companies in the negotiations.

g) The perspective of gains to Brazil was foreseen.

The first aspect, concerning the legal status of the agreement, has already been mentioned and will not be covered again. However, one should point out the fact that the new agreement would not be an appendix to the GATT, as the US wanted, but subordinated to the Multilateral Trade Organization (MTO). Brazilian negotiators felt some relief, because they always supported the view that the GATT had some institutional problems due to its peculiar legal status and for this reason it was inadequate to deal with international trade. The creation of an organization to deal with trade answered a very old Brazilian demand and certainly eased Itamaraty's resistance to an agreement dealing with services, even though it may have a very strong GATT inspiration.[186]

Second, Brazil pressed for and obtained a redefinition of the principles to be used in the agreement on services. The GATT's main principles (MFN, reciprocity, etc.) were all redefined to fit trade in services. This was Brazil's aspiration and one of its initial main requests. Even the concept of services was agreed beforehand in order to answer Brazilian concerns. This also avoided the mere transposition of GATT principles to the new agreement. The differences between the old definitions of principles and the new ones were not big, but they gave Brazil a feeling of participation and that helped it to negotiate other parts of the agreement.[187]

Third, one of the main objections of Itamaraty concerned the matter of national sovereignty. Brazil did not want to undertake any commitment that implied the cancellation of any of its national legislation, because it would generate serious domestic problems. On this issue, Brazil had the support of the EC and for this reason it was not very difficult to convince the US to modify its position. It was shown that even the US would have to change its national legislation if the agreement was to be strictly adhered to, in order to adapt itself to deregulation and liberalization in services. Trade in financial services and shipping are two cases in point. Thus, the acceptance of the concept of national legislation assured Itamaraty that it need not worry about sovereignty.[188]

Fourth, Brazil had strong reservations concerning the concept of 'rights of establishment'. Itamaraty argued that the concept of right of establishment if applied without restriction would imply loss of the ability of a country to use FDI as a tool to stimulate growth in certain fields. It also meant that Brazilian legislation would have to be adapted to it. Brazil declared that DCs wanted to introduce freedom for FDI through the back door. But when the concept of national legislation was accepted, Itamaraty noted that Brazil would not have to change its law on foreign investment. Moreover, when Itamaraty studied domestic law, it noted, with surprise, that Brazil had a liberal legislation on FDI.[189] Thus, Itamaraty stopped being afraid of discussing FDI because Brazil was quite open-minded regarding the entry of foreign capital, when compared to other countries. When this discovery was made it had a positive impact on Itamaraty's position in the negotiations and on Brazil's acceptance of the concept of rights of establishment.[190]

Fifth, Itamaraty also feared that the international agreement was a way of trying to limit the service exports of LDCs such as Brazil. Itamaraty did not want to see Brazilian firms lose markets to international competitors because of the agreement. For this reason, the proposals to be used in the agreement were all tested beforehand in two sectors: telecom, which was of special interest to DCs, and engineering, which was of great interest to Brazil, South Korea, Pakistan and India. The conclusion was that there was nothing in the agreement that could jeopardize or limit the performance of Brazilian firms. At this point, a prospective agreement received a green light from Brasilia and from the main negotiators.[191]

Sixth, the participation of Brazilian private firms, when the tests started, gave legitimacy and an impetus to the negotiations: legitimacy because Brazilian firms would be the main objects of an agreement. When they started taking part in the negotiations with Brazilian diplomats, they could not claim that the agreement had been planned without consulting them. Moreover, Brazilian firms started to carry out their own technical studies in order to join international negotiations and take part in them. This fact gave an impetus to these negotiations because when they were taking part in the elaboration of the sectorial studies and tests, the firms realized that they had everything to gain from an agreement - in terms of increased market access - and they started to press Itamaraty to go ahead and finalize the agreement.[192]

Seventh, the perspective that Brazil had something to gain from an agreement in services also took Itamaraty by surprise. Used to making speeches about how the international division of labour jeopardized the LDCs, and accusing the US of trying to use an international agreement in services to perpetuate the situation of poverty of LDCs, Itamaraty saw itself in a difficult situation. To admit that Brazil had something to gain, at least in some sectors from an agreement in services, would imply a serious review of many principles and guidelines that had determined the attitude of Itamaraty for many years. In particular, it would be very difficult for Itamaraty to refuse to sign an agreement on services if Brazil had something to gain from it, and even more so, if it benefited the Brazilian firms. Some Construction, Engineering and Design (CED) firms, and Rede Globo, a Brazilian firm in the audiovisual sector, supported the view that Itamaraty should be willing to offer to open Brazil's market in that sector, if it was included in a final agreement in services.[193]

Conclusion: Brazil changed its perception of the GATT

The main conclusion that can be drawn from this chapter is that domestic factors did have an influence on the Brazilian position in the GATT. Due to the peculiar 'division of labour or functions' existent in Brazil, the decisions concerning domestic trade policies were taken by economic ministries and decisions relating to international trade policy, such as the adherence of Brazil to international agreements like the Code of Subsidies, were decided by Itamaraty. The latter also makes decisions regarding Brazil's participation in economic conferences. This is the case because, according to Brazilian law, Itamaraty has the monopoly on Brazilian representation abroad.[194]

Therefore the discussions which occur inside Itamaraty help to explain the position of the Ministry abroad. Of course, if there is a change in Brazil's position in an international organization abroad it is expected that there is a change in the position of Itamaraty. There must be an agreement between the view which prevails at Itamaraty in Brasilia, and in the Missions maintained by Brazil abroad. When this is not the case, as during the period between 1986 and 1988 concerning the Brazilian Mission in Geneva, there must be a kind of compromise otherwise one side will have to alter its original point of view. If the Mission abroad has a different position from the Secretariat of State in Brasilia, the main negotiator may be replaced by a new one with clear instructions to adopt new directions. This is what explains the replacement of Batista in 1987 by Ricupero.

Intellectuals play an important role in perpetuating old values and ideologies. However, in the Brazilian case, the arrival of a new generation of intellectuals formed abroad - in particular in the US - and thus with an international view, helped to develop a discussion about protectionism and trade policies in general. Although this group did not have a direct influence on Brazil's position in Geneva, since GATT was not a subject of internal debate, they did contribute to breaking the domestic consensus against imports and in favour of protectionism which had prevailed in Brazil until the 1980s. They also emphasized the growing cost to Brazil of keeping its markets closed.

One of the main factors which opened the discussion about protectionism and industrial policy in Brazil was the Law on IT. For the first time Brazilian consumers could note how protectionism could have a direct influence on their way of life. The growing awareness of consumers that they had to pay more for a product of lower quality continuously undermined support for the Law of IT. In the end, public opinion in Brazil towards the Law changed from unanimous support when it was adopted to strong criticism when the expectations were not met and results failed to materialize. Members of Parliament were of no great consequence in explaining Brazil's position in the GATT, but they were very important actors in the outcome of the power struggle in Brasilia.

In the last instance, it can be said that the group led by Tarso had the support of the President of the Republic to assume control, remain in power and impose its view. The last victory of this group was the removal of Batista and his replacement by Ricupero, a diplomat of great political skills, who had absolutely no technical experience in the field. It was the first time since the GATT was created that Itamaraty sent an inexperienced man to head Brazil's negotiations in the Uruguay Round.[195]

Certainly external factors also contributed to the change in Brazil's position. Among them the most important is probably the threat of sanctions by the US. The US threatened to use sanctions on the matter of Brazil's Law of IT - unsuccessfully - and also against the lack of software protection - very successfully. In the field of IPRs the results of the use of sanctions were certainly achieved by the US, since IPRs had been approved by the Brazilian Parliament. There is no doubt that Brazil's position on IPRs in the Uruguay Round changed because of the use of sanctions.[196]

However, in services, the threat of sanctions by the US, in particular the threat of removing Brazil from the US General System Preferences (GSP) had the effect of strengthening the group led by Tarso, who favoured conducting negotiations with the US. Thus, the threat of sanctions by the US increasingly isolated the nationalist group led by Batista, but did not affect the negotiations directly in a first stage. However, sanctions should not be considered the only external factor which had an influence on Brazil's change in the Uruguay Round. Other factors, such as the threat by the US of the creation of a Super-GATT without Brazil and the need felt by Itamaraty for a set of multilateral rules to govern international trade in services, were also important. Moreover, with the emergence of a new group in power within Itamaraty after 1987 there was also a significant change in Brazil's perception of the world. First of all, this group led by Tarso did not see the US as an enemy of Brazil. Some of its members had lived in the US as diplomats and had a profound admiration for the US industrial power. They did not see the GATT as an instrument created by DCs to exploit LDCs. They saw the GATT as a forum for negotiations, where all actors could win. As a result, it can be said that they did not regard trade negotiations as a zero sum game, as the group led by Batista did. There was also a perception that as all countries had changed their original positions, Brazil should not be afraid of doing so as well. Indeed the US, for instance, accepted that national laws would be respected and that the goal of an agreement on services should not be trade liberalization. Liberalization would only be a means of achieving development and trade growth.

This kind of flexibility displayed by the US had to be reflected in Brazil's position too. Furthermore, Itamaraty realized that its concerns about sovereignty and respect for national law, and about rights of establishment of foreign firms had no foundation. Brazil's position became more flexible and Brazilian negotiators adopted a more constructive approach to the negotiations. The participation of Brazilian firms and other agencies at the end of the process also eased the path to an agreement since they could discuss any technical subject more easily with their foreign counterparts. Subjects that could have had an explosive impact in Brazil, such as liberalization of FDI, could be discussed without any of the ideological constraints that some Brazilian negotiators had.

End Notes

1. The main daily newspapers sell around 500,000 copies. The number is declared by the newspapers. According to Wilkie, Brazil had around 322 daily newspapers in 1986 (against 1,657 in the US). Moreover, most of them had only a local circulation. A proof of this fact is that circulation in Brazil was equivalent to 48 PTI in that year, less than one fifth of the US, which was 259 (PTI). The consumption of daily newspaper in Brazil in 1989 was only 2.5kg/PI, while in the US it was 52kg/PI. Wilkie, J. (ed.), 1993, *Statistical Abstract of Latin America.* v.30. Los Angeles, UCLA, pp.82-83.

2. This was possible due to TV. Brazil had 25 million TV sets in 1985, which increased to 30 million in 1989. Wilkie, 1993, *op.cit.*, p.92. IBGE estimates that 24,9 million houses in Brazil admitted having a TV set, against 9,3 million who

denied having one. BRAZIL. IBGE., 1991, *Anuário Estatístico*. Rio de Janeiro, IBGE. p.377. IBGE also found out that 43 million husbands or wives watch TV (against 15 million who do not watch it), while only 19,6 million read newspapers, against 38,7 million who do not read them (IBGE, 1991, *op.cit.* p.445). Data for 1989.

3. Nau, H., 1989, "Bargaining in the Uruguay Round". In Finger, J.M., & Olechowski, A. (eds.), *The Uruguay Round. A Handbook on the Multilateral Trade Negotiations*. Washington, IBRD. p.23.

4. In 1986 about 140.000 computers were sold in Brazil. In 1987, it is estimated that more than 100.000 computers were sold (Wilkie, 1993, *op.cit.*, p.97). The sales of smuggled computers were not less than that amount.

5. US was supporting sanctions against Brazil because the law did not reduce support for IT policy at first. However, later on, the political and economic costs of the law started to exceed its perceived benefits. See: Bastos, 1992, *The Interplay of Domestic and Foreign Political Constraints on the Information Policy of Brazil*. Maastricht, United Nations University/ Institute for New Technologies. pp.14-15.

6. Many Brazilian intellectuals and professors had studied in the US in the 1970s and the 1980s. As a result, they understood the US position better and some academics even sympathized with it.

7. The role of these US intellectuals trained was important because they turned the debate along less ideological lines, and they refused to put the dispute in terms of Brazil versus US. The main critic of the protectionist measures in Brazil was R. Campos, a Member of the Brazilian Parliament and a widely known economist.

8. For a synthesis of the discussion. see: Martone, C. and Braga, C., 1988, *Brazil and the Uruguay Round*. São Paulo, FIPE/USP.

9. If the President had sent a new draft-law to Congress it would seem a capitulation from Brazil, which did not interest either party. The US and Brazil worked inside three parameters: 1) non-renewal of the law after 1992; 2) flexible application and 3) non extension of the reserve to other sectors. Bastos, 1992, *op.cit.* p.15 and Odell, 1992, International Threats and Internal Politics: Brazil, the European Community and the United States. In Evans, P. & Jacobson, H. & Putnam, R. (eds.) *International Bargaining and Domestic Politics: An Interactive Approach*. Berkeley, University of California Press.

10. Ibid.

11. The rationale was the same: infant industry argument.

12. The Midterm Review of the Uruguay Round Negotiations. See GATT, *Focus*, January/February 1989.

13. At this point, Brazil's position had already changed in Geneva. Batista had already been removed from Geneva and replaced by Ricupero. See Chapter 1.

14. See: Flecha de Lima, Paulo Tarso, 1991, "The Multilateral Trade Negotiations and Brazilian Trade-Policy Reform". in Shepherd, G. & Langoni, C. (eds.).

Trade Reform: Lessons from Eight Countries. San Francisco, ICS Press (pp. 11-14).

15. Flecha de Lima, 1991, *op.cit.*, p.11.
16. Confidential interview with a Brazilian Ambassador.
17. An example is Brazil's initial position on tariffs, where it refused to offer any tariff concession. See Brazil.MRE., 1988a, *O Contexto de Acessos a Mercados na Rodada Uruguay*. Brasilia, MRE.
18. Confidential interview with a Brazilian Ambassador.
19. Finlayson, J. & Weston, A., 1990, *Middle Powers in the International System*. Ottawa, North-South Institute. p.40.
20. See Batista's version of the alliance in Tachinardi, 1991, *A Guerra das Paten-tes. O Conflito Brasil x EUA sobre Propriedade Intellectual*. São Paulo, Paz e Terra.
21. See Bastos 1992, *op.cit.*, p.15, about articles in the press putting the protection-ist policies into question.
22. For the evolution of the structure of Itamaraty, see Brazil. MRE., 1989, *Re-latório*. Brasilia, MRE.
23. An example of this was the creation of the Under-Secretariat of Economic Af-fairs, headed by Barbosa, supporter of Tarso.
24. Bastos, 1992, *op.cit.*, p.34.
25. See Kennedy, J. & Fonseca, R., 1989, "Brazilian Trade Policy and the Uruguay Round. In Nau, H.(ed.), *Domestic Trade Policies and the Uruguay Round*. New York, Columbia University, p.41.
26. Ibid.
27. See GATT Documents. Communications from Brazil.
28. See: Batista, 1987, *op.cit.*
29. See Chapter 4.
30. See Batista, 1987, *op.cit.*
31. Confidential interview with a GATT official.
32. Confidential interview with a Brazilian Ambassador.
33. See Batista in Tachinardi, 1993, *op.cit.* (Appendix).
34. Confidential interview with a Brazilian diplomat.
35. Confidential interview with a Brazilian diplomat. The Brazilian Mission in Ge-neva represents Brazil both in the GATT and in the United Nations.
36. See GATT Documents. Communications from Brazil. 1987/1988.
37. See Chapter 5.
38. See Ricupero, R., 1988, *Brasil e o Comércio International*. Brasilia, MRE.
39. See Ricupero, 1991, *op.cit.*
40. A history of Brazil in the GATT is beyond the scope of this book.
41. See Declaration of Nogueira in Tachinardi, 1993, *op.cit.*
42. See Chapters 2, 3 and 4. This blocking strategy is considered here as non-cooperative behaviour.
43. A complete victory for the US would be the launching of the Round with serv-

ices under GATT aegis, and no commitment to ending the MFA, VERs or roll-back. The Super-GATT would be the second best solution for the US and an absolute defeat Brazil.

44.   According to the perspective of the pro-UNCTAD group.

45.   Confidential interview with a Brazilian Ambassador.

46.   See Finlayson, J. & Weston, A., 1990, *Middle Powers in the International System*. Ottawa, North-South. p.XI.

47.   Confidential interview with a Brazilian Ambassador.

48.   See; Higgott, J. & Cooper, A., 1990, Middle Powers Leadership and Coalition Building: Australia, the Cairns Group and the Uruguay Round. In *International Organization 44*(3): pp. 589-632.

49.   Oxley, 1990, *The Challenge of Free-Trade*. London, Harvester Wheatsheaf. p.70.

50.   Ibid. Oxley, *op.cit.*, p.70.

51.   Confidential interview with a Brazilian Ambassador.

52.   Interview of Ruy Nogueira, Itamaraty's spokesman with Maria Tachinardi, from *Gazeta Mercantil* 15/09/1986. He said that Brazil had same interests in a new Round, because its foreign trade is extensive (about US$ 42 billion) and Brazil needs more and more market liberalization (market access).

53.   Ibid.

54.   Wilkie, 1993, *op.cit.*, pp.850-852. Data for 1985. In 1990 US accounted for 23.4% of Brazil's exports and the EU, 30.9%.

55.   See GATT. Secretariat., 1993a, *Brazil. Policy Trade Review Mechanism*. Report by the Secretariat. Geneva, GATT.

56.   The rationale for this process is that the importer sees its supplier as unstable and he looks for another 'safer' supplier.

57.   See Brazil's Communications after 1988 in the GNS.

58.   In 1984 a law was approved authorizing the US President to sign bilateral free-trade arrangements. In 1985 the US-Israel Free Trade Agreement was approved. A treaty with Canada followed.

59.   Aho, M. & Aronson, J., 1986, *Trade Talks: America Better Listen*. New York, Council on Foreign Affairs. p.123.

60.   Aho, 1986, *op.cit.*, p.131. Aho affirmed that in 1985 Reagan proclaimed that he had authorized U.S. negotiators to explore regional or bilateral agreements with other countries.

61.   This can be noted through a comparison of content of Brazilian communications to the GATT from 1985 to 1991.

62.   Batista, P.N., 1987, Trade in Services: Brazil's Perspective on the Negotiating Process. In *Sela Capitulos 16*. p.61.

63.   Chapter 4.

64.   Whalley, J.(ed.), 1989, *Developing Countries and the Global Trading System. Thematic Studies from a Ford Foundation Project*. (v.1). London, Macmillan. p.1.

65.   Cornford, 1993, "Some implications for banking of the Draft General Agreement on Trade in Services of December 1991." In *UNCTAD Review* n.4. p.32.

66.   Hussain, A., 1992, *The Chinese Economic Reforms in Retrospect and Prospect*. London, LSE.

67.   See Jackson S., 1992, *Chinese Enterprise Management: Reforms in Economic Perspective*. Berlin/New York, W. de Gruyter.

68.   Byrd, W., 1991, *The Market Mechanism and Economic Reform in China*. Armonk, Sharpe.

69.   See: Li, H., 1991, *Sino-Latin American Economic Relations*. New York, Praeger.

70.   See the interview in the Brazilian Magazine *VEJA* n.527 of February 1991. pp.1-4.

71.   Recent studies have suggested that the Brazilian industry can benefit from the end of the MFA. See for instance: Hamilton, C., 1990, *Textiles Trade and Developing Countries: Eliminating the Multi-fibre Arrangement in the 1990s*. Washington, IBRD.

72.   Both ISI and Infant Industry argument reject the principles of free-trade.

73.   Adam, W. & Brock, W., 1993, *Adam Smith Goes to Moscow: a Dialogue on Radical Reform*. Chichester (Sussex), Princeton University.

74.   Brazil has a very strong socialist party(PT). For Russia-Latin America relations, see Varas, A., 1991, *De la Komintern a la Perestroika: America Latina y URSS*. Buenos Aires, FLACSO.

75.   Brabant, J., 1991, *Economic Reforms in Centrally Planned Economies and their Impact on the Global Economy*. London, Macmillan.

76.   The differences between economic reforms in Eastern Europe and Latin America are in: Pereira, L.; Maravall, J. & Przeworski, A., 1993, *Economic Reforms in new Democracies: a Social-Democratic Approach*. Cambridge, Cambridge University Press, and Przeworski, A., 1991, *Democracy and the Market: Political and Economic Reforms in Eastern Europe and Latin America*. Cambridge, Cambridge University Press.

77.   This was possible because the group led by Tarso took control of the Secretariat of Administration of Itamaraty, which was in charge of promoting and removing diplomats from their positions.

78.   Data calculated from 1963 to 1969 based on the growth of Korea and Singapore. See IMF, 1994, *IFS Yearbook 1993*. Washington, IMF. p.148.

79.   The average of Korea remained 9% but the average of Singapore increased to around 10.5% per year. IMF, 1994, *op.cit.*, p.148.

80.   The average fell in Singapore to around 7% per year, but it was higher than 8% in Korea. Ibid.

81.   In Industrial countries the average was about 5%, 3% and 2.5% in respectively 1960s, 1970s and 1980s. IMF., 1994, *op.cit.* pp.148-149.

82.   See: Deyo, F., 1987, *The Political economy of the New Asian Industrialism*. Ithaca, N.Y., Cornell University.

83. In 1963, Brazil's exports were US$ 1.4 billion and Korea's exports were US$ 0.087 bi. In 1985, for the first time, Brazil's exports were less than Korea's with US$ 25.6 billion against Korea's exports of US$ 26.4 billion. IMF, 1994, *op.cit.* pp.243 and 452. Exports of merchandises only. If services were included Korea would have even higher exports than Brazil.

84. The GDP of Korea was around US$ 92.9 billion in 1985, while Brazil's was around US$ 227.9 billion. IBRD, 1991, *Trends in Developing Economies.* Washington, IBRD. p.58 and p.306. See also: Colombato, E., 1988, *International Trade: a Comparison of the present situation and prospects for the NICs and Italy: Argentine, Brazil, The Philippines, Hong Kong, Indonesia, Malaysia, Singapore, South Korea and Taiwan.* Turin, Fondazione Giovanni Agnelli.

85. In 1980, Korean GDP was US$ 62,6 bi, while Brazil's GDP was US$ 235,3. In 1990 Korea's GDP was US$ 239,6 bi, while GDP was only US$ 521,6 bi. See IBRD, 1991, *op.cit.*, p.58 and p.306.

86. Chile grew at an average rate of 3.2%, while Brazil grew at an average rate of 2.8% in the 1980s. See IBRD, 1991, *op.cit.*, p.57 and p.108.

87. Chilean GDP was around US$ 25.6 billion in 1980 and US$ 16 billion in 1985. In 1990 it passed the value of 1980 and reached US$ 27.8 billion. IBRD, 1991, *op.cit.*, p.109.

88. Noronha, D., 1993, *GATT, Mercosul & NAFTA.* São Paulo, Observador Legal.

89. See: Pereira, Maravall & Przeworski, 1993, *op.cit.*

90. See Meller, P., 1992, *Latin American Adjustment and Economic Reform: Issues and Recent Experiences.* Geneva, UNCTAD.

91. See Kumar, 1993, Developing countries coalitions in International Trade Negotiations. In Tussie, D,. & Glover, D. *The Developing Countries in the World Trade. Policies and Bargaining Strategies.* Boulder, Lynne Rienner. He says that the disbanding of the G-10 coalition at the Uruguay Round negotiations had an adverse effect on the working of the G-77 at UNCTAD. pp.213-216.

92. See Fukuyama, F., 1992, *The end of History and the last man.* London, Hamish Hamilton.

93. See: Bell, D., 1965, *The End of Ideologies: The Exhaustion of Political Ideas.* Free, Clier Macmillan.

94. Although Tarso was not a free-trader, as mentioned before.

95. Pragmatism is not exclusively Brazilian. See Ming Y., 1993, Pragmatism vs. Ideology: some Reflections on the Cold War Era. In Lundestad, G. & Westad, O. *Beyond the Cold War: New Dimensions on International Relations.* Oslo, Scandinavian University (pp. 39-44).

96. If a question of national interest was involved, the US and ex-USSR never were an isolated voice in international fora, such as the United Nations, if a question of vital national interest was involved.

97. Confidential interview with a Brazilian Ambassador.

98. Itamaraty's lack of confidence may be a result of inertia. Many diplomats mention inertia to explain some positions of Brazil in international fora. Itamaraty is

conservative and traditionalist and difficult to persuade to change its opinions.

99.   Confidential interview with a Brazilian Ambassador.

100.   No country can base its negotiating positions on blocking strategies, because in the long run, the costs outweigh the benefits. The only exception would be in the case of superpowers who do not depend on the support of other countries.

101.   Confidential interview with a Brazilian Ambassador.

102.   Confidential interview with a Brazilian Professor.

103.   Confidential interview with a Brazilian Ambassador. See Chapter 1.

104.   Confidential interview with a Brazilian Ambassador. Maciel had sent its first report about the Meeting of UNCTAD in Santiago (Chile) in the 1970s.

105.   Confidential interview with a Brazilian Ambassador.

106.   Confidential interview with a Brazilian Ambassador. In the 1970s and the 1980s virtually all heads of the Economic department and its divisions supported pro-UNCTAD policies.

107.   A free-trade approach or an Export-Promotion strategy.

108.   As proposed by the model of shared values and beliefs.

109.   The decentralized system which prevails at Itamaraty allows Heads of Departments and Divisions to 'interpret' superior orders.

110.   See for instance: Mantega, G., 1982, *Economia Politica Brasileira*. São Paulo, Paz e Terra.

111.   In Brazil, Friedman and the economists from Chicago, in general, were associated with the military in Chile. They were called derogatively 'Chicago boys'.

112.   Such as the dispute Brazil-US in I.T., in IPRs, and the conflict over whether services should be included in the GATT.

113.   Tarso and his Group always emphasized that they favoured a positive agenda with the US, while Batista and his group were only an obstacle to getting things done. Confidential interviews with two Brazilian Ambassadors.

114.   All the persons interviewed noted that Tarso was seen at Itamaraty as an entrepreneur. Confidential interviews with official from Itamaraty.

115.   See Flecha de Lima, Paulo Tarso, 1991, *op.cit.*

116.   Such as market access, exports of textiles under the MFA and steel under Multi Steel Agreement.

117.   Ibid. Flecha de Lima, Paulo de Tarso, 1991, *op.cit.*

118.   Position also supported by Macmillan, 1989, A Game Theoretical View of International Trade Negotiations: Implication for Less Developed Countries. In Whalley, J.(ed.), *Developing Countries and the Global Trading System. Thematic Studies from the Ford Foundation Project.* v.1. London, Macmillan. p.38. He notes that the size of the market is an important aspect of the bargaining power of any country.

119.   For an analysis of Brazil's attitude in UNCTAD see Nye, J., 1974, "UNCTAD: Poor Nation's Pressure Group". In Cox, R. & Jacobson, H. *Anatomy of Influence: Decision Making in International Organizations.* New Haven, Yale University. (pp.334-370).

120. See the statement of Batista in Tachinardi, 1993, *op.cit.*
121. Tarso comes from the State of Minas Gerais famous in Brazil for its conservatism. The politicians from this region are well-known for the adoption of Machiavellian tactics.
122. Confidential interview with officials from Itamaraty.
123. Confidential interview with a Brazilian Ambassador.
124. See Maciel, 1978, "Brazil's Proposal for the reform of the GATT System. in *The World Economy 1*(2) January.
125. See Oxley, 1990, *The Challenge of Free-Trade*. London, Harvester Wheatsheaf.
126. See Tachinardi, 1993, *op.cit.*, p.240. There was a pact between Brazil and the EC. Brazil would decrease its demands on agriculture, while the EC would support Brazil in services.
127. The service negotiations in the Uruguay Round agreed the creation of the GATS, which is a kind of 'compact' in services.
128. See GATT Documents. TNC.GNS of 1988.
129. The advantages of a service agreement are in OECD, 1989, *Trade in Services and Developing Countries*. Paris, OECD.
130. See Sacerdotti, 1990, *Liberalization of Services and Intellectual Property in the Uruguay Round of the GATT*. Fribourg, University Press Fribourg.
131. For the link of services and the international economy see: Summers, 1985, "Services in the International Economy". In Inman, R. (ed.) *Managing the Service Economy: Prospects and Problems*. Cambridge, Cambridge University Press (pp.27- 48).
132. Batista accepts that a multilateral forum gives more room for manoeuvre. See Tachinardi, 1993, *op.cit.*, p.246.
134. Certainly Batista, as a supporter of Brazil's IT policy, considered that an agreement might jeopardize it.
135. There was only one comprehensive study about services. It was carried out by an Inter-ministerial Group which included members of the Ministries of: Finance, Science and Technology and Economic Planning. Moreover, officials of the National Security Council, of the Brazilian Institute of Intellectual Property (INPI) and of the Trade Department (CACEX) were also present. The objective of the Group, as it can be concluded by its content, was only to make a study of the issue in Brazil. Brazil wanted to learn about its legislations, in order to be able to establish a dialogue with DCs. *Gazeta Mercantil* 4/04/96. In fact, this group only analyzed how Brazilian law would have to be changed in the case of an agreement in services. No economic study was carried out.
136. Interview with Tarso. In Tachinardi, 1993, *op.cit.*, p.234.
137. Bastos noted that only the threat of imposing sanctions by the US in 1988 led to the cancellation of some orders by American buyers (Bastos, 1992, *op.cit.*, p.8).
138. Batista, in Tachinardi, 1993, *op.cit.*, p.245.
139. See Lima, M., 1986, *The Political Economy of Brazilian Foreign Policy: Nuclear Energy, Trade and Itaipú*, Nashville, Vanderbilt University. p.414.

140. Helleiner, 1993, "Protectionism and the Developing Countries" In Salvatore, D.(ed.) *Protectionism and the World Welfare*. Cambridge, Cambridge University Press. p.404.
141. The policy of the U.S. was to withdraw Brazilian and Indian products discreetly from its General System of Preference (GSP).
142. The analysis of Brazil-US dispute in pharmaceutical or in IT lies outside the scope of this study. What is important is only its possible link with the service negotiations. The IT dispute is in Bastos, 1992, *op.cit.* and in Odell, 1991, *op.cit.* and the US-Brazil dispute on pharmaceutical is in Tachinardi, 1993, *op.cit.*
143. See: Bastos, 1992, *op.cit.*, and Odell, 1991, *op.cit.*
144. Due to the approval in 1984 of Brazil's Law on IT which created a market reserve for Brazilian producers of mini computers.
145. In *O Estado de Sao Paulo. 31/03/85* (My translation). The US Deputy representative Michael Smith made this statement in a closed circuit of TV to journalists from Sao Paulo, Caracas, Cidade do Mexico and Sao Jose. It was published by *O Estado de Sao Paulo* in Portuguese in indirect speech. It was translated by the authors, who also took the liberty of rephrasing from indirect to direct speech. Michael Smith also made an indirect link to the situation in the textile sector, which he considered very sensitive.
146. Bastos, 1992, *op.cit.*, p.9.
147. Bastos, 1992, *op.cit.*, p.9.
148. See Bastos, 1992, *op.cit.*, p.6.
149. Bastos, 1992, *op.cit.*, p.8.
150. Odell, 1991, *op.cit.*, p.23.
151. Bastos, 1992, *op.cit.*, p.6.
152. Bastos, 1992, *op.cit.*, p.18.
153. Odell, 1991, *op.cit.*, pp.25-26.
154. Bastos, 1992, *op.cit.*, p.18.
155. Bastos, 1992, *op.cit.*, p.19.
156. Bastos, 1992, *op.cit.*, p.8.
157. Bastos, 1992, *op.cit.*, p.6 has a chronology of the dispute.
158. Based on Tachinardi, 1993, *op.cit.*.
159. Tachinardi, 1993, *op.cit.*, p.110.
160. Ibid.
161. Ibid.
162. Ibid p.111.
163. Odell, 1991, *op.cit.*, p.25.
164. Confidential interview a Brazilian researcher.
165. Tachinardi, 1993, *op.cit.*, p.111.
166. See GATT documents of the GNS of 1988.
167. Kumar, 1993, *op.cit.*, p.210.
168. There was no agreement on the content of the panel. The U.S. wanted the panel

to examine Brazilian legislation on IPRs, and Itamaraty wanted to learn about the US right to use section 301. It was agreed that the panel would examine the compatibility of the US action with the GATT later on. See: Abreu 1993, "Trade Policies and Bargaining in a Heavily Indebted Economy: Brazil. In Tussie & Glover, D. *The Developing Countries in the World Trade. Policies and Bargaining Strategies*. Boulder, Lynne Rienner, p.147.

169. Ibid.
170. Abreu, 1993, *op.cit.*, p.147.
171. Finlayson & Weston, 1990, *op.cit.*, p.34.
172. See Martone, 1988, op.cit., p.36.
173. Odell, 1991, *op.cit.*, pp.24-25.
174. *Folha da Tarde* 10/10/86.
175. Ibid.
176. Tarso declared that the obstructionist position after the launching of the Uruguay Round would lead Brazil nowhere. In Tachinardi 1993, *op.cit.*, p.232.
177. As Curzon & Curzon (1974) have noted, to be influential a country has to take part in the negotiations. Curzon & Curzon, "GATT: Trader's Club". In Cox, 1974, *op.cit.* pp.298-333.
178. See the Declaration launching the Uruguay Round in GATT, 1987, *GATT Activities 1986*. Geneva, GATT.
179. Many Brazilian diplomats interviewed by this author shared the view that the US was not aware of the complexities of the issue he was getting involved with. Interviews n. 5, 18 and 26.
180. Brazil insisted that the objective of the service negotiations were growth and development of LDCs. Balasubramanyam, 1991, "International Trade in Services: The Real Issues". Greenaway, D. *Global Protectionism*. London, Macmillan. p.145.
181. Many EU countries had companies which enjoyed monopoly status, as telecom in France.
182. In this respect the replacement of Batista was fundamental, since he was seen as a troublemaker or a person who creates confusion. Confidential interviews with Brazilian Ambassadors.
183. Brazil had been promised since the beginning of the Round that it did not have to join a final agreement. See Batista, 1987, *op.cit.*, for his view of the negotiations.
184. When Batista was the main negotiator, Tarso's positions were not taken into account in Geneva. This is possible, due to the decentralized system which prevails at Itamaraty, and due to support for Batista from the head of Divisions in the Economic Department at Itamaraty. Confidential interview with a Brazilian Ambassador.
185. The view of Batista is that Brazil supported the Uruguay Round as part of the process of alignment with the US. This position is rejected here because it is based on ideological premises only and does not take into account possible

gains Brazil could have with a service agreement. See: Tachinardi, 1993, *op.cit.*, p.244.

186.   About Brazil's reservations towards GATT see: Maciel, 1979, *op.cit.*, p.15.

187.   Hoekman, 1993a, *Developing Countries and the Uruguay Round: Negotiation on Services.* Washington, IBRD. He says that Brazil accepted a broad definition of service in exchange for the adoption of a positive list.

188.   This also defended Itamaraty from domestic criticism that it had adhered to U.S. positions. The acceptance of national goals allowed Brazil to keep its industrial policies in IT, for instance.

189.   Except in some sectors such as telecom, IT and oil.

190.   Balasubramanyam, 1991, *op.cit.*, discusses these concepts.

191.   Confidential interview with a Brazilian diplomat.

192.   After 1988, when officials from other Ministries and from the private sector joined the technical negotiations, Itamaraty lost some of its influence and the benefits of liberalization could be seen more clearly. Confidential interview with officials from Itamaraty.

193.   Confidential interviews with Brazilian diplomats.

194.   Kennedy, J. & Fonseca, R., 1989, Brazilian Trade Policy and the Uruguay Round. In NAU, H. (ed.), *Domestic Trade Policies and the Uruguay Round.* New York, Columbia University. pp.29-43.

195.   This point was stressed by an anonymous source, to whom the author is most grateful. Confidential interview with a Brazilian diplomat.

196.   See Tachinardi, 1993, *op.cit.*

6.   Summary and Conclusions

Summary

This book proposes that Brazil had an aversion to the GATT until the 1980s. In Brazil, the perception of the Ministry of Foreign Affairs was that the GATT was a 'rich men's club'. This perception of Itamaraty, wrong as it might be, was the main individual factor for explaining Brazil's refusal to discuss services under the umbrella of the GATT or in the Uruguay Round.

Chapter One gave an overall view of the preliminary discussions on services before the launching of the Uruguay Round. It began with the discussions at the 1982 Ministerial Meeting and continued until the GATT Meetings of 1985. It was concluded that Batista's radical opposition to the discussion of services prevailed. He successfully managed to delay the launching of a new Round for a couple of years. The opposition of Batista also had some irrational elements. Batista refused to prepare any study about Brazil's service sector or about the impact of trade liberalization in services for Brazil's economy as a whole. This fact put Brazilian negotiators in a very difficult position, since they did not know the impact of what they were negotiating.

In Chapter Two, the book discussed the Decision Making Process (DMP) at Itamaraty. The best model to characterize Itamaraty's DMP is the single agency model, since Itamaraty prevails over other agencies in Brazil, on international trade policy issues. However, Itamaraty followed a pattern set by previous experience and repeated past ideological behaviour. For this reason we concluded that shared beliefs and values were also an important feature of Brazil's DMP in international trade policy.

The book also noted that the DMP of Itamaraty is highly hierarchical, though it is very decentralized as well. Thus, the role played by individuals in the outcome of the process becomes very important. This means that although the system is based, in principle, on a hierarchy, in practice it is possible for individuals to impose their views on the DMP. This was the case with Brazil's representative in the GATT, Batista. He did not follow instructions in their entirety, and finally he was invited to vacate his position as Brazilian Ambassador to the GATT. We also demonstrated in Chapter Two how the General Secretary of Itamaraty, and *'de facto'* Minister of Foreign Affairs, Paulo Tarso, took control of the apparatus of Itamaraty through the nomination of individuals of his group to the most important positions in the Ministry. He exploited his position as General Secretary of Administration to do so. It was control of this key position that made it possible to *convince* Batista to leave Geneva to represent Brazil in the United Nations in New York. The control of Itamaraty by Tarso was the main explanation for Brazil's sudden conversion to free-trade after 1988.

Chapter Two also discussed Brazil's participation in coalitions in the Uruguay Round. We described the purposes of the main coalitions of which Brazil was a member. These are the Latin American Group, the Brazilian-Indian Alliance, and the Group of 10 (the G-10). The G-10 was very narrow in terms of membership, since it included only LDCs. The G-10 aimed to abolish trade barriers in the field of clothing and textiles, and in the agricultural sector. The G-10 also adopted an obstructionist position to the inclusion, or even the discussion, of services in the new Round. In the Uruguay Round, the G-10 used filibuster tactics to delay the discussions about trade liberalization in services. It was found that Batista was the mentor of the G-10. Basically, Batista saw the G-10 as a mechanism to try to impose his views in the trade negotiations. The Cairns Group, on the other hand, only sought trade liberalization in agriculture. However, Batista had ideological reservations against the Cairns Group because it included DCs and LDCs. Only when Batista relinquished the position as Brazil's Ambassador to the GATT, and was replaced by Ricupero, could Brazil take full part in the Cairns Group.

Chapter Three summarized the launching of the Uruguay Round at Punta del Este (1986). It also discussed in more detail the reasons which Brazil used that opposed the discussion of services and their inclusion in the new Round. For analytical purposes only, these arguments were divided into political, technical, legal and economic ones. However, it was shown that they were in fact a smoke screen for Batista's personal aversion to the discussions of services in the Uruguay Round and the introduction of services in the GATT. At the end of the Punta del Este Ministerial Meeting, Brazil managed to include a dual-track system, where services would be discussed formally outside the GATT aegis.

Chapter Four described the evolution of Brazil's position in the Uruguay Round. It demonstrated how Brazil after 1988, when Ricupero became Brazil's representative in the GATT, Itamaraty started to adopt a more constructive position in the multilateral trade negotiations. It outlined the development of the negotiations from the Brazilian, Indian and the US perspectives. The presence of members of the Brazilian private sector in Geneva was positive because they could realize that they did not need to fear the GATT negotiations. Chapter Five described the reasons for the changes in the Brazilian position. It is divided into two parts: the domestic reasons (Part I), and the external reasons. The domestic reasons were divided into cultural, political, economic and internal (from the DMP of Itamaraty itself). Externally, we mentioned many factors which may have affected Brazil's position, such as the threat by the US of plurilateral solutions (a Super GATT), sanctions, changes in the international political environment, etc. No less important was the perception of Itamaraty that it was in Brazil's best interest to support a multilateral agreement to prevent future unilateral action from the US (Section 301 and Super 301).

Under a Brazilian perspective, the change in Itamaraty's position during the Uruguay Round seemed to be the most interesting episode of that Round, after forty years of strong support for protectionism. For this reason, we will discuss in more detail the main lessons to be drawn from Brazil's conversion to free-trade. Before that, we shall see what happened to the Uruguay Round.

The Uruguay Round

In the 1988 Mid-Term Review at Montreal, Brazil formally agreed with the principles which would guide a future agreement in services. This represented a U-turn in Itamaraty's initial opposition to discussing services. After the Montreal Meeting, the service negotiations advanced quite quickly, more rapidly than most analysts would expect. It advanced more quickly than in many other sectors of the Uruguay Round, such as Intellectual Property Rights and Agriculture. The only problem which happened in the service negotiations were caused, surprisingly, either by the US itself or by the EC. The US refused to liberalize further its market of telecom, because the US considered that it was necessary that the EC liberalized its market first. Special interests also put strong pressure on the US government not to liberalize its maritime rules to allow the access of foreign companies. On the other hand, the US was disappointed with the proposals of trade liberalization by other countries/areas, in particular by the EC, in the field of financial services and insurance. This led the US government to talk about *conditional MFN*, which would go against the principles and foundations of the GATT. Needless to say that this caused a strong reaction from the trade negotiators and the US withdrew the 'offer' (or the threat). Also, some shortcomings occurred in the field of audiovisual trade, where the US could not convince the EC - due to French pressure - to withdraw the subsidy and quotas linked to cultural productions.

Despite these shortcomings, there was a kind of *understanding* in services. The main block to a final agreement was definitely agriculture. The lack of agreement in agriculture in what was supposed to be the final meeting of the Uruguay Round led to a paralysis of the trade negotiating process. To overcome the deadlock, Dunkel prepared a draft proposal with what was considered to be the 'bottom' proposals of each unit/country. This was the Draft Final Act (DFA), submitted by Dunkel at the end of 1991. Brazil accepted the DFA immediately after its formal submission by Dunkel. This showed Brazil's new commitment to trade multilateralism, and apparently to free-trade. However, the DFA was rejected by the EC (read France), and the US had to enter into parallel discussions with the EC to find a common position. Only at the end of 1993, after more than two years of discussions between the EC and US and many threats of sanctions by the US, did the EC accept a new agreement to replace the agricultural section of the DFA. This agreement was called 'Blair House'. In spite of the support of the EC to the 'Blair House' agreement, France continued to reject it. As a result, it was necessary to 'clarify' the agreement to please France. In fact the 'clarifications' of the 'Blair House', change in the year used as a basis and the limit of export subsidies, were almost equivalent to a new Agreement. But the 'clarifications' allowed France, and as a result, the EC, to support the signature of the Uruguay Round. The position of Brazil was that the DFA was not a perfect document, but it was what could be achieved and Itamaraty was very happy with it. As a result, Itamaraty would support it as it was submitted. However, if each country requested new negotiations, Itamaraty would ask to open new negotiations as well.

Conclusions

On the issue of the changes in the Brazil's position , which is the main aim of this book, many conclusions can be drawn.

Domestically, the arrival of a generation of intellectuals who were trained in the US started to lend a new insight to the issue of protectionism and ISI policies. This new elite did not hesitate to question existing dogmas, such as ISI policies and infant industry arguments. The right to diverge from prevailing views received a boost with the end of the military regime in Brazil. Military rule in Brazil (1964-1985) had been characterized by extreme protectionist measures and a deepening of the ISI process. An increase in the discussion of the objectives and goals of Brazilian society following the military rule, placed in question many dogmas, the most important of which was the cost of protectionism. Brazilians became more critical of the values shared by its old elite. In fact, the Brazilian elite itself came to question more, and the press started to play a more important role and to discuss not only values but also practices and ideologies, such as the consensus view which opposed imports. These later policies had become part of the state's apparatus, particularly within the Brazilian bureaucracy. With the departure of the military from power in 1985, an era of Brazilian history ended and the search for a new economic model became apparent. This new model would probably have to reflect the emerging pluralism that was a characteristic of Brazilian society.

During the Sarney Administration there was an intense debate in the press about alternative models of development. LDCs which were recording an impressive economic performance, such as the Asian Tigers in Southeast Asia, Mexico and Chile in Latin America, not to mention China, were often mentioned as possible models for Brazil. However, the more important aspect is that a new mentality was being developed within Brazilian society which would probably be reflected in the state apparatus.

Another reason for change in Brazil's position was political. Some groups within the Brazilian economy, in particular exporters, became more active in the 1980s and this resulted in a realignment of domestic forces which had previously opposed imports. This group became more vocal and supported concessions to the US in the area of IT. But, more importantly, they started to put pressure on Brazil's decision-makers in order to abandon ISI policies. Therefore, their view had to be considered in the decision-making process in trade policy.

However, the economic aspect is also important to explain the change in Itamaraty's position in the Uruguay Round. If Brazil wanted to service its debt it had to export more in order to obtain a trade surplus. Brazil faced two main obstacles to increasing exports. First, Brazilian products were losing competitiveness abroad due to the lack of imports of modern and efficient infra-structure equipment, in telecoms and computers to mention but two examples. This obstacle could be solved simply by increasing Brazilian imports. Second, Brazil was facing difficulty increasing its exports because markets in DCs were becoming less open due to domestic protectionist pressures in those countries. This was particularly true for Brazilian exports of steel, orange juice and shoes. Therefore, it would be extremely difficult for Brazil to increase its exports to other countries without opening its market (for both goods and services) to imports of DCs. The result of the accumulation of these domestic factors was the end of the nationalist consensus which had prevailed from the 1940s to the 1970s. In short the consensus against imports dictated that imports were basically bad and should be replaced by domestic production. In other words, the ISI process in Brazil collapsed at the end of the 1970s, or perhaps even before.

However, external factors also contributed to undermine the nationalist consensus against imports and, as a result, to change Brazil's position in the GATT. First, Brazil was becoming isolated in the GATT system. Since Brazil had been defeated on the issue of whether services should be introduced in the GATT, Itamaraty had only two options. The first was for Brazil to try to participate in the discussions which were taking place in the Uruguay Round in a positive way. The second option was to continue to take part in the GATT as it had done from 1947 to 1988 as a country with some influence but which could not increase its bargaining power due to the lack of commitment to free-trade. This was the free-rider option. However, it appeared that the free-rider option would imply a growing cost for Brazil that it was not prepared to pay - for instance complete isolation on trade negotiations, as had happened in the Kennedy and the Tokyo Rounds. In this sense, the Uruguay Round would repeat Brazil's experience in the two previous Rounds. Also, the changes in Eastern Europe taught Brazil a hard lesson. There was only one viable economic system in the world, and this was the capitalist system. This economic system was based on several principles, among them interdependence, international competition and free-trade. There was no place for autarkies in the world of the 1990s. Brazil suddenly found out that economic nationalism belonged to the nineteenth century. It was necessary to adapt to the new economic reality.

Itamaraty realized that its pro-Third World approach and the support of the G-77 in UNCTAD had been one of the biggest mistakes of Brazilian diplomacy. The dream of a New International Economic Order (NIEO), although still sought, was no nearer by the end of the 1980s than it was in the 1960s, when the UNCTAD was created. Itamaraty also abruptly noted at the end of the 1980s that all Brazilian international economic diplomacy - based in the Group of 77 and eventually in the Group of 10 in the GATT - had been ineffective in achieving its goals. If the objective of Brazilian diplomacy had been to create a NIEO it failed. Likewise, if Itamaraty's goal was to improve Brazil's participation in the world economy it also fell short of achieving it, since Brazil was still accounted responsible for a very low proportion of world trade.

Moreover, Itamaraty would have to establish its own goals in its foreign economic diplomacy, outside and independent of the G-77. Brazil's international trade interests had much more in common with those of the Cairns Group and the US, in cereals trade for instance, than with most LDCs from Africa. Brazil would have to abandon its pro-LDCs rhetoric and work together with DCs when Brazil's interests so required. This would demand a more creative diplomacy and the establishment of new alliances. This already happened in the Uruguay Round, when Brazil joined the Cairns Group, a coalition of grain exporters. All the above mentioned factors seem to have played a significant role in changing Itamaraty's perspective on international trade questions. They certainly contributed to the decrease in the significance of the nationalist consensus bias against imports and to the critical reappraisal of ISI.

From a theoretical point of view, this book has come to some important conclusions. First, it seems that middle powers have some influence in trade negotiations. This confirms the work of Higgott & Cooper (1990) in Australia and Canada, which was elaborated in Cooper, Higgott & Nossal (1993). Similar work has been carried out for Canada and the Nordic Countries by Pratt and demonstrated similar results.[1] This book suggests, however, that the influence of middle powers is not limited to DCs, but also applies to LDCs, such as Brazil. This also confirms the pioneering work of Curzon & Curzon (1974) and of Finlayson & Weston (1990) on Middle Powers and the International System.

This book contributes to filling a gap which Cooper, Higgott and Nassal (1993) identified in their study of middle powers. This thesis, however, goes beyond the study of Brazil's participation in the Uruguay Round to analyze how Brazil's participation affected the outcome of the negotiations in a specific field: trade in services. We consider that it is necessary to use both a neo-realist and neo-liberal approach to understand the change in Brazil's stance in the Uruguay Round. Neo-realist theory, for example, the work of Krasner (1985), explains why Brazil opposed the introduction of services in the Uruguay Round. However, we argue that he fails to explain the change in Brazil from one of opposition to acceptance. Neo-realist theory supposes that changes in power, or the use of power by the hegemony, the US, through sanctions, is the main explanation. Nevertheless, it seems that sanctions only partially explain the change in Brazil's position. We suggest, based on the concept of perceptions and expectations, as suggested by Keohane (1984), that Brazil changed its position mainly due to domestic factors, including the Decision Making Process of the agency which represents Brazil abroad: Itamaraty. In fact, Brazil's position in the GATT has changed for many reasons, one of which is cultural: the collapse of the nationalist consensus against imports which was reflected in the change in Itamaraty's position.

The main conclusion which can be drawn from a study of Brazil's participation in the GATT is that the single most important explanation for Itamaraty's change of position was internal: its decision-making process. This contradicts neorealist theories which assume that the position of a country should reflect the distribution of international power. However, to discuss Itamaraty's Decision-Making Process one should be able first to answer the following question: how could a country maintain an ISI policy, if the signs of its failure were apparent for so long? This is a complex question since it involves different perceptions and notions of the common good.

Brazilian society has always analyzed the advantages of protecting its industries in terms of jobs and production. The social and economic costs of protectionism were never studied. Likewise, the increasing cost that Brazilian consumers had to pay for domestic products when cheaper imported products were available was never considered a relevant factor for decision-makers.[2] The ISI process enjoyed the support of economists, influential politicians, army officers and well-placed diplomats. They managed to keep the Brazilian economy partially isolated from the world economy. The concept of autarky and infant industry also received the support of intellectuals and gained respectability in academic circles. As a result, an inward-looking mentality was developed in Brazilian society. The consequences of this inward-looking approach were negative for Brazilian consumers, since they would be the main beneficiaries of trade liberalization. Furthermore, the ISI process also created a difficult network to defeat. The industries created during the ISI process, for instance, became strong supporters of protectionist measures. Tariffs guarantee a high rate of profits to the companies that operate inside the Brazilian economy, without mentioning the fact that they were free from foreign competition.

In the Brazilian society process these companies were very influential and used all their bargaining power to prevent trade liberalization. However, since this book explores Brazil's position in the GATT, it placed more emphasis on the role played by Itamaraty. First, it seems that Itamaraty did not perceive the advances made by the Asian Tigers. The process of trade liberalization in those countries was quite visible in the 1970s and while Brazil's participation was constant or even declining, their market share in world trade was steadily increasing. Instead of deepening these contacts, Itamaraty chose to increase its contacts with African countries, because this was considered to be politically more rewarding.

Secondly, Batista, and the Group pro-UNCTAD at Itamaraty, overestimated the prospects of UNCTAD acting as a forum to discuss services. Although it is necessary to recognize that there were voices in Itamaraty raised against the concentration of efforts in UNCTAD, such as Ambassador Maciel's, the fact that the two former Ministers of Foreign Affairs (Azeredo da Silveira and Saraiva Guerreiro) were strong supporters of UNCTAD did not help advance the negotiations in GATT.

Thirdly, Brazil with the G-10 (in the 1980s) repeated the same errors it had committed in the G-77 in the 1960s and the 1970s. Brazil allied itself in the G-10 with countries which had completely different economic, political and trade interests. The only common goal was to try to prevent the introduction of new issues in the GATT. No study was carried out to determine Brazil's true interests - trade, economic and political in the long term. Brazil's refusal to conduct a study of its service sector and to analyze the impact of a service liberalization in terms of gains in production and jobs determines the force of ideological factors.

Therefore, it would not be wrong to say that ideology and inertia were important explanations of the Brazilian attitude, since no analysis of costs and benefits to Brazil of such behaviour was ever discussed. This policy cost Brazil a lot in terms of lost political effort and capital in a dispute which Itamaraty could not win. Brazil could not defeat all the DCs. It also had other costs in terms of potential economic and social gains that a trade-off between concessions in services and advantages in goods could have brought.

Itamaraty has learnt important lessons about the rules of the game of international trade. Itamaraty has learnt that the GATT is not based on S&D treatment, unilateral concessions or non-reciprocity, as many in Brazil would like. Quite the contrary, it is based on bargaining and mutual concessions (reciprocity). Although GATT mentions S&D treatment, countries which only relied on it were marginalizing themselves in tariff discussions, as Brazil did between 1947 and 1987. This lack of understanding is not surprising, since the Uruguay Round is the first Round where Brazil's strategy cannot be described as asking solely for S&D treatment for LDCs only.

S&D treatment gave Brazil the bad habit of waiting to benefit from concessions negotiated among DCs, taking advantage of them due to the principle of MFN in the GATT and then asking for S&D not to commit itself to any of the agreed tariff reductions. In short, it acted as a free-rider. This policy seems to have come to an end. Any concession obtained now will depend on concessions granted. Brazil has to be a trade player, whether it likes it or not. Brazil has a big market and can exchange tariff concessions for market access for its products.

Important findings in this book are related to the Decision Making Process (DMP) relating to trade issues. In Brazil external negotiations are a monopoly of Itamaraty and not of the Finance Ministry. It is still very closed and is entirely an issue for Itamaraty in which Congress rarely take part. President Sarney, through lack of experience on trade issues, did not interfere in the trade negotiations in Geneva making the GATT almost an independent domain of Itamaraty. At Itamaraty the process is also concentrated in a few hands, where no more than two or three individuals can impose their view on the trade negotiations, as occurred when Maciel and Batista were Brazil's representatives in Geneva.

The DMP at Itamaraty is extremely decentralized which allows the Brazilian representative to pursue his own views, even when they differ from the directives given by Itamaraty. Batista 'manipulated' the DMP in order to make policy coincide with his personal views. This was possible because he had support from key decision-makers in Brasilia, who held crucial positions in the State apparatus. When this support vanished, due to a process of co-opting support of diplomats by General Secretary Tarso, Batista started to 'interpret' the instructions as he believed they should be read. This shows that the DMP at Itamaraty is extremely subjective, where the influence of an individual diplomat is decisive in determining a certain policy.

The result of five years of obstructionist policy by Itamaraty against the inclusion of services in the GATT prevented a rational discussion about the service sector in Brazil, and its international competitiveness. Brazil, believing it was taking a wise decision, refused to present studies on services. If it had done so, Brazil could have learnt that, if it really wanted to attract FDI, it could also gain from trade liberalization in several service sectors. Examples of these sectors were financial services, telecoms, tourism, audio-visuals, software and CED. Nonetheless, Brazil won a 'victory' at Punta del Este, from Itamaraty's perspective, by separating goods from services. With this dual-track procedure Brazil wanted to prevent concessions in services being exchanged for concessions in goods. The separation had the positive effect of creating rules for services, but on the other hand it created an artificial barrier between trade in services and goods which no longer exist in practice.

However, it is ironic that Brazil's objective was to prevent trade-offs between services and goods whilst by the end of the negotiations, although it was not successful, Brazil was proposing such trade-offs in order to obtain concessions in market access for orange juice.

As suggestion for other studies, I would propose that other researchers concentrate on the issue of trade in services, a subject which has not yet been properly explored. There is only one author in Brazil who has written about this issue, but he adopts a purely economic perspective and does not consider the interplay between politics and concessions which are very important in trade negotiations. This is especially true in the case of Brazil, whose external attitude is based on coalitions or alliances. Brazil's participation in the G-10 and the refusal to accept the inclusion of services in the Uruguay Round almost led to the breakdown of the GATT system. On the other hand, the Cairns Group due to its sectoral interest in agriculture, seemed to attend Brazil's interest better than the G-10. The Cairns Group had also a more constructive approach than the G-10. However, as Batista dismissed the importance of agriculture in Brazil's exports, the role of Brazil in the Cairns Group was initially very limited. Only with the strengthening of Tarso's position as the *de facto* Minister of Foreign Affairs was it possible to alter Brazil's priorities in the Uruguay Round.

Regarding the significance of the threat of sanctions on Brazil's trade policies, it can be considered very powerful and influential when used to gain leverage on specific issues, such as IPRs or on the question of the absence of a law to protect software in Brazil. Sanctions were also important in undermining the consensus against imports which existed in Brazil until the 1980s. However, they were not very effective when used to oppose a national policy, or when there is a consensus against making concessions, as the Law on IT illustrates.

New studies

More studies on the effectiveness of sanctions on Brazil's negotiating position need to be conducted. There are some studies about the case of IT and about pharmaceuticals. However, with the exception of the study of Odell (1993) they fail to include an international perspective of what was happening with other countries. In the case of services, it was difficult to impose sanctions because services are such a broad area that sanctions tend to be less effective. Moreover, the attempts to link negotiations on services with sanctions in IT did not give the expected results.

Another field which warrants more study is the Decision-Making Process in Brazil, in particular in relation to Itamaraty. There is no doubt that Brazil has has a very influential bureaucracy. However, the influence of Itamaraty is surprising for any standard of comparison. It is also necessary to study the reach (and desirability) of such a power. It seems that in the Brazilian case, some controls over the bureaucracy would cause more good than harm. It would be interesting to see in an international comparison how different systems of control of powerful bureacracies have worked in different countries. In the Brazilian case Itamaraty started not only to represent the country but also to formulate policy, which was not its main goal. The lack of existence in Brazil of a Trade Ministry explains how Itamaraty could infiltrate in an area which was originally out of its legal competence.

Another field of study still in need of exploration is the role of middle powers. Brazil, for instance, is a country which has not been analyzed in terms of international economic organizations, such as the GATT, UNC-TAD and IMF. This concentrates in the field of services. It is necessary to develop studies in other areas, such as Intellectual Property Rights, Tariffs, Trade Related Investment Measures, etc.

Furthermore, the studies about middle powers tend to emphasize the role of DC middle powers, such as Canada, Australia and Nordic countries. There are few studies about the roles which LDC middle powers, such as Brazil, India, Mexico, play in international economic negotiations.

End Notes

1. See: Pratt, C. (ed.), 1990, Middle Power Internationalism; The North-South Dimension, Kingston, Mcgill-Queen's University and 1989, Internationalism under Strain: The North-South Policies of Canada, Holland, Norway and Sweden. Toronto, University of Toronto.
2. It was beyond the scope of this thesis to discuss the costs of protectionism. Nevertheless, we do point out that some advantages could be reaped from trade liberalization of services.

Interviewees

1.	Mr. Djalma Abreu	(Official Itamaraty)
2.	Prof. Marcelo de Paiva Abreu	(Brazilian Researcher)
3.	Ms. Sebastiana M. Azevedo	(Itamaraty Official)
4.	Ambassador Rumbem Barbosa	(Brazilian Diplomat)
5.	Ambassador Barthel-Rosa	(GATT Official)
6.	Secretario Luis Balduino Carneiro	(Brazilian Diplomat)
7.	Secretaria Glivania Coimbra	(Brazilian Diplomat)
8.	Secretario Carlos Marcio Condenzey	(Brazilian Diplomat)
9.	Mr. Eduardo Guerra Coutinho	(M.Finance Official)
10.	Dr. Jose Carlos Dias	(Brazilian Researcher)
11.	Dr. Willy Faro	(GATT Official)
12.	Ms. Mariana Ferrer	(Itamaraty Official)
13.	Ambassador Gelson Fonseca	(Brazilian Diplomat)
14.	Mr. Aluisio Tupinamba Gomes	(Itamaraty Official)
15.	Mr. David Hartridge	(GATT Official)
16.	Dr. R. J. Krommenacker	(GATT Official)
17.	Ministro J. Graca Lima	(Brazilian Diplomat)
18.	Ambassador George Maciel	(Brazilian Diplomat)
19.	Mr. Mario Marconini	(GATT Official)
20.	Prof. Dr. Celso Martone	(Brazilian Researcher)
21.	Ministro Pedro L. C. de Mendonca	(Brazilian Diplomat)
22.	Ms. Cassia Moraes	(Official Itamaraty)
23.	Mr. Nusrat Nazeer	(GATT Official)
24.	Ministro Joao Gualberto Porto	(Brazilian Diplomat)
25.	Secretario Victor Luis Prado	(Brazilian Diplomat)
26.	Ambassador M. Raffaelli	(GATT Official)
27.	Ms. Barbara Ribeiro Santana	(Itamaraty Official)
28.	Ambassador John Shakespeare	(British Diplomat)
29.	Ambassador Paulo Tarso Flecha de Lima	(Brazilian Diplomat)
30.	Mr. David Woods	(GATT Official)
31.	Ambassador J. Zutschi	(Indian Diplomat)
32.	Reinaldo Salgado	(Brazilian Diplomat)
33.	Vilmar Coutinho	(Brazilian Diplomat)
34.	Luis Gilberto	(Brazilian Diplomat)

Bibliography

Abreu, M. 1993. Trade Policies and Bargaining in a Heavily Indebted Economy: Brazil. In Tussie, D & Glover, D. The Developing Countries in the World Trade. Policies and Bargaining Strategies. Boulder, Lynne Rienner Publishers. HF 1413 D48.

Abreu, M. 1992. *O Brasil e o GATT*. Rio de Janeiro, Catholic University (PUC)/Economics Dept., 1992.

Abreu, M. 1990. *Brazil - EC Countries: Trade in Services*. Rio de Janeiro, Catholic University (PUC)- Economics Dept.(mimeo).

Abreu, M.P. & Fritsch, W. 1989. Market Access for Manufactured Exports. In Whalley, J. (Ed.). *Developing Countries and the Global Trading System. Thematic Studies from a Ford Foundation Project* (v.1). London, Macmillan, 1989 (112-131).

Abreu, M.P. & Fristch, W. 1988. *Obstacles to Brazilian Export Growth and the Present Multilateral Trade Negotiations*. Paper given at the Conference on Trade Policy and the Developing World. Ottawa, 16-22 August, 1987. Rio de Janeiro, Catholic University (PUC) Economics Dept.

Adler, E. 1987. *The Power of Ideology: the Quest for Technological Autonomy in Argentina and Brazil*. Berkeley, University of California.

Adler, E. 1986. Ideological Guerrillas and the quest for technological autonomy: development of a domestic industry in Brazil. *International Organization* 40 (3).

Agathise, E. 1990. Services and the Development Process: Legal Aspects of Changing Economic Determinants. In *Journal of World Trade 24* (5): 103-113. October.

Aggarwal, V. 1985. *Liberal Protectionism. The Organized Politics of Organized Textiles Trade*. Berkeley, University of California.

Almeida, Paulo Roberto de. 1990. The 'New' Intellectual Regime and its Economic Impact on Developing Countries. In Sacerdoti, G. *Liberalization of Services and Intellectual Property in the Uruguay Round*. Fribourg, University of Fribourg.(74-86).

Arruda, Mauro (Co.) & Ferraz, J.& Roncisvalle, C.A. 1991. *A Internacionalização da Rede Globo. Mudanças Organizacionais e Novas Estratégicas*. Caribe, Cepal (mimeo).

Avery, W. & Rapkin, D. (ed.). 1989. Hegemony and US Foreign Economic Policy in the 'Long Decade' of the 1950s. In Keohane, R. *International Institutions and State paper: Essays in International Relations Theory.* Boulder, Westview.

Baer, M. 1989. *Algumas Notas sobre a Presença do Capital Estrangeiro no Sistema Financeiro Brasileiro.* Rio de Janeiro, MRE. Paper presented at the seminar: Brazil   and   International   Trade   of   Services   organized   by MRE/BNDES/UNCTAD/PNUD/CEPAL in Rio.

Balassa, Bela. 1971. The Structure of Protection in Brazil. In Balassa, Bela.(Ed.) *The Structure of Protection in Developing Countries.* Baltimore, The John Hopkins Press for the IDB.

Balasubramanyam, V. 1991. International Trade in Services: The Real Issues. In Greenfield D. *Global Protectionism.* London, Macmillan. (119-143).

Baldinelli, Elvio. *Argentina y Brasil: Dos Estrategias para la Exportacion.* Buenos Aires, Fundacion de Investigaciones Economicas Latinoamericanas, 1985.

Barboza, M. Gibson. 1992. *Na Diplomacia o Traço todo da Vida.* Rio de Janeiro, Record.

Bastos, M. 1992. *The Interplay of Domestic and Foreign Political Constraints on the Informatics Policy of Brazil.* Maastricht (NH), United Nations University/Institute for New Technologies (UNU/INTECH W.P. n.6).

Batista, P.N. 1987. Trade in Services: Brazil's perspective on the negotiating process. In *Sela Capitulos 16*:61-66.

Berg, T. G. Trade in Services: Towards a Development Road of GATT Negotiations Benefiting both Developing and Industrialized States. In *Harvard International Law Journal 28* Winter 1987.

Bhagwati, J. 1987a. Economic Costs of Trade Restrictions. In Finger, J.M. and Olechowski, A.(Ed.) *The Uruguay Round. A Handbook on the Multilateral Trade Negotiations.* Washington, IBRD.

Bhagwati, J. 1987b. International Trade in Services and its Relevance for Economic Development. In Giarini, Orio. *The Emerging Service Economy.* London, Pergamon Press. (Services World Forum).

Bhagwati, J. 1987c. Services. In Finger, J. & Olechowski, A. (ed.) *The Uruguay Round. A Handbook on the Multilateral Trade Negotiations.* Washington, World Bank.

Bhagwati, J. 1985. *Trade in Services and Developing Countries.* London, LSE. (Xth Annual Geneva Lecture, London School of Economics, 28 November 1985).

Bhagwati, J. 1984. Splintering and Disembodiment of Services: Implications for Developing Countries. In *The World Economy* 7:133-144.

Bhagwati, J. & Ruggie, J. 1984. *Power, Passions and Purposes*. Cambridge (MA), MIT Press.

Bifani, Paolo. 1989. Intellectual Property Rights and International Trade. In UNCTAD. *Uruguay Round: Papers on Selected Issues*. New York, United Nations.

Binmore, K. *Bargaining and Coalitions I*. 1983. London, LSE. (Pamphlet Collection).

Braga, C.A. Primo.1990. Brazil. In Messerlin, P.A. and Sauvant, K.P.(Eds.) *The Uruguay Round: Services in the World Economy*. Washington/New York, The IBRD/UNCTC, 1990.(197-209).

Brams, S. 1990. *Negotiation Games. Applying Game Theory to Bargaining and Arbitration*. New York, Routledge. HD58.6B81.

Brams, S. 1975. *Game Theory and Politics*. London, Free Press/Macmillan.

Brandao, A. & Carvalho, J. 1991. *Trade, Exchange Rate and Agricultural Policies in Brazil*. Washington, IBRD. (The Political Economy of Agricultural Policing. World Bank Comparative Studies n.380/17/2).

Brown, W. 1950. *The United States and The Restoration of the World Trade. An Analysis and an Appraisal of the ITO Charter and the General Agreement on Tariffs and Trade*. Washington, Brooking.

Caldas, R. 1989. *A Política Externa do Governo Kubitschek e a Crise da Estratégia de Aliado Especial*. Brasilia, UnB. MA thesis.

Calvert, P.(Ed). 1991. *Political and Economic Encyclopaedia of South America and the Caribbean*. Harlow(Essex), Longman.

Carter, R. 1990. Insurance. In Messerlin, P. & Sauvant, K. (Eds). *The Uruguay Round: Services in the World Economy*. Washington and New York, The World Bank (IBRD) and United Nations Centre on Transnational Corporations (UNCTC), 1990.

Castro, M. 1992. *Uneven Development and Peripheral Capitalism: The case of Brazilian Informatics*. London, LSE. (PhD Dissertation).

Christopherson, S. & Ball, S. 1989. Media Services: Considerations Relevant to Multilateral Trade Negotiations. In United Nations. UNCTAD. *Trade in Services: Sectorial Issues*. Geneva, UNCTAD, (249-308).

Clark, C. 1957. *The Condition of Economic Progress*. London, Macmillan.

Cleary, D. 1987. *Local Boy Makes Good. José Sarney, Maranhão and the Presidency of Brazil.* Glasgow, University of Glasgow. F2538.22. S. C62.

Clemencon, R. G. 1990. *Perceptions and Interests: Developing Countries and the International Economic System. A Comparative Analysis of Statements Given to Plenary Meetings of UNCTAD in 1976, 1983 and 1987.* Bern, Peter Lang.

Clements, B. 1988. *Foreign Trade Strategies, Employment and Income Distribution in Brazil.* London/New York, Praeger.

Coes, D. 1991. Brazil. Papageorgeiou, D.; Michaely, M. & Choksi, M. (Eds). *Liberalizing Foreign Trade. The Experience of Brazil, Colombia and Peru.* Cambridge, Basil Blackwell. Vol.4 (pp.1-142).

Cohen, S. 1988. *The Making of United States International Economic Policy. Principles, Problems and Proposals for Reform.* New York, Praeger.

Cohen, S. & Meltzer, R. 1982. *United States International Economic Policy in Action. Diversity of Decision Making.* New York, Praeger.

Colombato, Enrico. 1988. *International Trade: A comparison of the Present Situation and Prospects for the NICs and Italy.* Turin, Fondazione Giovanni Agnelli.

Cooper, A., Higgott, R. & Nossal, K. 1993. *Relocating Middle Powers: Australia and Canada in a Changing World Order.* Vancouver, UBC.

Corden, W. Max. 1987. The Revival of Protectionism in Developed Countries. In Salvatore, D.(Ed.) *The New Protectionist Threat to World Welfare.* New York, North-Holland (45-68).

Cornford, A. 1993. Some implications for banking of the Draft General Agreement on Trade in Services of December 1991. In *Unctad Review n.4.*

Cox, R & Jacobson, H. 1974. *Anatomy of Influence: Decision-Making in International Organizations.* New Haven and London, Yale University.

Curzon, G. & Curzon, V. 1974. GATT: Trader's Club. Cox, R. & Jacobson, H. *Anatomy of Influence: Decision-Making in International Organizations.* New Haven and London, Yale University (298-333).

Cutajar, M.Z.(Ed.). 1985. *UNCTAD and the North-South Dialogue: the First Twenty Years.* New York, Pergamon.

Deardorff, A. 1984. *Comparative Advantage and International Trade and Investment in Services.* Michigan, University of Michigan.

Delfim Netto, A. 1980. *Manter o Desenvolvimento e Reduzir a Dependência Externa:*

Palestra na ESG. Brasília, SEPLAN.

Denton, G. and Laite, J. 1988. *The Uruguay Round: Freeing World Trade in Manu-facturing, Agriculture, Services and Investment.* London, HMSO Publications. (Wilton Park Papers n. 3 on Wilton Park Conference n. 320: 3-7 May 1988. Conference Report).

Desai, A.V. 1989. India in the Uruguay Round. In *Journal of World Trade 23*(6): 33-58.

Dewitz, W. R. 1988. Services and the Uruguay Round: Issues Raised in Connection with Multilateral Action on Services: A Comment. In Petersmann, E. & Meinhard, H. (Eds.). *The New GATT Round of Multilateral Trade Negotiations: Legal and Econonmic Problems.* Dauntree (Holland), Klewer Law and Taxation Publishers. Vol. 5.

Dias, J.C. 1993. *Intellectual Property Rights Protection and the Inflow of Foreign Technology and Direct Foreign Investment: The Brazilian Case.* Canterbury, University of Kent (PhD Dissertation).

Ehlerman, C. & Campogrande, G. 1988. Rules on Services in the EEC: A Model for Negotiating World Wide Rules? In Petersmann, E. & Meinhard, H. (Eds.). *The New GATT Round of Multilateral Trade Negotiations: Legal and Econonmic Problems.* Dauntree (Holland), Klewer Law and Taxation Publishers. Vol.5.

Erzan, G. & Holmes. 1990. Effects of the Multi-fibre Arrangements on Developing Countries' Trade: An Empirical investigation. In Hamilton, Carl. *Textiles Trade and the Developing Countries. Eliminating the Multi Fibre arrangement in the 1990s.* Washington, The World Bank.(63-102).

Erzan, G. et al. 1986. *The Profile of Protection in Developing Countries.* Geneva, UNCTAD.

Evans, P. Jacobson, H. & Putnam, R.(Eds.), 1993, *Double Edged Diplomacy: International Bargaining and Domestic Politics.* Berkeley, University of California.

Evans, P. & Frischtak, C. & Tigre, P. 1992a. *Informatica Brasileira em Transicao. Politica Governamental e Tendencias Internacionais nos anos 90.* Rio de Janeiro, IEI/IUERJ.

Evans, P. & Frischtak, C. & Tigre, P. 1992b. *High Technology and Third World Industrialization.: Brazilian Computer Policy in Comparative Perspective.* Berkeley, University of California (International and Area Studies. Research Series, n. 85).

Evans, P. Assertive industrialization and declining hegemony: US-Brazilian conflicts in the computer industry. In *International Organization*.

Ewing, A. 1985. Why Freer Trade in Services is in the Interest of Developing Countries. *Journal of World Trade Law 19*: 147-69.

Faust, P. 1989a. Shipping Services. United Nations. UNCTAD. *Trade in Services: Sectorial Issues*. Geneva, UNCTAD. (113-152).

Faust, P. 1989b. The United Nations Convention on a Code of Conduct for Liner Conferences. *UNCTAD Review 1*(1):1-15. Geneva, UNCTAD.

Feketekuty, G. 1988. *International Trade in Services*. Cambridge, American Enterprise Institute/Ballinger Publication, 1988. HD 9980.5 F 29.

Finger, J. & Olechowski, A.(Eds.). 1987. *The Uruguay Round A Handbook on the Multilateral Trade Negotiations*. Washington, IBRD.

Finlayson, J. & Weston, A. 1990. *Middle Powers in the International System*. Ottawa, North-South Institute. Brazil's influence p.XI.

Flecha de Lima, P. Tarso. 1991. The Multilateral Trade Negotiations and Brazilian Trade-Policy Reform. In Shepherd, G. and Langoni, C.G.(Eds). *Trade Reform. Lessons from Eight Countries*. San Francisco, ICS Press (11-14).

Fonseca, R. & Kennedy, J. 1989. Brazilian Trade Policy and the Uruguay Round. In NAU, Henry. (Ed.) *Domestic Trade Policies and the Uruguay Round*. New York, Colombia University (29-43).

Fontaine, R. 1970. *The Foreign PolicyMaking Process in Brazil*. Washington, John Hopkins University (PhD Dissertation).

Frischtak, C. 1992. O Mercado Internacional e o Potencial Competitivo dos Computadores Nacionais de Equipamentos e Sistemas. In Evans, P. & Frischtak, C. & Tigre, P. *Informática Brasileira em Transição. Política Governamental e Tendências Internacionais nos anos 90*. Rio de Janeiro, IEI, IUERJ.

Frohlich, N., Oppenheiner, J. & Young, O.(Eds.). 1971. *Political Leaders and Collective Goods*. Princeton, Princeton University.

Fuchs, V. 1968. *The Service Economy*. New York, National Bureau of Economic Research.

Gadbaw, R. & Richards, T.(Eds.). 1988. *Intellectual Property Rights. Global Consensus - Global Conflict?* Boulder, Westview.

Gelb, A. and Sagari, S. 1990. Banking. In Messerlin, P. and Sauvant, K. P.(Eds.). *The Uruguay Round: Services in the World Economy*. Washington and New York,

The IBRD and United Nations Centre on Transnational Corporations (UNCTC).

Gelb, A. 1988. *Liberalizing Banking and Financial Services: Costs and Benefits for Developing Countries*. Draft outline for CASIN Seminar (mimeo).

Gibbs, M. and Mashayekhi, M. 1988. Services: Cooperation for Development. In *Journal of World Trade Law 22* (2): 81-107. April.

Gilpin, R. 1987. *The Political Economy of International Relations*. Princeton, Princeton University.

Goldstein, J. & Keohane, R. 1993. *Ideas and Foreign Policy: Beliefs, Institutions and Political Change*. Ithaca, Cornell University.

Golt, S. 1978. *Developing Countries in the GATT System*. London, Trade Policy Research Centre.

Golt, S. 1982.*Trade Issues in the Mid 1980s A Policy Statement*. London, the British-North American Committee.

Golt, S. 1988. *The GATT Negotiations 1986-1990: Origins, Issues & Prospects*. London, British-North American Committee.

Goncalves, R. 1986. *UNCTAD, Structural Adjustment and Structural Change: in search of a Comprehensive Approach*. Geneva, UNCTAD (Discussion Papers n.20).

Grey, R. de C. 1991. *"1992". Financial Services and the Uruguay Round*. Geneva, UNCTAD.(Discussion Papers n.34)) UN.2237/34.

Grey, R. de C. 1990. *The Services Agenda*. Halifax (Nova Scotia), The Institute for Research on Public Policy.

Grey, R. de C. 1989. "1992". Financial Services and the Uruguay Round. In United Nations. UNCTAD. *1989. Trade in Services: Sectorial Issues*. New York, United Nations.

Grynszpan, F. 1990. Case Studies in Brazilian Intellectual Property Rights. In Rushing, F.W. & Brown, C.G.(Ed.). *Intellectual Property Rights in Science, Technology, and Economic Performance. International Comparisons*. Boulder, Westview, (99-112).

Guerreiro, R.S. 1992. *Lembranças de um Empregado do Itamaraty*. São Paulo, Siciliano. F 2538.25.G98.

Gunasekera, B.H., Parsons, D., & Kirsby, M. 1989. Liberalizing Agricultural Trade: Some perspectives for Developing Countries. In Whalley, J. (Ed.). *Developing*

Countries and the Global Trading System.Thematic Studies from a Ford Foundation Project (v.1). London, Macmillan.

Guzzini,S. The Continuing Story of a Death Foretold Realism in International Relations/International Political Economy. In *EUI Working Papers and Social Sciences 92/20. Florence, EUI.*

Haas, P. 1989. Do regimes matter? Epistemic communities and Mediterranean pollution control. *International Organization 43*(3): 377-403.

Hamilton, C. 1990. *Textiles Trade and the Developing Countries. Eliminating the Multi Fibre Arrangement in the 1990s*. Washington, IBRD.

Hamilton, C. & Whalley, J. 1989. Coalitions in the Uruguay Round. In *Weltwirtschaftliches Archiv (Review of World Economics) 125*: 547-562. HB5.

Haq, Khadija (Ed.) 1988. *Linking the World: Trade Policies for the Future.* Islamabad (Pakistan), North-South Round Table.

Helleiner, G. 1993. Protectionism and the Developing Countries. In Salvatore, D. (Ed.). *Protectionism and World Welfare.* Cambridge, Cambridge University Press. (396-418).

Helleiner, G. 1987. *The Uruguay Round: Issues for Multilateral Trade Negotiations.* Ottawa, North-South Institute.

Herman, B. and van Holst, B. 1981. *Towards a Theory of International Trade in Services.* Amsterdam, Netherlands Economic Institute.

Hicks, J. (1969). *A Theory of Economic History.* Oxford, Clarendon.

Higgott, R. & Cooper, A., 1990. Middle Power Leadership and Coalition Building: Australia, the Cairns Group, and the Uruguay Round of Trade negotiations. In *International Organization 44* (3): 589-632. Autumn.

Hillman, A.(Ed.). 1991*Markets and Politicians. Politicized Economic Choice.* Boston, Kluwer Academic Publishers (Studies in Public Choice).

Hindley, B. and Smith, A. 1984. Comparative Advantage and Trade in Services. In *World Economy 7* (4): 369-390.

Hoekman, B. (forthcoming). Conceptual and Political Economy Issues in Liberalizing International Transactions in Services. Deardoff, A. & Stern, R. (Eds). *Analytical and Negotiating Issues in the Global Trading System.* University of Michigan, Ann Arbor.

Hoekman, B. 1993a. *Developing Countries and the Uruguay Round: negotiation on services.* Washington, IBRD. (World Bank Policy Research Working Paper n. 1220).

Hoekman, B. 1993b. Policies Affecting Trade in Services: A Review and Assessment of Principal Instruments. In United Nations -IBRD. *Liberalizing International Transactions in Services: A Handbook.* New York, United Nations-IBRD.

Hoekman, B. 1993c. Safeguards Provisions and Internatioonal Trade Agreements Involving services. *The World Economy.* January.

Hoekman, B. 1992. Market Access and Multilateral Trade Agreements: The Uruguay Round Service Negotiations. *The World Economy.* October.

Hoekman, B. 1988. Services as a Quid Pro Quo for a Safeguards Code? In *The World Economy.* June.

Hoekman, B. & Karsenty, G. 1992. Trade Structure, Economic Development and International Transaction in Services. *Development Policy Review.* London, Overseas Development Institute, September.

Hoekman, B. & Leidy, M. 1991. Antidumping for Services? In Tharakan, P. (Ed.). *Policy Implications of Antidumping Measures.* North Holland.

Hogwood, P. 1990. *Playing to Win: Concepts of Utility and Partner Choice in Coalition Theory.* Glasgow, University of Strathclyde.

Hudec, R. 1990. *The GATT Legal System and World Trade Diplomacy.* New York, Butterworth.

Hudec, R. 1987. *Developing Countries in the GATT Legal System.* London, Trade Policy Research Centre.

Jackson, J. 1988. *International Competition in Services. A Constitutional Framework.* Washington, American Enterprise Institute for Public Policy Research. (AEI studies, n.478).HD 9980.6 J 11.

Jackson, J. 1990. *Restructuring the GATT System.* London, Pinter/Royal Institute of International Affairs.

Jones, R. & Kierkowski, H. 1990. The Role of Services in Production and International Trade. In Jones, R. & Krueger, A. *The Politocal Economy of International Trade.* Cambridge (MA), Basil Blackwell.

Kahler, M. & Odell, J. 1989. Developing Country Coalition-Building and International Trade Negotiations. In Whalley, J. (Ed.). *Developing Countries and the Global Trading System. Thematic Studies from a Ford Foundation Project* (v.1). London, Macmillan.

Kennedy, J. & Fonseca, R. 1989. Brazilian Trade Policy and the Uruguay Round. In Nau, Henry. (Ed.) *Domestic Trade Policies and the Uruguay Round.* New York, Colombia University Press. (29-43).

Keohane, R. 1984. *After Hegemony: Cooperation and Discord in the World Political Economy.* Princeton, Princeton University.

Kindleberger, C. 1978. *Government and International Trade.* Princeton, Princeton University/Department of Economics.

Kock, K. 1969. *International Trade Policy and the GATT (1947-1967).* Stockolm, Almqvist & Wiksell.

Koekkoek, K. 1989. *Developing Countries and the Uruguay Round. Some Aspects.* Rotterdam, Universiteits Erasmus Drukkerij.

Koekkoek, K. 1988. Trade in Services, the Developing Countries and the Uruguay Round. In *World Economy.* 151-156.

Koekkoek and De Leeuw. 1990. The Application of GATT to International Trade in Services: General considerations and LDCs In *Aussenwirstschaft 42*: 65-84.

Krasner, S. 1985. *Structural Conflict: Third World Against Global Liberalisation.* Los Angeles, University of California.

Krommenacker, R. 1984. *World Traded Services: the Challenge for the Eighties.* Dedham-MA, Artech House.

Krommenacker, R. 1988. Multilateral Services Negotiations: From Interest Lateralism to Reasoned Multilateralism in the Context of the Servicization of the Economy. In Petersmann, E. & Meinhard, H. (Eds.). *The New GATT Round of Multilateral Trade Negotiations: Legal and Econonmic Problems.* Dauntree (Holland), Klewer Law and Taxation Publishers. Vol.5.

Kumar, R. 1993. Developing Country Coalitions in International Trade Negotiations. In Tussie, D. & Glover, D. *The Developing Countries in the World Trade. Policies and Bargaining Strategies.* Boulder, Lynne Rienner Publishers. HF 1413 D48.

Kume, H. 1991. A Reforma Tarifária e a Nova Política de Importação. In Velloso, Joao Paulo (coord.). *O Brazil e a Nova economia Mundial.* Rio de Janeiro, Jose Olympio. (105-119).

Kume, H. and Piatini G. 1991. *The Politics of Protection in Brazil.* Rio de Janeiro, Coordenacao Tecnica de Tarifas (CTT).

Kuznets, Simon. 1971. *Economic Growth of Nations.* Cambrige (MA), Harvard University Press.

Lanvin, B. 1987. *International Trade in Services, Information Services and Development*. Geneva, UNCTAD (Discussion Papers n.23).

Lazar, F. 1990. Services and the GATT: US Motives and a Blueprint for Negotiations. In *Journal of World Trade 24* (1): 135-145. February.

Lima, M.R.S. 1986. *The Political Economy of Brazilian Foreign Policy: Nuclear Energy, Trade and Itaipú*. Nashville, Vanderbilt University (PhD Dissertation).

Ljspa Lyndon Johnson School of Public Affairs. University of Texas at Austin. 1983. *Foreign Economic Decision-making: Case Studies from the Johnson Administration and their Implications*. Austin, University of Texas at Austin.

Low, P. 1993. *Trading Free. The GATT and U.S. Trade Policy*. New York, The Twenty Century Fund.

Low, P. 1990. *The GATT System in Transition: The relevance of Traditional Issues*. Rio de Janeiro, PUC-Dep. Economia.

Maciel, G. 1986. O Brazil e o GATT. In *Contexto Internacional 3*: 81-91. January-June 1986.

Maciel, G. 1978. Brazil's Proposal for the Reform of the GATT System. In *The World Economy 1*(2). January.

Maciel, G. 1977. *The International Framework for World Trade. Brazilian Proposals for GATT Reform*. London, Trade Policy Research Centre.

Mack, J. and A. Wiston. 1989. The Havana Charter Experience: Lessons for Developing Countries in J. Whalley (Ed.) *Developing Countries and the Global Trade System*. Volume 1: Thematic Studies from a Ford Foundation Project. London, Macmillan.

Macmillan, J. 1989. A Game Theoretical View of International Trade Negotiations: Implications for Less Developed Countries. In Whalley, J.(Ed.). *Developing Countries and the Global Trading System. Thematic Studies from a Ford Foundation Project* (v.1). London, Macmillan.

Mallampalli, P. 1990. Professional Services. In Messerlin, P. and Sauvant, K. P.(Eds.). *The Uruguay Round: Services in the World Economy*. Washington/New York, IBRD/UNCTC.

Marconinl, M. 1990. Multilateral Negotiations on Trade in Services: General Concepts and the Test of Sectoral Application. In *Development & South-South Cooperation VI (10)*: 5-21. June. (Trade in Services- Special Edition).

Marconini, M. 1989. Services and Uruguay Round: Concepts and Negotiations. In

Comércio Internacional Banamex.I(2): 49-53. June.

Mark, J. and Helleiner, G. 1988. *Trade in Services The Negotiating Concerns of the Developing Countries*. Ottawa, North- South Institute.

Mark, J. 1984. *Trade and Investment in services: an Issue for the 1980s*. Ottawa, North-South Institute.

Martone, C. and Braga, C. 1988. Brazil and the Uruguay Round. São Paulo, FIPE/Universidade de Sao Paulo (USP) (Paper Prepared for Conference on The Multilateral Trade Negotiations and the Developing Countries-Washington (DC), September 15-16, 1988.

Mckee, D. 1988. *Growth, development, and the service economy in the third world*. New York, Praeger, 1988.

Melvin, J. 1989. *Trade in Services: a Theoretical Analysis*. Halifax (Nova Scotia), Institute for Research on Public Policy.

Messerlin, P. and Sauvant, K. P.(Eds.). 1990. *The Uruguay Round: Services in the World Economy*. Washington and New York, The International Bank for Reconstruction and Development(IBRD) and United Nations Centre on Transnational Corporations (UNCTC).

Nau, H. 1989. Domestic Trade Politics and the Uruguay Round: an overview. In Nau, H. (Ed.) *Domestic Trade Policies and the Uruguay Round*. New York, Colombia University (1-25).

Nau, H. 1987. Bargaining in the Uruguay Round. In Finger, J.M. and Olechowski, A.(Ed.) *The Uruguay Round. A Handbook on the Multilateral Trade Negotiations*. Washington, World Bank, 1987.

Nayar, D. 1988. Some reflections on the Uruguay Round and Trade in Services. In *Journal of World Trade* 22(5): 35-47. October.

Nayar, D. 1986. *International Trade in Services: Implications for Developing Countries*. (Eximbank Commencement Day Annual Lecture).

Nicolaides, P. 1989. *Liberalizing Service Trade. Strategies for Success*. London, Routledge-The Royal Institute of International Affairs.(Chatham House Papers).

Nicolaides, P. 1987. *Liberalizing Trade in Services: An overview of the Issues and the Difficulties*. London, Royal Institute of International Affairs. (Chatham House, Discussion Paper n.3, December).

Noronha, D. 1993. *GATT, Mercosul & NAFTA*. São Paulo, Observador Legal.

Nusbaumer, J. 1987. *Services in the Global Market*. Boston, Kluwer Academic Publishers.

Nye, J. 1990. *Bound to Lead. The Changing Nature of American Power*. New York, Basic Books.

Nye, J. 1974. *UNCTAD: Poor Nation's Pressure Group*. In Cox, R. & Jacobson, H. *Anatomy of Influence: Decision-Making in International Organizations*. New Haven London, Yale University (334-370).

Odell, J. 1992. International threats and internal politics: Brazil, the European Community and United States. In Evans, P.; Jacobson, H. & Putnam, R. (Eds.). *International Bargaining and Domestic Politics: an Interactive Approach*. Berkeley, University of California Press.

Ostry, S. 1987. Interdependence: Vulnerability and Opportunity, Washington, Canadian External Affairs. *Canadian Foreign Policy Series, Statements and Speeches*.

Oulton, N. 1984. *International Trade in Services and the Comparative Advantage of E.C. Countries*. London, Trade Policy Research Centre.

Outreville, J. 1989. Trade in Insurance Services. In United Nations. UNCTAD. *Trade in Services: Sectorial Issues*. New York, United Nations (153-184).

Oxley, A. 1990. *The Challenge of Free-Trade*. London, Harvester Wheatsheaf (Simon & Schuster International Group).

Papageorgiou, G. 1991a. *Liberalizing Foreign Trade. Brazil, Colombia and Peru*. Washington, Basil Blackwell. (vol.4).

Papageorgiou, D.; Michaely, M. and Choksi, A. (Eds.). 1991b. *Liberalizing Foreign Trade. Lessons of Experience in the Developing World*. Washington, Basil Blackwell (Volume 7).

Parakala, P. 1991. *Military regimes, security doctrines and foreign policy: Brazil, Indonesia and Ghana*. London, LSE.

Pereira, L., Maravall, J. & Przeworski, A.. 1993. *Economic Reforms in New Democracies*. Cambridge, Cambridge University Press.

Petersmann, E. & Meinhard, H.(Eds.). 1988. *The New GATT Round of Multilateral Trade Negotiations: Legal and Economic Problems*. Dauntree (Holland), Klewer Law and Taxation Publishers. (Studies in Transnational Economic Law. Vol.5).

Pipe, R. 1989. Telecommunications Services: Considerations for Developing Countries in Uruguay Round Negotiations. In United Nations. UNCTAD. *Trade in Services: Sectorial Issues*. Geneva, UNCTAD. (49-112).

Pratt, C.(Ed.). 1990. *Middle Power Internationalism: The North-South Dimension.* Kingston (Ontario), McGill-Queen's University Press.

Pratt, C.(Ed.).1989. *International System under Strain. The North-South Policy of Canada, Holland, Norway and Sweden.* Toronto, University of Toronto.

Raffaelli, M. 1990. Some Considerations on the Multi-fibre Arrangements: Past, Present and Future. In Hamilton, C. *Textiles Trade and the Developing Countries. Eliminating the Multi Fibre Arrangement in the 1990s.* Washington, The IBRD, (263-291).

Rego Barros Netto, S. 1987. O Gatt de Havana a Punta del Este. In *Revista Brasileira de Comércio Exterior.* n. 9 (January /February 1987).

Richards, T. 1988. Brazil. In Gadbaw, R.M. & Richards. T.J. (Eds.). *Intellectual Property Rights. Global Consensus Global Conflict?* Boulder, Westview, 1988 (149-185).

Richardson, J. 1987. A Sub-sectoral Approach to Services Trade Theory. In Giarini, Orio (Ed.). *The Emerging Service Economy.* London, Pergamon Press.(59-82).

Ricupero, R. 1988. *O Brasil e o Futuro do Comércio Internacional.* Paper presented in the seminar: "A nova era da economia mundial" (New phase of world economy), organized by Institute Fernand Braudel de economia Mundial, August.

Roche, D. 1989. *Building Global Security: Agenda for the 1990s.* Toronto, NC Press.

Roett, R. 1992. *Brazil. Politics in a Patrimonial Society.* Westport(Connecticut), Westview. 4th Edition.

Rojot, J. 1991. *Negotiating: From Theory to Practice.* London, Macmillan. HD58.6 R74.

Rothstein, R. 1979. *Global Bargaining: UNCTAD and the Quest for a New International Economic Order.* Princeton, Princeton University.

_____. 1977. *The Weak in the World of the Strong.* New York, Columbia University.

Ruelan, D. & Ruelan, A. 1989. *Le Brèsil.* Paris, Karthala.

Rushing, F. & Brown, C. (Eds.). 1990. *Intellectual Property Rights in Science, Technology, and Economic Performance. International Comparisons.* Boulder-London, Westview.

Sacerdoti, G.(Ed.). 1990. *Liberalization of Services and Intellectual Property in the Uruguay Round of GATT.* Fribourg, University Press Fribourg (Proceedings of the Conference on "The Uruguay Round of Gatt and the Improvement of the Legal

Framework of Trade in services", Bergamo, University of Bergamo, 21-23 September 1989, Italy - PUPIL, vol. 6).

Sachs, I., 1985. Trade and Development: A Prospective View of UNCTAD. In Cutajar, M.Z.(Ed.). 1985. *UNCTAD and the North-South Dialogue: the First Twenty Years* (243-259). New York, Pergamon.

Sampson, G. 1989. Developing Countries and the Liberalization of Trade in Services. In Whalley, J. (Ed.). *Developing Countries and the Global Trading System. Thematic studies from a Ford Foundation Project* (v.1). London, Macmillan, (132-148).

Sapir, A. and Lutz, E.1981. Trade in Services, Economic Determinants and Development Related issues. In *World Bank Staff Working Paper n. 480*, August.

Schneider, R. 1991. *Order and Progress: A Political History of Brazil*. Boulder, Westview. F2521 S35.

Schott, J. & Mazza, J. 1986. Trade in Services and Developing Countries. In *Journal of World Trade 20*(3): 253-273. May/June.

Schware, R. 1992. Obstáculos e Oportunidades pera os Produtores Brasileiros de Software. In Evans, P., Frischtak, C. & Tigre, P. *Informática Brasileira em Transição. Política Governamental e Tendências Internacionais nos anos 90*. Rio de Janeiro, IEI, IUERJ.

Sciamma, Guido. 1988. La Posizione del Brasile nell'Uruguay Round del Gatt con Particulare Riferimento al Commercio Internazionale di Servizi. Milan, Universita Commerciale Luigi Bocconi/Facolta di Economia e Commercio. (Tesis di Laurea in Economia Politica).

Selcher, W. 1981. *Brazil in the International System: The Rise of a Middle Power*. Boulder, Westview. Unctad p.231/group of 77 influence p.228.

Selcher, W. 1978. *Brazil's Multilateral Relations: Between First and Third Worlds*. Boulder, Westview.

Shelp, R.(Ed.). 1984. *Service Industries and Economic Development. Case studies in Technology Transfer*. New York, Praeger. (Sponsored and Administered by the FMME Fund for Multinational Management Education).

Shepherd, G. & Langoni, C.G.(Eds.). 1991. *Trade Reform. Lessons from Eight Countries*. San Francisco (US), Institute for Contemporary Studies(ICS Press).

Sherwood, R. 1990. *Intellectual Property and Economic Development*. Boulder, Westview.

Simonsen, M.E. *Trade, Debt and Protectionism - The Brazilian Case*. seggr. GATT.

Sjostedt, G. & Sundelius, B. (Eds.). 1986. *Free Trade - Managed Trade? Perspectives on a Realistic Trade Order*. Boulder (Colorado), Westview. (Westview Special Studies in International Economics and Business).

Soares de Lima, M.R. 1986. *The Political Economy of Brazilian Foreign Policy : Nuclear energy, Trade and Itaipú*. Nashville, Vanderbilt. (PhD Dissertation).

Soubra, Y. 1989. Construction and Engineering Design Services: Issue Relevant to Multilateral Negotiations on Trade In Services. In United Nations. UNCTAD. *Trade in Services: Sectorial Issues*. Geneva, UNCTAD. (185-214).

South America, Central America and the Caribbean. 1993. London, Europe Publication.

Strange, S. 1988. *State and Markets*. London, Pinter.

Sturmey, S. 1985. *Workbook on the application of the UNCTAD Code*. London, Seatrade.

Summers, R. 1985. Services in the International Economy. In INMAN, Robert (Ed.). *Managing the Service Economy: Prospects and Problems*. Cambridge, Cambridge University Press. (27-48).

Tachinardi, M. 1993. *A Guerra das Patentes. O Conflito Brasil x EUA sobre Propriedade Intelectual*. São Paulo, Paz e Terra.

Taylor, D. 1987. *UNCTAD and Trade in Services*. Geneva, Institute for Research on Public Policy, 1987 (Series on Trade in Services. Discussion Papers. March).

Thomas, V.; Matin, K. & Nash, J. 1990. *Lessons in Trade Policy Reform*. Washington, IBRD.(Policy and Research Series n.10).

Tigre, P. 1992. Dilemas Atuais e Opcoes Futuras para a Politica de Informatica. In Evans, P. Fritschtak, C. & Tigre, P.B. *Informática Brasileira em Transição. Política Governamental e Tendências Internacionais nos anos 90*. Rio de Janeiro, UFRJ/IEI.

Tigre, P.B. 1991. Política ou Não-política? Os Descaminhos da Informática no Brasil. Velloso, J.R.(Ed.). *Aquarella do Brasil. Ensaios Políticos e Econômicos sobre o Governo Collor*. Rio de Janeiro, Rio Fundo.

Trela, I. & Whalley, J. Taxes, Outwards Orientation and Growth Performance in Korea. *Policy, Research and External Affairs Working Papers: Public Economics*. WPS n.519. Washington, IBRD.

Tussie, D. 1993a. Holding the Balance: The Cairn Group in the Uruguay Round. In Tussie, D & Glover, D. 1993. *The Developing Countries in the World Trade. Policies and Bargaining Strategies*. Boulder, Lynne Rienner Publishers. HF 1413 D48.

Tussie, D. 1993b. The Uruguay Round and the trading system in the balance: Dilemmas for the developing countries. In Tussie, D & Agosin, M. (Eds). *Trade and Growth: New Dilemmas in Trade Policy*. London, Macmillan.

Tussie, Diana. 1987. *The Less Developed Countries and the World Trading System. A Challenge to the GATT*. London, Pinter.

Underhill, G. 1992. *The Politics of Expanding Global Markets:The Uruguay Round and Trade in Financial Services*. Conventry, University of Warwick (Dept. of Politics and International Studies. Pais Papers. Working Paper n. 108. April 1992).

Velloso, J.(Ed.) 1991. *Aquarella do Brasil. Ensaios Políticos e Econômicos sobre o Governo Collor*. Rio de Janeiro, Rio Fundo Editora.

Vittas, D. 1992. *Contractual Savings and Emerging Security Markets*. Washington, The International Bank for Reconstruction and Development(IBRD). (Working Papers n.33732).

Wallerstein, I. 1979. *The Capitalist World-Economy*. Paris, Maison des Sciences de l'Homme & Cambridge, Cambridge University Press.

Wallerstein, I. 1974. *The Modern World System: Capitalist Agriculture and the Origins of the European World-Economy in the Sixteenth Century*. Cambridge, Cambridge University Press & Paris, Editions de la Maison des Sciences de l'Homme.

Weiss, T. 1986. *Multilateral Development Diplomacy in UNCTAD. The Lessons of Group Negotiations: 1964-1984*. Basingstoke, Macmillan.

Whalley, J.(Ed.) 1989. *Developing Countries and the Global Trading System. Thematic Studies from a Ford Foundation Project* (v.1). London, Macmillan.

Wiener, J. 1994. *Making the Rules for Agriculture in the Uruguay Round of the GATT: A Study in International Leadership*. Canterbury, University of Kent. (PhD Dissertation).

Wilkie, J.(Ed.). 1993. *Statistical Abstract of Latin America. v. 30*. Los Angeles, UCLA-Latin American Center.

Williams, M. 1991. *Third World Cooperation. The Group of 77 in UNCTAD*. New York, St Martin Press (HF1413 W72).

Wilterdink. Where Nations Meet: National Identities in International Organization. In *EUI Working Papers and Social Sciences 92/20. Florence, EUI.*

Winham, G. 1989. The Pre-negotiation Phase of the Uruguay Round. *International Journal.*44 Spring. pp. 280-303.

Wolf, M. 1984. Two-Edged Sword: Demands of Developing Countries and The Trading System. In Bhagwatti, J. & Ruggie, G.(Eds.). *Power, Passions and Purpose: Prospects for North-South Negotiations.* Cambridge, MIT.

Zietz, J. and Valdis, A. 1986. *The Cost of Protectionism to Developing Countries. An Analysis for Selected Agricultural Products.* Washington, IBRD (World Bank Staff Papers n. 769).

Zini, A. 1990. *Brazil-France. Macroeconomic conditions and perspectives for trade in services.* (Coleção Documentos do Instituto de Estudos Avancados da Universidade de Sao Paulo USP).

Official Documents

Brazil. 1993. Brazil. 1992. Policy Trade Review. Geneva, GATT.

Brazil. IBGE. 1991. Anuário Estatístico do Brasil. Rio de Janeiro, IBGE.

Brazil. Itamaraty. MRE. 1988a. O Contexto de Acesso a Mercados na Rodada Uruguay. Brasilia, MRE.

Brazil. Itamaraty. MRE. 1988b. O Contexto dos Temas Normativos. Brasilia, MRE.

Brazil. Itamaraty. MRE. 1988c. Os Novos Temas da Rodada Uruguay. Brasilia, MRE.

Brazil. Itamaraty. MRE. Relatorio 19-. Brasilia, MRE, various issues.

Brazil. Itamaraty. Secretaria Geral de Politica Exterior. Departamento Economico. GETEC. Boletim de Diplomacia Economica.

GATT. 1993. Brazil. 1992. Policy Trade Review. Report by the Secretariat. Geneva, GATT.

GATT. 1992. The Uruguay Round. A Giant Step for Trade and Development, and a Response to the Challenges of The Modern World. Geneva, GATT.

GATT. 1986. The Text of the General Agreement on Tariffs and Trade. Geneva, GATT.

GATT. 1985. Trade Policies for a Better Future. Proposals for Action. Geneva, GATT. (Leutwiler Report).

GATT. Brazil. 1993. Brazil. 1992. Policy Trade Review. Geneva, GATT.

GATT. Trade Negotiating Committee (TNC). 1991. Draft Final Act Embodying the Results of The Uruguay Round of Multilateral Trade Negotiations. GATT, Geneva. (MTN.TNC/W/FA).

GATT. Trade Negotiating Committee (TNC). 1993. MTN./FA II-A1B. General Agreement on Trade in Services (GATS). Geneva, GATT.

GATT. 1974. Arrangement Regarding International Trade in Textiles. Geneva, GATT.

GATT. 1964a. The GATT and Economic Development. Geneva, GATT.

GATT. 1964b. The Role of GATT in Relation to Trade and Development. Geneva, GATT.

GATT. 1947-19- . Basic Instruments and Selected Documents (BISD) GATT, various issues.

GATT. 1947-19- . Focus Newsletter. Geneva, GATT.

GATT. 1947-19- . GATT Activities. Geneva, GATT.

GATT. 1947-19-. International Trade. Geneva, GATT.

GATT. 1987/93. News of the Uruguay Round (NUR). Geneva, GATT.

GATT. 19- . Press Release/ Communiqué de Presse. Geneva, GATT.

IBGE. 1991. Anuário Estatístico do Brasil. Rio de Janeiro, IBGE.

International Civil Aviation Organization. 1981. Memorandum on ICAO: the story of The International Aviation Organization. Montreal, ICAO.

OECD. 1989. Trade in Services and Developing Countries. Paris, OECD.

Trade Negotiating Committee (TNC). 1991. Draft Final Act Embodying the Results of The Uruguay Round of Multilateral Trade Negotiations. GATT, Geneva. (MTN.TNC/W/FA).

Trade Negotiating Committee (TNC). 1993. MTN./FA II-A1B. General Agreement on Trade in Services (GATS). Geneva, GATT.

Trade Negotiation Committee - Institute for International Legal Information (Eds.). 1992. "The Dunkel Draft". From the GATT Secretariat: Draft Final Act Embodying the Results of the Uruguay Round of Multilateral Negotiations. Buffalo, William S. Hein & Co.

Transnational Corporations and Management Division (TCMD)*. 1993. The Transnationalization of Service Industries: an Empirical Analysis of the Determinants of Foreign Direct Investment by Transnational Service Corporations. New York, United Nations/ Department of Economic and Social Development. (1448/103).

United Nations Conference on Trade and Development (UNCTAD). 1990 a. Statistical Survey on Insurance and Reinsurance Operations in Developing Countries 1984-1986. New York, United Nations.

UNCTAD. 1990 b. Technology, Trade Policy, and the Uruguay Round. Papers and Proceedings of a Round Table held in Delphi, Greece, from 22 to 24 April 1989. United Nations, New York. UNCTAD (140).

UNCTAD. 1990 c. Uruguay Round: Further Paper on Selected Issues. New York, United Nations.

UNCTAD. 1989 a. Services and the Development Potential; The Indian Context. New York, United Nations. UNCTAD. 10.

UNCTAD. 1989 b. Trade in Services: Sectorial Issues. New York, United Nations. UNCTAD (9).

UNCTAD. 1987. Revitalizing Development, Growth and International Trade. Assessment and Policies Options. New York, UNCTAD. (Report to UNCTAD VII)

UNCTAD. 1986. Protectionism and Structural Adjustment. Restrictions on Trade and Structural Adjustment. Report by the UNCTAD Secretariat. Geneva, UNCTAD. (TD/B/1081).

UNCTAD. 1985 a. Port Development. A Handbook for Planners in Developing Countries. Geneva, UNCTAD.

UNCTAD. 1985 b. Production and Trade in Services: Policies and their Underlying Factors Bearing upon International Service Transactions. Geneva, UNCTAD, 1985. TD/B/941/Rev.1.

UNCTAD. 1985 c. Services and the Development Process; Study by the UNCTAD Secretariat. Geneva, UNCTAD.

UNCTAD. 1983. UNCTAD Activities in the Field of Shipping. Geneva, United Nations (TD/278).

UNCTAD. 1981. The Set of Multilaterally Agreed Equitable Principles and Rules for the Control of Restrictive Business Practices. Geneva, UNCTAD. TD/RBP/CONF/10/Rev.1.

UNCTAD/UNDP. 1990. Round Table in Technology and Trade Policy:1989 delphos, Greece. New York, United Nations.

United Nations Center for Transnational Corporations (UNCTC). 1990a. Foreign Direct Investment and Transnational Corporations in Services. New York, United Nations. (1448/103).

UNCTC. 1990b. Transnational Corporations, Services and the Uruguay Round. New York, United Nations(1448/103).

UNCTC. 1990c. Transnational Service Corporations and Developing Countries: Impact and Policy Issues. New York, United Nations(1448/103).

UNCTC. 1989. Service and Development: The Role of Foreign Direct Investment and Trade. New York, United Nations. UN 1448/95.

United Nations. 1983. The Convention on a Code of Conduct for Liner Conferences. In United Nations Conference of Plenipotentiaries on a Code of Conduct for Liner Conferences. vol.II. Final Act (Including the Convention and Resolutions) and Tonnage Requirements. Geneva, United Nations.

* ex-United Nations Center for Transnational Corporations (UNCTC)

Newspapers Consulted (1982-1990)

1. Brazilian Newspapers

Estado de São Paulo
Folha de São Paulo
Jornal da Tarde
Jornal do Brasil

2. French Newspapers

Le Monde/Le Monde Diplomatique

3. Japanese Newspapers

The Japan Times

4. UK Newspapers

Daily Telegraph
The Financial Times
The Guardian
The Independent
The Times

5. US Newspapers

The New York Times
The Washington Post
International Herald Tribune

Index

271

For Product Safety Concerns and Information please contact our EU
representative GPSR@taylorandfrancis.com Taylor & Francis Verlag GmbH,
Kaufingerstraße 24, 80331 München, Germany

Printed and bound by CPI Group (UK) Ltd, Croydon, CR0 4YY
08/05/2025
01864430-0001